Dean Smith
A Tribute

by
Ken Rosenthal

SPORTS PUBLISHING LLC
www.SportsPublishingLLC.com

Director of Production: Susan M. Moyer
Cover design:Terry Hayden

ISBN: 1-58261-003-7

SPORTS PUBLISHING LLC
www.sportspublishingllc.com

Printed in the United States.

Acknowledgments

A book of this nature could not have been written without the cooperation of others—those who agreed to be interviewed, those who helped arrange the interviews and those who provided ideas and support.

First, I must thank Dean Smith for living a life and creating a career that made this project worthwhile and for allowing those close to him to participate.

This is not an authorized book. As far as I could tell, Coach Smith didn't encourage anyone to speak with me; on the other hand, he didn't discourage anyone.

Former Carolina greats Michael Jordan and James Worthy declined to be interviewed without a formal request from Coach Smith. Duke coach Mike Krzyzewski and Indiana coach Bob Knight did not participate for the same reason. Krzyzewski and former Clemson coach Tates Locke were the only ACC coaches, past or present, who were unwilling to share their memories.

Almost everyone else was extremely cooperative, starting with Dick Vitale, who graciously agreed to write the foreword.

Steve Kirschner, director of media relations for the North Carolina men's basketball team, probably was my most valuable resource; he always was pleasant, professional and helpful.

Carolina fans might find this difficult to believe, but Duke sports information director Mike Cragg and varsity club director Mary Dinkins were more than willing to aid and abet this collection of enemy propaganda.

Ditto for North Carolina State assistant athletic director Mark Bockelman, Virginia SID Rich Murray and Maryland assistant SID Chuck Walsh, Wake Forest SID John Justus, Georgia Tech SID Mike Finn and Clemson SID Tim Bourret.

Other SIDs who went above and beyond included Dean Buchan (Kansas), Brian Binnette (South Carolina), John Heisler (Notre Dame), Mike Gore (North Carolina-Asheville), Scott McConnell (Texas), John Lanctot (DePaul) and Kent Partridge (Auburn).

Now for the big question: How many media-relations types does it take to arrange an interview with an NBA player? Let's just say the book would not have been as complete without the help of Steve Schur, Bob Zink and Todd Von Ville (Cleveland), Bill Wickett (Detroit), Raymond Ridder and Kyle Spencer (Golden State), Dave Haggith and Matt Akler (Toronto), Karen Frascona and Rob Wilson (Philadelphia) and Maureen Lewis and Mike Gathagan (Washington). Thanks also to Natalie Knorr (Charlotte), Tony Fay and J.J. Carter (Dallas), David Benner, (Indiana), John Black (Los Angeles), Bill King (Milwaukee), Tim Donovan (Miami) and Joel Glass (Orlando).

Several of my colleagues at The Baltimore Sun offered ideas and more importantly, phone numbers. My thanks to Jerry Bembry, Molly Dunham Glassman, John Eisenberg, Ken Fuson, Don Markus and Paul McMullen for their assistance.

My friend, Baltimore college basketball expert Paul Baker, inspired me with his love for the game. Mike Littwin, one of my professional heroes, told me to call Doug Moe. Dick Jerardi of the *Philadelphia Daily News*, what can I say? I owe you a lot, pal.

One of the great pleasures of doing this book was interviewing colleagues like Peter Gammons, Dick Weiss and Mark Whicker, giants of the profession who have been kind to me at every turn. As always, John Feinstein was generous with his time, giving me encouragement, knowledge and friendship.

My agent, Steve Greenberg of The Dreaming Dog Group in Indianapolis, was the mastermind behind this project. It was the least he could do, seeing as how he hired me for my first newspaper job in York, Pennsylvania, then bolted for another job before I even arrived.

Finally, I must thank my children—Sammy, Hannah and Sarah—for putting up with daddy's long hours, and my wife, Lisa, for her love, support and especially her patience. We delayed one of our rare nights out while I interviewed Charlie Scott. The Rosenthal starting five lacks height, but I'll put it up against anyone's.

Ken Rosenthal, Baltimore, Md.

Author's Note

I am not a North Carolina fan. I am not a Duke fan. I am not even an ACC fan, at least not by birth.

Growing up on Long Island, I rooted for St. John's, then attended the University of Pennsylvania. It was just my luck that I started at Penn the year after it beat North Carolina in the NCAA tournament and made the Final Four.

Until writing this book, my only contact with North Carolina basketball was as a sports columnist who covered Maryland for *The Baltimore Sun*, starting in 1991.

I began this project with few pre-conceived notions. I attacked it from a journalist's perspective, trying to present the fullest possible portrait of the winningest coach in college basketball history.

This book is the product of more than 100 interviews—some in person, most by phone, one by e-mail (thank you, Terry Holland).

The words are not my words, but the words of the subjects. Any changes I made were for transition and clarity.

Dean Smith's accomplishments are well documented. But those who knew him best remember him as a man dedicated to civil rights and to his Baptist faith; as a teacher, career counselor and father figure.

And, oh yes, as a pretty fair basketball coach.

Contents

The Nineties

The Managers

Opposing Coaches

Opposing Players

Referees

Media

On the Perimeter

From the Inside

Foreword

by Dick Vitale

When I got the head coaching job at the University of Detroit in 1974, I went on an unbelievable campaign to recruit Tommy LaGarde. I put petitions out. I was trying to get some splash, some headlines. They hadn't gotten a lot of positive publicity at Detroit. I came in and said: "Here's the guy I'm going after. I know Dean Smith is after him. I don't care. I'm going after Tommy LaGarde." I went after him big-time. I tried to get Dave DeBusschere involved with the recruiting. But it was so late. Obviously, the kid went to North Carolina and became a starter.

As soon as he got down there, I got a call from Dean. He had that one policy where he was very loyal to his recruits about going back and playing in their home areas. He said: "I want to bring Tommy LaGarde back to Detroit." I was ecstatic. Obviously, our fans and alumni were going to go nuts, knowing we were able to get the University of North Carolina to come to Calihan Gym.

There was one stipulation, and the stipulation was very simple. If he came to Detroit, we'd have to play him twice at North Carolina. I said: "Amen!" Fortunately for me, I was gone by the time those games came up. The next coach had to go down there. But that told me about the dedication he had to his players, the relationships he had.

When I think about Dean Smith, when you look at his career over four decades, what amazes me is his consistency. He was always able to adjust his style to the rules, the shot clock, the three-point shot, whatever changes they made. He had such a creative mind. He was always one step ahead of everyone. And to be able to avoid any kind of controversy or NCAA violations with the amount of scrutiny there is today, that's just amazing. With that NCAA rule book as thick as it is today, there are so many things that can go wrong.

In my travels with the Jimmy V Foundation, I've met a lot of North Carolina players, from Charlie Scott to James Worthy. The relationships Dean has developed with his players are so special, so unique. I have never heard any of his former players utter a negative word in any shape or form about the man. That blows my mind. His reputation is just impeccable.

He always stressed "We" instead of "I." All you had to do was look at their stat sheets at North Carolina. Everyone was listed alphabetically, not by the number of points they scored. Everything was done to show, "We're a team." Minutes weren't shown. He didn't want that to be the individual desire of a player. When you think about creating the huddle at the foul line, players pointing at one another to recognize a great pass, the blue team coming in to create a spark, creating the Four Corners and passing game—he was just always one step ahead. The kids believed what he said. And he was a miracle worker in the last three minutes of games.

I'll never forget my departed buddy, Jimmy Valvano, pounding North Carolina pretty good one day, North Carolina State laying a whipping on them big time. There I am, saying: "This baby's not over! Dean Smith is Michelangelo! He can absolutely create a nightmare at the end of a game! Stay tuned!" We listed a bunch of their miracle comebacks. And the next day, I get a call. It's Valvano. And he's screaming: "I'm sick and tired of hearing about Dean Smith! There we are, we're pounding 'em, blowing 'em away, and all you're saying is: 'Dean this, Dean that. What about your buddy, your Paisan?" I said: "Jimmy V, you're right." But Dean had just developed that knack for keeping his team in games.

To see him so poised, the sartorial way he dressed, the way he carried himself, one word summarized Dean Smith—C-L-A-S-S. Class in every shape and form. Everything they did, from the uniforms they wore, to the layup drills, to the way they practiced, became a model for so many programs. Their players symbolized what student-athletes were all about. People look at it and say: "He only won two national championships." But if he had been more selfish, had tried to talk players like Bob McAdoo, James Worthy and Michael Jordan into staying, he would have won more. He always put the players ahead of the program. He was an amazing ambassador for basketball.

He's All-Rolls Royce. Solid gold.

Chapter One

THE SIXTIES

HUGH DONOHUE

Donohue, the women's basketball coach at the State University of New York at Purchase, played at North Carolina from 1959-60 to 1961-62.

I should have finished in the class of '61. But I had an injury, red-shirted and wound up on his first team in '61-'62. I was a carry-over from Frank McGuire.

He was a little laid-back when he first came. Those first couple of years, Frank still did most of the recruiting. When he would take his trips to New York, Dean would run the ballclub. He did a good job. He was different because he concentrated on defense. If Frank left for three or four days, those three or four days Dean would put a basket on the rim, so we couldn't score. Some guys disliked it, but it's like everything else with change. You had to get used to it.

McGuire's style was that every game was a battle. He was a magnificent motivator. In his pre-game talk he would reflect about the opponent, tell a story from when he was at St. John's or North Carolina. Those of us who played for him got lessons in life. He was a church-going man. His son had cerebral palsy, which I think a lot of people didn't know about. He was a great family man, and it carried over to the team. We all felt part of his family. He was Catholic; I was Catholic. Most of the guys were Catholic.

Dean was more stern. Coming from the Air Force Academy —we had forgotten that he had played at Kansas—we assumed he must be a military guy of some sort. I thought he was a Midwestern guy, sincere. He was very knowledgeable about the game. He had been a math major, and was pretty analytical. And he was very good at breaking down film, which back then was black and white. I enjoyed the film sessions.

That first year was the year after the (point-shaving) scandal in '61. We only got to play 17 games. Our record was 8-9—his only losing record. We had the fourth- or fifth-best talent in the league. He did a good job with us. He was very, very creative. Just looking at some films that (Carolina) broke down and sent me, you probably could still run the shuffle offense that we ran in '61-'62.

I've done the camp for 20, 25 years. I ran a business in Chapel Hill from 1985 to '90. I sat in on practice probably 50 to 100 times. I never saw much of a change in practice. The talent level was better, but it was always done in time sequence, always orderly. His teaching philosophy changed with the personnel he had. But it wasn't like a fear thing. (The players) believed he was a great teacher-coach. He was a teacher first. The term, "Coach," is used for wins and losses. But I really think he was a great teacher of the game of basketball.

We stayed close. He was always nice to me. He gave me a chance to come back and play that last year, which I'm eternally grateful for. He has been a friend of mine for years. Anytime we wanted to go to a ballgame, we were able to go to a ballgame. One of the great things about the guy is that those of us who had mediocre or non-outstanding careers could be as friendly with him as the guys who were stars. If there were 100 Dean Smith lettermen, we all felt like we contributed something. He made us feel that way.

I'm one of the guys who, toward the end, thought he would walk away from it. If you look back at the year he broke the record, I'm not sure if he would have retired if he had had a mediocre year. I don't think he ever set out to be the guy everyone would chase. I don't know if he's comfortable with that even now. I think he wanted to be a teacher more than a coach who had the most wins or outlasted everybody.

DONNIE WALSH

Walsh, a member of Dean Smith's first team at North Carolina, played in Chapel Hill from 1959-60 to 1961-62. He helped coach the freshman team while attending North Carolina Law School and later became associate head coach under Frank McGuire at South Carolina from 1965 to '76. He was named general manager of the Indiana Pacers in 1986 and team president in '88.

Donnie Walsh

When I got to Carolina, he was an assistant coach, the guy I was closest to. I felt right away that he was talking to me about things I hadn't really heard about, particularly on defense. I can remember being at a gym on campus that we called the Old Tin Can, being with another guy, Yogi Poteet. Dean was the freshman coach. He was teaching us individual defense. It was the first time I had ever been exposed to anything like that.

In those days, Frank McGuire was such a monumental figure. But I didn't see that much of a change at all when Dean became coach (in Walsh's senior year). I really respected Dean because he had pride about the way he wanted to play. Early in his career, he wasn't as successful. We didn't have the same kind of players we had before. His game was a lot different than Frank McGuire's. He got a lot of criticism for that. But he always stood up to it. I admired him for that.

Frank played a lot of zone, and his system was really geared around star players like Doug Moe and York Larese. Without him saying it, we knew those were the guys who were supposed to get the ball. Dean came out playing a five-man offense and a tremendous pressing defense. He played a passing game rather than a more structured offense. The idea was to share the ball—whoever got the best shot, got the best shot. He didn't single out any players.

If you knew Dean's defense, then you knew all defenses— that's how thorough his defensive scheme is. If you could do what Dean taught in the NBA, it would flat-out work. But it would be very difficult. There are a lot more games. It's hard for players to do that. We play 48 minutes. But his multiple-defense concept is a great concept. The way he teaches it, he builds from basics, makes it real easy to step to more exotic defenses. Offensively, he likes to run the ball, which I think would work in the NBA. Dean can coach. He's such a smart guy. He thought up all these things. I know he could have adjusted to the pro game. But I always felt he was the perfect guy to coach a college team.

He wants to win. He's extremely competitive. But he keeps everything in great perspective, with the individual and the team. The way he disciplines a team, it's all through peer pressure. If you make a mistake, if you mess up, the whole team has to run, rather than him just screaming at you. If you were running sprints at the end of practice, and weren't doing them as hard as you could, then everyone had to run again. Believe me, it works.

He isn't bringing you there to use you. He has your best interests at heart. He knows that even on his team there are only three or four players with a chance to play pro ball. Then everyone has to go out and have a life. He encourages that. He's straight about it. And he follows up on it.

Being around him when I was in law school, talking about the four corners, talking about the passing game, I didn't know it at the time, but he was kind of the innovator of all these things, the trademark things that everyone copies. In hindsight, I realize how special he was. I didn't know it at the time.

Still, my feelings about him are more off the court than on the court. He never wanted to hurt anybody. I just thought he was a terrific guy. After he got big, he was, "Oh, that guy at North Carolina," like he was trying to manipulate everything. I never could put that together with the guy I knew.

CHARLES SHAFFER

Shaffer, an attorney at Atlanta, played for North Carolina from 1961-62 to 1963-64.

He placed great emphasis on man-to-man defense. That's the first thing I remember. He also placed great emphasis on unselfishness on offense. One of his main principles is that if you play great man-to-man defense, you have a chance to win even if you don't shoot well. That's a great philosophy. You're going to have nights when you shoot very well, and nights you don't. But if you play great man-to-man defense, you can stay in the game.

Back in those days, the early '60s, our goal was to try to hold the other team in the 50s. If they got 60, we felt we had not done our job on defense. Under Coach McGuire—and he was a great coach—we played a lot of zone defense, not as much man-to-man. But right off the bat, Coach Smith established man-to-man defense as the way we would do it. He took great pride in taking the other team out of its offense. It would be a great thrill for us to do that, to take the opponents out of their set offense, prevent them from making a pass when they wanted to make it.

Psychologically, it had the effect of taking the pressure off you on the other end of the court. The other aspect of it was to take good shots: Don't come down and throw up wild shots after two passes. It was part of being unselfish. Those two coaching philosophies—one defensive, one of-fensive—really worked very well in the building of an incredibly sound bas-ketball program. He didn't deviate from either of those philosophies. He put them in on Day One in 1961, and stayed with them for 34 years.

I didn't play for Coach McGuire. I played on Coach Smith's first team as a sophomore. A lot of guys on that team had been recruited by Coach McGuire. He used a lot of zone defense. I don't think his teams were quite as worried about taking good shots. If you were hot, you took the shots. But Dean put those two philosophies in, and to some degree, they were changes from the way Coach McGuire did things. It took some of the players a little time to adapt. I don't think there were any dissidents, but it was just a change, a change in the way we practiced, a change in the way we played. Coach followed Frank McGuire, who was a god. He won the national championship in 1957. There was a period of adaptation.

It all came together in the Kentucky game my junior year, Coach Smith's second year. Ironically, it was a game he won against Adolph Rupp—and he ended up breaking Rupp's record 34 years later. But his philosophies early on came together in that game. The first year we were 8-9. The second year, we had Billy Cunningham, Larry Brown. We had a good basketball team. We were not tall. Duke had a couple of 7-footers back in '63, if you can believe that. Billy Cunningham was our tallest player, and he was 6-foot-5.

We went up to Indiana and played Indiana on a Saturday afternoon in Bloomington (December 15). They had the Van Arsdale twins (Dick and Tom). The previous Friday their picture had been on the cover of *Sports Illustrated*. They were considered the two best sophomores in college. Indiana had Branch McCracken as coach, and Jimmy Rayl, one of the great shooters. They beat us pretty good (90-76). But that was Billy's first great game. We went back to our hotel in Bloomington, and we already had the films. We looked at the films and tried to figure out why it had not clicked. We really had not gotten used to the system yet. We were tentative. We went back and saw what we were supposed to do offensively and defensively. And on Sunday we got on the bus for Lexington.

Kentucky had Cotton Nash, a preseason All-American. We shot a little bit on Monday afternoon. We got to the arena at six o'clock Monday night. The freshman game had just started. The place was packed. We looked up, and all of a sudden, the score was 25-5. The Kentucky freshmen were beating the heck out of somebody. It was a really awesome place to walk into. And we hadn't played well against Indiana.

We go into the dressing room, and Coach Smith said not to worry, to assume we were playing Tennessee. He said: "Look at their jerseys, and pretend they have 'Tennessee' on them. You're not playing Kentucky, just put it out of your minds." To me and the rest of the team, that had a great psychological impact. It took the pressure off. We focused on what we had to do.

The system he put in was a box-and-one on Cotton Nash. He put Yogi Pateet, 6-foot-1, on Cotton Nash, who was 6-foot-5. The rest of us played a four-man zone. The whole philosophy of Dean's defense was, "Don't let the offense make the pass they're used to making, that they expect to make." They always wanted to get the ball to Cotton Nash. Yogi Poteet stayed right with him. They couldn't get the ball to Nash. By the end of the game, Kentucky became so frustrated that someone 6-foot-1 was able to keep the ball away from him. Everywhere he went, there was someone to help Yogi. It was a masterful defensive strategy. At the end of the game, their offense had broken down. We had taken them out of their offense, which is exactly what Coach wanted to do.

Then, on the offensive end, Coach put in what later became the Four Corners. We didn't call it the Four Corners. Dean put it in, and we called it "The Kentucky Play." Larry Brown was the point guard. The play was, he would back up toward halfcourt, and the other four of us would spread out to the four corners. Larry would drive into the middle, or come back out and dish it to one of us. We ran that play, and Larry drove to the foul line. I came from the corner and made a lay-up. It may have been the first basket out of the Four Corners. It was all working. It was all clicking. Everyone was taking good shots. If you look at the film of that game, nobody took a bad shot.

After the game, we were just ecstatic. We had beaten Kentucky (68-66), beaten Adolph Rupp, in Kentucky. I don't think we had more than ten people there from Carolina. We came in the dressing room, and I looked at Coach and said, "Coach, that's the finest game that anyone has ever coached." We knew it then. We knew he was a great coach. He was 29 years old. We were like puppets out there doing what we were supposed to. And by golly, it worked. That, to me, was the significance of the Kentucky game. I don't think he's ever coached a better game. I don't think anyone could coach a better game than he did that night in Lexington, Kentucky, in 1962.

When I was in law school, I was an assistant freshmen coach. I would come over in the afternoon and work with the freshmen. I remember one time playing over at North Carolina State. State was pretty good then. Press Maravich was their coach. We held the ball, but they had a real good team, and ended up beating us. The State fans were really rough on Coach Smith. There were two or three very tough years. But he is so incredibly principled. He knew the systems he was putting in were the right systems. He would just stay focused on his principles, and try to block everything else out.

It had to have a real adverse impact on him, but you never saw it. Those of us who were fortunate enough to be there knew the program was sound. His mind was like a computer when it came to basketball. He just kept focusing on defense, good shots on offense. It was just a matter of getting players, getting established. Once he got Larry Miller, then Charlie Scott, he was off and running, putting good athletes into the system that he had in place, with him as the coach. It just took off.

I remember the press conference when he broke Rupp's record. It was against Colorado in Winston-Salem (North Carolina). All of the former players who could get there did. There must have been 30 or 40 of us. There would have been 100 if they could have gotten there. After the game, all of the players went down to the hallway outside the dressing room. That's all we could do—there were so many of us. He got out of the press conference, and all he saw was 30 or 40 of us, lined up in the hallway. He never wants to be in the limelight. He shies away from that. But here, he couldn't avoid this great affection of 30 or 40 players who played for him. It was a very touching moment, to be in that line, see him come down that line, talking with every player.

I got back to Atlanta, and saw the clips of the press conference. Someone asked Dean:0 "What impact is this having on you? How are you reacting?" He said: "The first thing I'd like to do is thank the University of North Carolina for hiring me. The next thing, I'd like to thank all of the coaches who coached with me over the years"—and he named all of them. Then he said: "I would also like to thank all of my players who played for me. I don't have time to name them all, but I want to thank each one personally." Then he made this incredible comment. "I want to thank everyone for this moment" —then he kind of paused and added: "if indeed it is a moment." I thought: "Coach, you just broke the all-time record, you could at least call it a moment." I'll never forget that. I wrote that up, my recollections of that day, and sent it to him. It was one of the richest basketball afternoons any basketball alum could ever have.

I was shocked when he retired. I was just so sentimental about it. Our youngest child was a junior at Chapel Hill when he retired. She had heard about Coach Smith. She met him. He was a good friend to her through the years. She felt like she really knew the man, because she did. She called up the afternoon she found out in tears. This was my20-year-old daughter. The impact on her was significant. She said: "How could this happen?"

I knew it was going to come at some point. I didn't think it would take place when it did. But I think back on it, and it was just like Coach Smith. Beautifully planned. Everything considered. It was just like putting in a play to score the winning basket when the buzzer goes off. And it was based on loyalty. Bill Guthridge is a fantastic coach. Bill Guthridge deserved to be a head coach. And Dean made sure Bill Guthridge was a head coach.

When I watched the press conference, I thought: "Maybe it's not that surprising." It was planned to a t. He was in total control of the whole process. His loyalty to Bill Guthridge, talking to all of the other assistants . . . it was just like scouting a team getting ready to play a game. I continue to be sentimental about it. That's a 34-year era in college basketball that will never be matched.

DOUG MOE

Moe played at North Carolina from 1958-59 to 1960-61 before becoming a three-time ABA All-Star and a head coach for 15 seasons with the San Antonio Spurs, Denver Nuggets and Philadelphia 76ers.

Doug Moe

The thing that makes Smitty so great is that not only is he a great coach, but he just cares about the people that he's been involved with. I never actually played for him—he was my assistant coach. But he was always telling me that I had to go back to school when I was out and hadn't finished. And I was always saying: "No sweat, Coach. I'm going back to school."

It just so happened I was working in Durham, North Carolina, selling insurance. He called on a Monday morning and said: "Look, I've got you an interview with Bill Miller, the coach at Elon College." He told me what time to be there. He said: "Wear a coat and tie and be on time." Then he hung up the phone.

I went over and met with Coach Miller, then the president, and ended up an assistant coach while I finished school, which I would have never, ever done on my own. It was one of those things he did on his own. I didn't know. I didn't ask him to. I never thought about going back at the time.

He did that, and then I was at Elon College, finishing up after two years. A couple of representatives from the Italian League came over. They wanted to bring (Billy) Cunningham to Italy. Well, Dean knew that Cunningham was going to the NBA. He said: "Forget Cunningham, you've got to get Moe." They flew me to Italy that spring, and I ended up playing there two years. It was an unbelievable experience.

A few years later North Carolina was in the NCAA Final Four in Louisville. I got a call from Coach Smith. I was in Italy. It was after the season. He said that the ABA was starting up. Larry Brown was his assistant coach. Babe McCarthy was in the room. So was my father, who followed North Carolina. This was before the Final Four, the day before, two days before. I talked to Larry. I talked to Babe McCarthy. I ended up in the ABA.

That's not unusual, what he did for me. He does it for everyone. That's just the way he is. He tries to help all his players. He doesn't make a big deal about it. He just does those things.

There's no telling how much I owe him. I have no clue to this day where I'd be had he not called and made me go back to school. That was the number-one thing. Finishing school gave me confidence. I don't know what would have happened if I hadn't—I can only speculate. But I know I wouldn't like to find out, either. I'm very happy with the way things turned out. I'm sure it would have been different. I can't imagine my life being as good as it has been without him.

BILLY CUNNINGHAM

Cunningham, a star at North Carolina from 1962-63 to 1964-65, was inducted into the Basketball Hall of Fame in 1985, and named one of the NBA's 50 greatest players of all-time in 1997. He recalls the events of January 6, 1965—the night Dean Smith was hung in effigy.

We were struggling as a team. We played at Wake Forest and got beat (107-85). We came back on the bus, and when we got in front of Woollen Gym, there in the tree was Dean Smith hanging in effigy.

Initially, we didn't know what the devil it was. Then someone explained it. We were very upset. We made sure it came out of the tree. I would guess it was about four feet tall. There was no crowd—it was late in the evening. I was part of the group that took it down.

We were mostly upset because we realized it wasn't his fault. It was the way we were performing. I realized that he was limited because the school was basically on a form of probation.

We had great success under Frank McGuire. Everyone expected things to be the same, even though we were on probation. As we know, it just doesn't happen that way.

He was limited with regard to recruiting. He couldn't recruit outside the state. At the time, there was still segregation. I would say the level of play in the state was fair, at best. We had several guys on the team—starters, guys who were factors on the team—who were walk-ons. That's something you didn't find very often. Maybe there would be one at what you would consider a big-time program.

To say I knew at the time that he would be a special coach, no. I didn't know that. I knew he was an excellent coach, but who would know at that time that he was special? His greatest quality that he was able to develop through the rough times was his concern for all of his players. He was concerned even when he didn't have the opportunity to recruit the players who were there. He was concerned about the sixteenth player as much as he was the first.

I was recruited by Frank McGuire. He went to coach the Philadelphia Warriors when I was a freshman. I did have second thoughts about staying. But I decided to stick with my decision. We were very good my freshman year because there were a lot of players in place. Larry Brown was there. The only bad year really was my junior year—that's when Dean was hung in effigy. We got better my senior year, won seven of our last eight games.

I could see as my career at Carolina went on that he was such a detail person, such a teacher. I could see how we would work, how practices were

Billy Cunningham

broken down to the minute. I could see how much I was learning as a player, how much better we were getting as a team. I realized at the end of my career that things were going to be better at Carolina after I left.

After you're away from something and have a chance to watch from the outside, after you're away from the forest, you could see the growth. It's the old story: He needed talent, but once he had some talent, how he developed it was just beautiful. He was a great coach, a brilliant man. He would have been successful at anything he did. He had a passion. He just loved it. He still loves it, but not at the level he demands of himself. Knowing him, if he couldn't give everything of himself to his players it was time to move on.

I was a little surprised he lasted as long as he did. What was it, more than 35 years? That's a long time to coach, a long time to recruit—I know he never enjoyed that part of it, going out and recruiting the kids. And to still have that passion, that's beautiful.

I used to go down every summer and spend time with him when I was coaching. I'd look at his films. He'd look at my films. We'd talk about different things, possible changes to help our teams, both ways. We'd spend a couple of days doing that. He had a very good feel for the pro game. He was a basketball person. The 24-second clock, dealing with different types of personalities — that might have been something he didn't understand or grasp. He wasn't around those players all the time. But he was very helpful.

Getting hung in effigy, if something like that happened today with a coach, I don't know if he would have lasted. It's on ESPN, the alumni are up in arms. But he got through that. It just shows you, you can't listen to the fans.

BOB LEWIS

Lewis, a 6-foot-3 guard, averaged 27.4 points per game as a junior, the highest total in Dean Smith's 36 years as Carolina's head coach. He scored 49 points against Florida State on December 16, 1965, a Carolina record. Smith reached the Final Four for the first time in 1966-67, Lewis' senior season. Lewis, a resident of Edgewater, Maryland, is a theatrical technician at the John F. Kennedy Center in Washington, D.C.

If I'm not mistaken, I was Coach Smith's first recruit, coming out of St. John's in Washington, D.C. Billy Cunningham, of course, was the big star. But he was recruited by Frank McGuire. The guys before him—Doug Moe, Larry Brown, those guys—were also recruited by Frank McGuire.

It was in 1963 when I headed down to North Carolina. Not only was I a young man, but Coach Smith was a young man, in his early 30s. He came up here with Donnie Walsh. Billy Cunningham and Larry Brown also helped recruit me, and Ken Rosemond—an assistant at that time—was there, too. He was just a great guy.

I had visited Kentucky, six or seven other schools. Carolina at that time was a very small school. There are something like 24,000 students now. But I think there were less than 10,000 at that time. The campus was tiny. The gym we played in, Woollen Gym, only seated 5,000. We practiced in a thing called the Tin Can that was built in 1924. I remember at Woollen, students A to L could go to one game, L to Z could go to the next. It was just different. Basketball was big back then, but nothing like it is today. Those guys are like rock stars now.

Coach Smith was very influential when talking to my parents. Education is his game. He said that if I came to North Carolina, he would do everything possible to make sure I got a degree. That, of course, is what every parent wants to hear. I went down there. The campus was gorgeous. I had a great time. I decided, "Hey, this is the place I want to go." I met Tom Gauntlett in August. We were roommates all four years. And we're still friends 36 years later.

Our freshman team was very, very good. We even played the varsity a few times and gave them a pretty good run. At that time, Billy Cunningham was the big star, of course. The other players were good, but most were from down in North Carolina. And of course there were no blacks. They weren't allowed. In Washington D.C., I had played against only blacks. It was a big difference going there.

The program was just starting to build. My sophomore year, Billy was a senior. That's when everyone thought, "Here we go. We're going to do this. We're going to do that." But we didn't. Billy was, is and always will be a great player. Everyone thought, there was only one ball, here are Bob Lewis and Billy Cunningham, there's going to be a problem. But Billy and I really played well together.

Coach Smith brought me along very, very well. I was just a kid. A very thin kid. There was a big difference going from freshman to varsity, physically. I watch these kids go today from high school to the NBA, they're phenomenal. We struggled that year. Billy and I had a pretty good scoring average together, probably 50 points a game between us. But we couldn't get over the hump.

I remember the night Coach Smith was hung in effigy. I didn't see it right away. The buses weren't luxury liners like they are now. They had these little two-inch windows. But we pulled up, and it was right dead in front of Woollen Gym. I remember getting off. Billy was the senior. He was the leader. Most of the other guys were sophomores and juniors. We were sort of stunned. Billy got out, went over and pulled it down. We were all just shocked about it.

Bob Lewis

The talk was that Coach Smith might have been in some kind of trouble with the alumni or administration. Basketball was important down there. We weren't winning. Billy and I were there. We were expected to do better. And we knew from then on it was important for us to win. There might not have been any problem. The president of the university might have called Coach Smith in his office and said everything was fine. But we didn't know that.

We never doubted him. Whatever he told us to do, we did. I never remember a huddle where Coach said he wanted us to do something and we were like: "No, that won't work." It's not the coach. It's the people on the court. We were giving everything he had. But it was more of a balanced league at that time. If you don't have the players, you can't win. I don't want to reflect badly on anybody on the team. We were doing our best.

When Ken Rosemond left for Georgia, there was talk of some of us transferring, because that freshman team was so close. Ken was my freshman coach. I spent 90 percent of my time with him, not Coach Smith. He was with the varsity. I would only go to him if I had to. He would speak to me going back and forth to practice, but I didn't deal much with Coach Smith. Ken Rosemond was my man. We had a great freshman team. All the guys on that team were close. Then, all of a sudden, this thing came up about Ken going to Georgia.

As kids back then, you didn't think about that. You thought, "He's here for life, I can always go to him, talk to him like my dad." There was, at one time, talk of transferring. Nobody ever did. Ken Rosemond was not involved in any of that. He was as loyal as he could ever be. And Coach Smith, I'm sure, was influential in getting him his job. It was a good move for everyone. As far as transferring, nothing happened.

The next year, Billy left, and Coach Smith recruited Larry Miller. He was a sophomore when I was a junior, and we started playing pretty well. The following year, we got Rusty Clark, Dick Grubar, Bill Bunting, that great class. That was my senior year. That's when it took off. Coach Smith brought along a very young team. I was the only senior who started. Larry was a junior. Everyone else was sophomores.

That first Final Four, we all knew about UCLA with Lew Alcindor. And everyone had heard about the great Elvin Hayes. We knew those teams were there. We thought: "All right, we're going to play Dayton." But Donnie May was a darn good player. We didn't play well. We struggled and lost (76-62). But we had come a long way. And we had Charlie Scott coming. The year before, I went down with Coach and recruited Charlie at the Laurinburg Institute.

Going to Carolina, it was the first time I had ever experienced segregation. It had never entered my mind. I never thought about it. It was just strange. Recruiting Charlie, I wanted to get anyone who could help Carolina win. He was a great guy, and also a terrific player. We became friends. He was a freshman when I was a senior. Myself and Tom Gauntlett, we kind of took him under our wing. I had helped recruit a lot of people, like everyone does. But Charlie was pretty special.

Coach Smith was always on top of every single person's classes. We had people that made sure everyone was going to class and working toward getting their degree. He kept a very watchful eye on all the students. We were young kids. We wanted to party. And Carolina is a pretty nice place to party. We did our partying. But we put it all together. Coach Smith was the man in charge, and he had the respect of everyone. You did not want to disrespect him. We dressed properly. We were pretty decent young guys back then.

When I was there, Coach Smith wasn't a big superstar, wasn't THE coach, wasn't an 800-win guy. He was just a young guy trying to get into the business. But he was exactly the same person he is today. It was 37 years ago. And every year for 37 years, he has sent me a team brochure and a letter. It's a form letter now—so many people have gone through the program. But at the bottom of each letter, he writes a little note.

The one I just got said, "Bob, I'm late with the brochure this year. I started with 1998 seniors and went back to 1962." That's every player on the team. Not just Bob Lewis, Larry Miller and Billy Cunningham. Every single person. They're all treated the same.

The note continues, "Hope your daughter is enjoying Vanderbilt, and will do well there academically and athletically. Best wishes in 1999 and always to B.J." — that's my wife — "and your mom. Call me if you could use a couple of tickets to our Maryland game. Best, Dean."

Now, c'mon. Thirty-six years have passed. I'm 54 years old. And I'm still getting these letters. There's nobody in the world like that. That's how he is. And you know what? I called him and went to the Maryland game.

LARRY MILLER

Miller, a 6-foot-4 guard from Catasauqua, Pennsylvania, was believed to be headed for Duke before he chose North Carolina. He scored in double figures a school-record 64 consecutive games and helped lead the Tar Heels to ACC tournament championships and Final Fours in his final two seasons, 1966-67 and 1967-68.

Back then, they didn't contact you until usually your junior or senior year. Duke started recruiting me as a freshman.

I got to know Coach (Vic) Bubas and his wife real well. They used to come up to Pennsylvania in the summertime. I was probably the most recruited player that year. At the time, not all of the colleges were integrated. You still had some that were not recruiting black athletes. I was recruited by everyone. I got letters from the Kennedys, suggesting Ivy League schools. It got to be pretty hectic at the end.

I only visited Duke, Carolina, Michigan and Michigan State. The day I was at Michigan was the day President Kennedy got shot. Needless to say, that wasn't a good trip. I got all kinds of offers. Cash offers. Cars. One school gave me a blank piece of paper and said write in what you want. Another school offered me a clothing account, a car when I was a sophomore— you couldn't have one as a freshman—free airfare for me and my family and a summer job making more than my dad was making at the time working for Mack Truck.

I'd feel these people out. I'd never ask for anything, but I'd see what they would suggest, just to see where they were coming from. I'd just listen, and they kept on talking. I knew I never was going to take anything. That wasn't part of the plan.

It came down to Duke and Carolina. I was going to decide before my graduation on June 8. I told Coach Bubas and Coach Smith that I would make my decision, invite one of them to my graduation and sign a letter-of-intent. But the truth was, even that day I wasn't sure.

I liked both those guys. I had really grown fond of Coach Bubas. So, I asked my parents. They didn't finish high school because of the Depression. I said: "What school do you like better?" They liked both. I said: "Which coach do you like better?" They said both were perfectly nice gentlemen. And they said I was going to have to make the decision, and live with it the rest of my life.

Carolina had a great reputation, but was sort of in a down period. Duke had been in the NCAA final the year before. They called me before the start of the national-championship game. But I just had a feeling that Carolina was the place for me. I felt like maybe we could do something.

Duke had a feeling toward the end that I was leaning toward Carolina. Bucky Waters was Coach Bubas' assistant. They came up to Pennsylvania. We were talking in their motel room, and they almost had me in tears. But Coach Bubas, he was a gentleman. He wrote me a letter when I signed with Carolina that I swore I wouldn't open up until after I graduated. I knew I'd break down in tears. Coach Bubas came up to me after we beat them in my final game in the ACC tournament and shook my hand. I told him about the letter. It was incredible. He wished me all the best. He wished me all the best, even though he knew I'd be only about eight minutes away.

I get too much credit (for Smith's breakthrough). It was a combination of things that all had to converge. Coach Smith had to be the right headmaster, had to know what he was doing. He was an innovator. And he had to recruit a second class behind me—Dick Grubar, Bill Bunting, Rusty

Clark, those guys. That had to happen. If that didn't happen, I would have led the nation in scoring, but we wouldn't have won. And we also had a great player named Bob Lewis. He was one of the reasons I came there. I saw him play in high school. I knew that if I could compete with him, I could become a good college player.

Everything had to fall into place. Maybe those guys came because I was there, but then, we had to get Charlie (Scott), too. He had already committed to Davidson when he visited Chapel Hill. We took him to dinner, he and his advisor. He was from New York, but he was going to school in Laurinburg, North Carolina. Charlie didn't say a word at dinner. I was thinking: "This guy doesn't like us." Dick Grubar and I took him out after, and got him to open up. We told him that we could have a chance for the national title. He was the key guy. He was not only the first prominent black player, but a great basketball player. He was a smart, intelligent person. He opened up the door at Carolina for black athletes. A lot of things came into place back at that time.

The kids in my recruiting class were good in high school. But as freshmen, we went to Duke, and they had seven high school All-Americans on their team. By my senior year, I was the only one who actually had playing time. But our freshman team beat them at Duke. I told Coach Smith it was one of the greatest wins we ever had. The students at Duke showed no mercy. They used to say that I used so much grease in my hair, I needed an oil change every 30 days. To win over there, against that team, was an incredible upset.

He promised the parents that he would look out for the kids, and that included religion. I was a Catholic, and we used to have to go to St. Thomas More. We'd have to bring back programs from each Sunday's service. At that time, I was kind of disenchanted with the church. I just told him I wasn't going to go anymore. He said: "What about your parents?" I said if I was home, I wouldn't be going, I'm not going to be hypocritical and go here. I guess I was the first one to challenge that. Billy Cunningham was a senior. He used to wake us up and take us to church every Sunday.

Coach Smith was very flexible with things like that. But he was also very, very strict. He was inflexible on certain things, missing practice, missing class. There weren't any excuses. If you had a class scheduled or a lab scheduled during practice, you went to the lab or the class. If he heard you were missing class, he brought you in. The on-time thing, if you were one minute late for the bus, the bus was gone. If you were one minute late for practice, you'd run the stairs. I remember one time during the holidays, Charlie came in like an hour late. All of us were thinking: "This is not going to be good." Charlie got there, and Coach told him to put on the weighted vest and start running the stairs. It seemed like he ran the rest of practice. He had a better workout than we did.

When I was a sophomore, Bob Lewis and myself became the key players. We went to Ohio State and ran the Four Corners, ran it in a way for Bob and I to isolate ourselves in the middle. We utilized every resource we had available to us. I remember that game quite well. We went to Ohio State and won on their court (82-72) Between us, we must have had 60 to 70 points. We only missed four or five field goals. It was a lot of layups. It was like shooting ducks.

That same year, we were playing Duke in the finals of the ACC tournament. They had the best team in the country. We could have beaten them. We played a solid game. But they didn't want to come out and guard us. We were going to try the same strategy, isolate myself and Bob Lewis. But we lost (21-20).

The next year, we changed our style—Grubar, Clark and those guys were now sophomores, and they joined the team. The offense no longer isolated me. We started running fast breaks, pressing defenses, traps, a motion offense. All these things were new to the game at that point. All of a sudden, we went from a team winning 16 games in a season to one of the top four teams in the country. We became the favorites, overtook Duke.

You could see things were changing. And you could see that Coach Smith was very confident. Every situation that could come up in a game, we worked on in practice. Back then, we had the jump ball. We had to cover every jump-ball situation. One game against Georgia Tech my junior year, we ran a play with one second left. We had to throw the ball the full length of the court. He designed a play almost exactly like the play Grant Hill and Christian Laettner did against Kentucky. It just so happened that Rusty couldn't hit the shot. But this was 30 years ago.

We went to the Final Four my last two years, but back then, the ACC tournament was king. The NCAA tournament was almost a letdown. The ACC was such a big event in the south. You had to win three straight games in three days. You couldn't lose, or you went home. The pressure was enormous. My stomach was in knots for three days. My parents didn't come down because it would be a distraction. I wanted to totally focus on that thing.

I wasn't surprised the program became what it did. You had all the ingredients covered. It was a great school, number one. It won a national championship in '57. You could see the recruits starting to come visit. By the time I was there, some great players were coming to look at the school. And with Coach Smith being there, there was a lot of support from the University. The fans were excited about everything. It looked like it would take something awful to go the other way. Now that you had that recruiting built up, high-school kids noticed. Now they get to see everyone on TV. The pros enter into it now, and money becomes a big issue. But back then, it was built on reputation on success.

We still keep in touch. I just got a letter from him two days ago. He said to make sure that I said hello to my sister and mother. We try to get together at least once a year for lunch. We usually contact each other about four or five times a year. The former players get a media guide every year of the current team. It's 260 pages thick, as big as any publication in the country.

To this day, I consider it my second home. It's just like it was yesterday.

DICK GRUBAR

Grubar, a 6-foot-4 guard, was part of Smith's breakthrough 1965 recruiting class that went on to reach three consecutive Final Fours. He was an assistant coach at Virginia Commonwealth and Florida for seven years, then returned to North Carolina to enter the real-estate business. He was a city councilman in Greensboro from 1989 to '97.

You knew all the pieces were in place. The key to the puzzle was having the 7-footer in Rusty Clark. I thought the size was there. We had two superstars already in the program—Bob Lewis and Larry Miller. I thought there was an opportunity to be very good.

At the time I was being recruited I was 6-3 or 6-4. I played every position in high school. Most other colleges recruited me as a small forward. I had no interest in being a forward in college. I knew I'd be banging heads with guys much bigger. He indicated to me that he needed a point guard, and that he would give me a good shot at playing point guard. That's what I wanted to do.

I had handled the ball in high school. And I knew he was telling me the truth. He had already signed Rusty Clark, Bill Bunting and Joe Brown—they were all forwards and centers. I was the only guard. He signed Gerald Tuttle after me. I signed late, the end of April, or early May. It was an opportunity to play the position I wanted. And I felt good about Coach Smith. He was a very believable person. And he has proven that to be the truth.

It was the best choice I've made in my life, without a doubt. I came from a Catholic high school, and was considering Notre Dame and Boston College—(Bob) Cousy was the coach at Boston College at that time. Then Kentucky—Pat Riley was from my area (Schenectady, N.Y.) He was three years ahead of me. I looked at Kentucky very seriously. I was going there until December of my senior year. But Coach Rupp, I never met the guy even when I visited in the fall. He came to visit me. But it was not about basketball. It was about Coach Rupp.

Dick Grubar

We had a freshman team. That spring, while I was being recruited, Dean hired Larry Brown to be his assistant. He was one heck of a recruiter, very personable. He was our freshman coach. He was go-go Carolina. But he also was a really good teacher. He worked with us pretty much exclusively. Coach Smith worked with the varsity. We played them, the freshmen vs. the varsity—and we beat 'em, before a crowd. I think it was the last time he did that. For Coach Brown, it was like winning the national championship. Maybe the sophomores, juniors and seniors weren't there yet. We played later in the season, and they beat us—but not in front of a crowd. We went on to go 15-1 as freshmen. Our only loss was to Virginia Tech at Virginia Tech.

A defining moment for us as sophomores was when we had to go play Kentucky at Kentucky. It was our fourth game of the season. They were coming off their loss in the national championship game to Texas Western. They had Louie Dampier and Pat Riley. They were ranked in the top five in the country. But we beat them (64-55). The confidence Dean gave us to win at Kentucky gave us the confidence to carry it from there. It gave us an opportunity to say: "We've got something special here."

Dean is probably the king of masking his emotions. He never really got very high. I've never seen him very low. He's as good as anybody at keeping a level course. But you've got to put it in perspective. The NCAA tournament wasn't as big then as it is today. There was more interest in the ACC tournament than the Eastern Regionals or the Final Four, especially from the fans. The pressure was to win the ACC tournament — you had to do that to move on. We won three regular-season titles, but we still had to win the tournament. That's where the pressure was. We kind of let up after that, going on to the Eastern Regionals, then the Final Four.

The first year, we were a very good team. We got to the semi-finals, and got beat by Ohio State—Donnie May went 13-for-16. It was a game we thought we should have won. The next year we did get to the final, but we lost to UCLA. Kareem was the greatest player there was then, no doubt about it. (But) Coach changed our game. He decided he wanted to hold it early so they didn't get away. The feeling on the team was, we were ready to play, we didn't want to hold the ball. We ended up not doing either well, and getting demolished. The third year, I got hurt in the ACC final. I didn't get to play at all in the Regional or the Final Four. All I remember is walking out on crutches.

He was a guiding light in getting me into coaching. I thought that was a natural progression for me. He was a big reason I did that. I respected him, what he tried to do. But back then, there were no (recruiting) rules, like there are today. You were active seven days a week, 24 hours a day, 12 months a year. You never caught a break, especially as an assistant. You were recruiting, scouting—or recruiting. You could go away on trips for 15 or 20 days. I'd come in for a game, then go back on the road. I got to be 27 or 28 and said: "Is this what I want to do my whole life?" People see the grandeur of

Dean Smith or Bobby Knight. But a lot of coaches have tough lives. It got to the point where I wanted to move on.

He was influential in that, too. Most people get caught up in trying to make as much money as they can. His whole philosophy was, that's fine, but you also need to enjoy what you do, and over the course of time, everything will take care of itself. That's very truthful. Any career decisions that I thought about making, it's not that he told me what to do, but I'd run it by him. As I got further away, it got harder for him. He had more and more players doing that.

He always talked to us about giving back, needing to give back to the community. That was why I became a city councilman. I thought that was an area where I could give back to my community. He was very big on using basketball to take you to some other level. Basketball wasn't the end-all, be-all. At school, be a part of the student body. He talked about sacrifice. Working to make your community better.

RUSTY CLARK

Clark, a 6-foot-10 center from Fayetteville, North Carolina, also was part of the 1965 recruiting class that helped transform North Carolina into a national power.

I've heard him say that he might have been fired if he hadn't recruited me. He's mighty nice to say that, but Dean always gave me far more credit than I ever deserved. I think that if I had never gone to Carolina, he still would have had the same record. He had good teams, a nucleus of really good athletes. He was fortunate to have a couple of superstars. But what made it work was chemistry. What was unique about Dean was his ability to draw from the talent pool he had. If he had five kids on the floor, they worked better as a team than they did individually. That, to me, was a great coach. He raised us to a different level than we ever could have reached individually. It was like having an extra person on your team.

I had pretty strong family ties to Chapel Hill. My parents had both gone there. I grew up a Tar Heel fan. I looked at some other schools, too. I thought I was going to go to Davidson for a long time. Lefty Driesell was there. They had a real good program. I looked at Virginia, too, for a while, but not too seriously. I had a Morehead scholarship to Carolina, a nonathletic scholarship. It was a combination of things that made me go there. The scholarship had a lot to do with it.

He was very nice. I liked him. He always said the right things. And it impressed me that he was very sincere about my education. That was very important to me. I never dreamed of being a professional ballplayer. I was a zoology major, pre-med. He convinced me and my parents that basketball would not interfere with my ability to do my coursework, that he would do everything he could to make sure there was no conflict. And he did that. I had a pretty demanding workload. With most coaches, it would have caused a great conflict. If it did with Coach Smith, he hid it well.

He adjusted practices. He adjusted times. He did all kinds of things, not just for me, but other guys, too. But he probably did as much for me as anybody else—my schedule happened to be demanding. I had a lot of labs. He made sure that practice started a little later the days that I had labs. He did some really nice things to keep me involved with the team. And anytime someone needed help, maybe some tutoring, he always seemed to offer that. He said that he would do that during recruiting. But it's one thing to say it, and another thing to do it. He did that beyond what I even expected.

They had some guys before us. No one ever talks about that. They had Billy Cunningham, Larry Brown. They were winning 15, 16 games a year. It's not like he had a losing record when we came. He just hadn't won an ACC tournament. But he had some very competitive teams and some All-Americans. He got a lot of mileage out of those guys. He had some mighty good ball teams. They were not the bottom of the league. And the program was still under recruiting restrictions then. They were at a disadvantage. I think a lot of people forget that, give our team a little more credit than we deserve. He fosters that to some extent. He's very generous when he talks about us.

I don't know that when you're 18 years old you think you're going to be part of taking a program to another level. It's not something you can conceptualize. I don't think I did, anyway. I knew we had some talented guys—Coach would let you know what was going on, the people he had recruited. And he had some North Carolina guys coming in. I had played with Bill Bunting in some All-Star games. Joe Brown and I had gone to basketball camp together. It was exciting to play with people you knew.

At that time, Duke was the hot team. They had been winning. They had Art Heyman and Jeff Mullins. They were the top team in the country for several years. We were just a bunch of little sophomores. Of course, we had Bob Lewis and Larry Miller. Lewis was a senior then, Miller a junior. They were All-Americans. But we started three sophomores. It was like starting three freshmen today. We certainly were not favored to win everything. And even after we won the ACC tournament and went to the Final Four, the sportswriters still picked Duke in our junior year. Dominant as Duke was, it took a while to change opinions.

We won the ACC tournament, went to the Final Four and were ranked in the top two or three each of my three years. At that time, UCLA was pretty dominant. With the exception of them, we could play with anyone in the country. He had raised the program to a national level. But I'm not sure when you were our age that you had a chance to view it the way you do now. You just look at it differently now.

Coach Smith is an extremely intellectual person. He has a Master's in statistics. If you've ever taken statistics, that would let you understand how his mind works. He had this value system, points for scoring, points for rebounds. Offensive rebounds were different than defensive rebounds. Turnovers were in there. You could go through a game and have 25 points and 10 rebounds, but if you had enough turnovers, screwed up enough, you could be negative four. Likewise, if you scored four points and played a real good fundamental game, you could have a plus number. It was a very complex system. We had a fairly complex defensive system. It kind of set the tone for a lot of defenses of the day. He was quite a scholar in developing defenses and offenses. And he had a tremendous ability to teach us his system. It was a real privilege to play for him.

The whole four years, I never heard him say a cuss word, which is almost unheard of in the sports arena. We had some tense moments. But he was a different kind of guy. I remember my junior year, I was taking a philosophy course, comparison of religions. We got into some very interesting philosophies. Then the team went to L.A. for the Final Four. He had dinner lined up for me with a philosopher, whom I had studied. The philosopher autographed a book for me. That's not what you usually do when you go to the Final Four.

He thinks as a full person. It's not just run, sweat, shoot, score. There's a great deal of depth to him. I appreciated that. He allowed me to grow. He didn't try to limit me to organized athletics. He stressed that, did everything he could to encourage you. But he was very concerned with your mental growth, your well-being. The whole person.

CHARLES SCOTT

In 1966, Scott became one of the first black athletes to earn an athletic scholarship at a southern school, heading to North Carolina after attending Laurinburg (North Carolina) Prep. He led the Tar Heels to their second and third straight Final Fours in 1968 and '69, earned the ABA Rookie of the Year award with the Virginia Squires in 1971 and won an NBA championship with the Boston Celtics in 1976.

He is president of a sports marketing company in Atlanta.

The obstacles I faced, I expected. If you were in the South in the '60s, you expected to be called "nigger". When it happened, there wasn't anything new about it. You go to Clemson or Alabama, and they're playing "Dixie," you expected that. They weren't going to be singing, "Glory, Hallelujah!" When I made the choice, I knew there would be some problems, I knew these things were going to happen. I do not compare myself in any shape or form to Jackie Robinson. But the correlation was, when Jackie Robinson went to play baseball, the names he was called didn't surprise him. When it happened, it was not unexpected.

Coach Smith said that if I came there, I'd have to understand the situation. I'd have to deal with it, and deal with it in a certain way. He also said that there were probably some people at North Carolina who didn't want me to go there. But he made me feel very comfortable about coming and playing. He felt he had a good program. He said I could be part of it, part of starting the North Carolina tradition.

It was necessary. It had to be done. Someone had to break that barrier. It was going to be done sooner or later. Taking on that responsibility, I knew there would be hardships. And I knew I could not respond to them. Those were things I accepted. They were not wanted. But they were understood.

I originally wasn't planning to go to North Carolina. I had verbally committed to signing with Davidson and playing for Lefty Driesell. I was not planning on making any changes. I wanted to sign a letter of intent at the earliest time possible. But my high-school coach wanted me to wait. I looked at other schools to honor his wishes.

He used to take me up to North Carolina all the time—Laurinburg was only an hour-and-a-half from Chapel Hill. We used to go watch the games. My first contact was probably with Larry Brown. But I remember meeting Coach Smith for the first time. He always wanted to know what you wanted to be called. Everyone called me Charlie. He asked me: "What do you want me to call you?" I told him, and he called me "Charles." He always has called me "Charles." That makes an impression on you.

The other thing I remember is that he took me to church with him. You've got to remember that was at a time when blacks weren't going to church with whites. For the choice I was making, that had a great impression on me. I had been to 20 or 30 other schools. I hadn't been to church with any of the other coaches. I had seen Lefty seven or eight times. I never went to church with him. It was a personal thing. In the South, it was a very personal thing. It showed me a lot about Coach Smith's church, his whole approach. What he was doing was not just a singular thing. He didn't want me to come just to play basketball. He felt I was part of the whole community.

Those were the first things that really stood out. Carolina wasn't a top school at the time. Coach Smith was not as revered. This was at a time when he was just trying to build. The thing you remember about him was his personality. He has always been a paternal type of individual, a father-type figure. He is a no-nonsense person. You first meet Lefty Driesell, he's more a friendly figure. When you meet Bobby Knight, you don't think of him as that. Coach Smith is not mean, but he's not a guy you joke with. We still call him, "Coach." That in itself speaks of his impact.

When Coach Smith recruited me, the biggest thing was that I didn't stay with one player. I had meetings with the players I'd be playing with—Dick Grubar, Larry Miller. That to me was a key. I thought: "If they accept me now, when I come later, it won't be a big change." The guys at Davidson were graduating. You didn't know how you would fit in. I knew how I'd fit in at Carolina. And Coach Smith gave me the feeling that he was someone who would watch out for you.

Lefty was very upset. I don't think he ever got over it. It was like: "Just think, if you had gone to Davidson, it might be me and not Coach Smith they're talking about." I was the first black in the South all the other blacks had to look up to. That's why they all followed—Bob McAdoo, Walter Davis, Phil Ford. They all followed one another. They all felt Carolina was the school to go to, because it was the one that had opened up to blacks. That was a time of rebellion, too. I could rebel, but I still understood that I had a responsibility to make sure other blacks came to North Carolina.

I remember the ACC tournament final against Duke in 1969. The biggest thing about that game, Dick Grubar was hurt. We were down nine to Duke at halftime. At that point, everyone was emotional. Coach Smith never lost faith in us. He kept us doing the same things, over and over again. There were times he allowed me to take control. He felt that was where the game would be going. He showed that faith in me. Coach Smith didn't do that too often with players. When he showed that faith, I felt I had to respond in similar fashion. (Scott scored 40 points, and Carolina won, 85-74.)

Without Dick, we were actually changing our team in the middle of the NCAA tournament. We had to readjust. We had played together for so long, spent two years together. All of a sudden, we lost a key player, our point guard. It was tough. The game against Davidson (in the Eastern Regional final) was tougher. And not just because it was against Lefty, and that whole thing.

John Roche had just been voted ACC Player of the Year. I was extremely disappointed. I thought there were racial connotations. At one point, I thought about not playing the game. At another point, I thought it would be better to prove my point than not to play. That was the day of the game.

It had all gotten out in the open after I was asked about it. It was festering inside all along. When someone asks you about it, then you vent how you feel. If someone hadn't asked, I wouldn't have vented. When someone asked me, it gave me a forum to say how I felt. Especially when you're 18, 19 years old, you want to react.

I didn't make the team bus. Coach Smith called a team meeting. He told them exactly what it was. He told them I had a right to do it. More than worrying about the team, he was worrying about how I felt. He told the other guys that I had a right to feel the way I felt. I eventually came over with an assistant coach, John Lotz, who had been trying to talk me into playing. The game vindicated me in my own mind, gave me satisfaction (Scott hit a long jumper at the buzzer to give Carolina an 87-85 victory). But I never got the award.

Coach Smith's coaching style is Coach Smith's philosophy on life. The first thing he always told us was, play every game like it's your last. Therefore, when you look back on it, you won't say: "I wish I would have done that." If you did the best you could, no one could ask any more. That's something you took into life. The loyalty he taught us—he had undying loyalty. He never blamed us for anything. He was always behind us. He always said: "Don't worry." His coaching philosophy was his life.

Your relationship gets better with him after you leave, mostly because you're older. After you leave school, you understand what he's saying, what he's trying to do. When you're playing, and you're 17, 18 years old, you want to play. "Why is this guy restricting me? Why is he not playing me?" You're an athlete. But when you get out, when you get married and especially when you have children, you understand that he was not just teaching us about basketball. He was teaching us how to be good husbands, good parents, good businessmen. How to be successful in life.

Eddie Fogler is a perfect example. Eddie Fogler's father gave Coach Smith hell for three years. Eddie came out of New York City. He was all-city. He went to Carolina, and the first two years he didn't start. Dick Grubar started. His father gave Coach Smith hell. But Eddie Fogler is where he is because of Coach Smith. Look at Roy Williams—he never played. Jim Delany was another one. These guys never even got to play.

I was really Coach Smith's first ballplayer. Larry Miller and Bob Lewis came before me, but they didn't have great pro careers. Larry Brown and Billy Cunningham weren't really recruited by Coach Smith. I was his first recruit to do a lot of things—Olympic team, NBA, All-Star teams, Rookie of the Year. I look at myself today, I am a product of his teachings. I'm very thankful. These things got me to where I am today.

Everyone's success was directly intertwined with Coach Smith's involvement. My values on life, my values on family, they all came from Coach Smith. These are the things that make me happy. And I didn't have those values before I met Coach Smith. Our relationship was built more on longevity than what we did while we were in school. Our lives—everyone's lives at North Carolina—would not be the same if not for Coach Smith. All of us would have to say that.

He has always been a father figure. Look at Michael (Jordan) when his father died—Coach Smith was the first person he tried to reach. It's impossible to measure this man's value to his players. I remember when we used to make fun of him. No one liked their coach in college—he disciplined you. But no one had any idea the type of influence that Coach Smith would have on so many people over a long period of time.

Chapter Two

THE SEVENTIES

BILL CHAMBERLAIN

Chamberlain, the second black to play at North Carolina, is a teacher at the East Laurinburg (North Carolina) Alternative Learning Academy and the high-school basketball coach at the Laurinburg Institute.

I came to Carolina in '68. Being from the same neighborhood as Charles Scott, I didn't know a lot about the rest of the country. I hadn't traveled much, for sure. But Charlie put North Carolina on the map to me. And so did the Laurinburg Institute. A lot of guys from Harlem had gone to Laurinburg—Earl Manigault, Skipper Hayes and Charlie Davis; George Frazier, Billy Avery, Al Williams and many others. The state of North Carolina opened up via the Laurinburg Institute for a lot of kids from the city.

I was very fortunate to have two solid parents, and a great high-school coach at Long Island Lutheran—The Rev. Ed Visscher. He was a mentor to me. With all the attention I was getting, from 100 some-odd colleges, I decided to narrow it down. Of course, I wanted to stay in the East. (Lou) Carnesecca and St. John's were interested. So was Syracuse. My high-school friend, Dean Meminger, had gone to Marquette. It came down to Princeton and North Carolina. I enjoyed my visit to Princeton. Academically, I had done pretty well. Bill Bradley came to our apartment. That kind of helped. My mother wanted me to go to Princeton. But I really liked Coach Smith, Coach Guthridge and John Lotz, who was from Long Island.

Going down south wasn't a factor to me. I attributed that to my spending time at Long Island Lutheran with blacks and whites. My parents always taught me you get along with people regardless. It didn't matter where you were. As long as you had that comfortable feeling, that was the important thing. People were friendly. They would speak to you on the street. It's where I live now, where my children are.

The Carolina coaches were very upfront. There were no behind-the-scenes offers. My parents saw to that. They helped me in the decision-making process. And when I whittled it down, North Carolina was the best in many respects. Coach Smith was a guy I wanted to be involved with. He was a dedicated Christian who really didn't take a lot of junk, a very straightforward man. He was there for you on and off the court. He was a lifelong friend.

We went through the whole range of things at Carolina. If you remember the '70s, there were a lot of things going on in the country that were volatile. What people didn't know about Coach Smith was that he was consistently dedicated to integration and equality. He wanted to integrate the ACC, and he did so with Charlie Scott. Before that, he was involved in the civil-rights struggle in the South. That's one thing about him that has been consistent all his life. That's how he lived. It impressed me quite a bit. I was really happy he won the Arthur Ashe Award a few years back. That was just a beautiful ceremony. I was blessed to watch it on television. He was surprised to see all his former players. It was good to see other people realize that he was a solid humanitarian, a champion of civil-rights issues his whole life.

There were things on campus that needed to be addressed. I was active with the black student movement. He signed petitions that I brought to his desk without hesitation. And he was happy to do so. A lot of factions didn't care for him to do that. He wasn't necessarily popular for that with the University community. But on the whole, Chapel Hill had a reputation for being liberal. In that respect, he was consistent with the community in general.

There were not any internal problems on the team, none at all. A lot of guys on the team were understanding of what the issues were. They might not have been vocal about those concerns. But they understood that race was an issue that could not continue to be a factor in the evaluation of people. The South had a problem with that in general, then more so than now. Some of the strides that were made back then at Carolina are still in effect today. My teammates were great. Steve Previs was my roommate my second year, Craig Corson from New Hampshire was my roommate my freshman year. Those guys are as dear to me as Charles Scott and Bob McAdoo are.

It was a good group of guys. We respected each other. Race was not an issue. At least it wasn't for me. My junior year, I was the only black on the team, and we won the NIT. Everyone was happy for me. It was a team victory. The attitude came through Dean to us. He wouldn't allow prejudice, and the reverse was true as well. Charles and I weren't walking around talking about "Whitey this" and "Whitey that." We believed that people should be judged as people. Coach Smith really fostered that.

We were close the whole time, even though there were some things we differed on philosophically. He was the coach. I was just a young guy. He knew what was right. But we could discuss things. Some people in authority positions, they don't give you that flexibility. But Coach would always talk to you about what was going on. I really appreciated that.

As for basketball, I just learned to think about the game, work hard, play team defense. Defense is not the fun side of the game. I don't care who you are. Everyone wants the ball in their hands. Everyone wants to shoot the ball. The reality is, if you don't stop your opponent, you're in trouble. Coach Smith was not about to trade basket for basket. We were aggressive defenders. I liked that. I liked changing someone else's philosophy, making a team do what we wanted them to do, creating turnovers, things like that. Multiple defenses, changing defenses in transition, it caught other people by surprise. Which, of course, is a great element to winning.

As a coach, the interesting thing for me is realizing how difficult it is to implement what he had going on. A lot of things Carolina accomplished was because they had a really successful organization. It's hard to take that and transfer it somewhere else. You don't have that kind of organization. You talk about building a program, that should be the blueprint. I'm biased. There are great programs across the country. This just happens to be the best one. He learned to meet the academic needs of his players, help them make decisions socially, stay out of trouble. You have to preach and teach judgment. He did that as well. He did as much as anybody could do to ensure that the student-athlete was prepared for the future.

In 1988, my wife of 17 years passed five weeks after having a little boy. We were happy with the birth of our second son. Then she died from a cerebral aneurysm five weeks later. I was living in Raleigh, working for the state government. Coach Smith was there. He came over. He spent time. We talked. The last thing we were thinking about after the birth of our child was losing her. But he helped me through that.

He came to me, gave me material to read, Bible passages. He didn't have time to do it. He was still coaching. It was November. It wasn't that he didn't have anything else to do. But he was concerned about me and my sons, William Jr. and Carlton. A year and a half later, he and I were together when Bob McAdoo's wife passed. A slice of life, whatever it is, he's not going to shy away from it. If someone needs him, he's there. You can't say that about a lot of people, but you can say it about him.

He's like another father figure. He's there for you 24, seven. He doesn't carry you. He helps you learn how to stand up on your own. Even if you do stumble, he's there to help you get back on your feet. I just don't know any program or any person as helpful to their former student-athletes. A lot of kids go off after four years, and they can't get a ticket to a home game. It's not like that at Carolina. They don't forget you.

I've raised my boys myself with the help of family and the grace of the Lord. That's another big factor in his life. He's shown us all by how he lives. He's a dedicated Christian gentleman. It's easy to talk that way, but when you actually walk your talk, that's something special. He's a true witness to Christ.

BOB MCADOO

McAdoo, the only junior-college transfer ever awarded a scholarship by Dean Smith, played the 1971-72 season at North Carolina. He became the first Carolina player to enter the NBA draft with eligibility remaining and was named the league's Rookie of the Year in 1973 and Most Valuable Player in 1975. He was a member of the Los Angeles Lakers' championship teams in 1982 and '85 and joined the Miami Heat as an assistant coach in 1995.

I was recruited heavily by them when I was in junior college. I had always known of Dean's record before. And I was impressed as a youngster that the University of North Carolina had gotten Charlie Scott—the first black at Carolina. I remember Bill Chamberlain also going there. I knew they had never had a junior-college player. I knew it was something special for them even to recruit me. John Lotz did most of the recruiting. But I did meet Coach Smith. We talked. I was very impressed.

He had the nerve to recruit and go after black athletes, which was not too popular at that time. When I think back, it's kind of funny. I know my parents being in close proximity (in Greensboro) was part of the reason I went there. But I remember when people used to recruit me in high school and junior college. Everyone was stressing the social part of college life. I happened to be down at Carolina on a recruiting visit around Christmas. There was nobody on campus. I didn't see anyone. I didn't see any black females, nothing. Later on, I'd ask myself, "Why did I go here?" There was really no social contact with anyone. I met Bill Chamberlain, the only other black on the team at that time. It came down to my parents being able to see me play, the sincerity of Coach Smith and John Lotz. And the campus was beautiful.

There weren't any blacks there at that time. It took some getting used to after being in an all-black environment all my life. I could go home if I wanted to be into the dating scene at North Carolina A&T, or over to North Carolina Central in Durham. But my main concern at that time was getting an education and being the best basketball player I could possibly be. Once school started, I ended up seeing a few girls on campus, and dating them.

Bob McAdoo

Dean was great about it. What really impressed me is that he just came right out and said: "If you dated my daughter, I wouldn't have a problem with that one iota." That showed me the man didn't have a racist bone in his body, which meant a lot to me at the time, as a young black kid coming out of the environment I came out of. I was really skeptical of whites. But he was just there for you.

Playing was really the easy part. When I got there, there was all this mystique about Carolina — it was a great program; would I fit in; how hard it was. It was the exact opposite to me. Nobody believed me at the time, but the junior-college team I came off was a lot more talented than the Carolina team that got to the Final Four. We were just freshmen and sophomores, but there was no comparison in talent.

Just playing in Carmichael was a dream. It was tight, packed, hot in there. It was definitely a lot of fun. It was the hardest work I've ever done in my life as a basketball player, the conditioning and everything. It helped me get to the level I got to. You learned a lot. You learned how to play basketball. You learned how to play basketball the right way.

When I decided to leave for the NBA, Dean was the main guy I consulted. People don't know that. I caught a lot a flak being the first one. But it probably paved the way for Jordan and James Worthy when they left. He said: "If they offer you this, you can have some financial security, and I would go too." He put a figure out there. And it came to pass. That's what happened. I had all his blessings. And I caught hell because of that from alumni and fans.

I know that it was a while before he recruited another junior-college player. From my observations, as a young player at that time, I think the problem came with other players. Guys expected to move up. You look at other guys, guys coming off the freshman team, they expected to play. Here I was coming from junior college, and some guys were knocked down on the depth chart. Some guys didn't like it. I'd hear some grumblings—"I thought I was going to be playing this year, here he comes and takes a spot."

The only thing I could see is that I immediately helped the program. UCLA was the number-one school at the time. They had been doing it (recruiting junior-college players) for a while. John Wooden won championships with it. I don't know. He might have gotten flak from people who said: "Look, this guy is leaving after one year."

Even to this day, he constantly keeps in contact, sees how I'm doing. He was at my father's funeral. He was at my wife's funeral. I didn't call him and tell him. He found out and he was there. My boys went to his basketball camp. He made sure my mother went to games when she wanted. He helped us find lawyers and accountants once we got to the pros. He's been a good friend.

Looking back, he was a brave man, with the climate where it was back then. I remember Charlie Scott caught hell being the first black. I'm sure Dean got catcalls and everything for recruiting him. Charlie paved the way for Bill Chamberlain and me, being second and third. I was the first black player from the state to play varsity—Bill and Charlie were New York guys. He started recruiting blacks from the state after that. It kind of opened up the floodgates. Jordan came from Wilmington. James Worthy was from Gastonia. Ray Harrison was from Greensboro. The recruiting in North Carolina for blacks started opening up after I came through.

DAVE CHADWICK

Chadwick, a player at North Carolina from 1968-69 to '70-'71, is senior pastor at the Forest Hill Presbyterian Church, Charlotte, North Carolina, and the author of It's How You Play the Game, *a book about 12 life and leadership principles embodied by Dean Smith.*

What has impressed me the most would be the fact that he's a principle-centered person. That's the bottom line for me. It's what I get into in my book. His major concern—the principle that guides his life—is that he cares more for other people than he does for himself. That guides him in everything he does.

All that Carolina family stuff is true. His goal is to make us better basketball players and better people in the four years that we're there, so that we'll become better citizens when we graduate. If that includes professional basketball, that's fine. I played in Europe for three years. It was a great experience. He helped me to get to both teams.

His deal is that he cares more for us as people. What happens as a result is that you have so much loyalty to him, you play your heart out. When you have great talent willing to play its heart out for you, you're going to win a lot of games. I believe in all my heart —and he has said this to me—that he was never concerned about wins or losses. He wanted us to get to be better players and better people. As a result, the wins and losses occurred.

He led by principle, not by his own ego-centered development. We caught that. We knew that. You saw it all around you. The obvious examples were when he told Antawn Jamison to go pro, J.R. Reid, Michael Jordan. If he just wanted to win national championships, he would have counseled those guys to stay. But he was more concerned with them being financially secure, and he counseled them to go.

He made an indelible mark on my life. I've never been the same. In the book I've written, I'm trying to identify 12 life and leadership principles by which he lives, and pass them on to the next generation. When you have a principle-centered life, your purpose is to live by conviction, not convenience.

Dave Chadwick

You make your decisions in life according to principle. The team took on the nature of that. That's why we won. It's as easy as that.

When I was at Carolina, there was a stirring inside that this was a very unique man and special person. But I don't think any of us—especially those of us who played in the '60s and '70s—knew that he was quite as great as he became. The years have proven him to be even bigger than we understood. I've had to assume two responsibilities in my life—being the father of three children, and being the leader of a church. Those life and leadership principles, I became very cognizant of them. I began to institute them in my own life and leadership style. I've probably imbibed more of them than I realize.

My father is a pastor, a Christian minister. I was basically a good kid from a suburb of Orlando. I was fairly unassuming. I had good skills. I wasn't very aggressive—that usually was the knock on me. I had some talent, but I wasn't a superstar. We got along very well. He was larger-than-life even then. But I had such an awesome respect for him.

There's a gradation that occurs at Carolina. When you're a freshman, you're scum. When you're a sophomore, you're scum with purpose. By your junior year, he begins to like you. And by your senior year, you're good friends. It really is a gradation system. As a freshman, you're nothing. I started to have a purpose as a sophomore. By my junior year, I was the seventh man. By my senior year, I started eleven games, and was the sixth man. I moved up the ladder.

People kid me and say I lead this church like Dean Smith coached the Carolina basketball program. There's probably some truth to that. The obvious one would be with the staff and the rest of the leadership team—my greatest concern is to treat them right as people. It's like the old commercial—people are the most important product. I really believe that. My job is to make the people on my staff successful. In that principle-centered approach, the church has been very successful. The church desires to serve more than to be served.

GEORGE KARL

Karl, a native of Penn Hills, Pennsylvania, played at Carolina from 1969-70 to 1972-73. He began his coaching career as an assistant under fellow Tar Heel alum Doug Moe with the ABA's San Antonio Spurs in 1978, and later became head coach of the NBA's Cleveland Cavaliers, Golden State Warriors, Seattle SuperSonics and Milwaukee Bucks.

They recruited me very late. I played in the Dapper Dan Roundball Classic in late March, maybe early April. I played very well. They came to my high school the next Monday. I was already signed, sealed and delivered to Maryland. I was going to go to Maryland. I felt pretty sure Lefty Driesell was going to get me. It was his first year at Maryland.

I actually asked the guy counseling me, my junior-high coach, Roger Brobst, if I should even waste Carolina's time and go visit. He told me I should fulfill my obligations. I had one more visit to Carolina, and one to Duke. I remember Coach when we were driving in from the airport. He picked me up, and we drove the 30 minutes to Chapel Hill. He asked me what I thought my chances were of going to Carolina. I said: "Not that good." I think I put a number on it, said one in ten. It might have been closer to one in 100. He said: "I like those odds. That's not a problem to me."

I had a very good weekend with Steve Previs and Dennis Wuycik. The first priorities were team and family—that was very evident to me. I guess in a lot of ways, that's probably what I was searching for. The players were more honest and direct. I felt real comfortable in Chapel Hill. It was a good trip. He drove me to the airport and said: "What are my chances now?" I said: "I think about 50-50." The process really started that weekend. I made my decision the day Bill Russell played his last game—I remember watching the NBA Finals that Sunday in 1969. I told Roger Brobst: "I'm going to Carolina." It was probably the best decision I ever made.

Coach is a better teacher of life than he is of basketball. It's a very comfortable arena of development. There's a lot of pressure, but the pressure is motivational and stimulating more than it is negative and heavy. The whole program, the whole school, it was a glorious four years. You look back on it and think: "I'm part of a fraternity that is highly regarded, that a lot of people are jealous of." You're talking about love for a program, a school and a person that you would basically do anything in the world for.

I came out of high school as a scorer. I turned into a point guard. There was some shock treatment in that process—"I'm not allowed to shoot? Whoa, hold it. I'm used to scoring 30 points a game." I didn't even know what defense was. Defensively, I figured you hustled and played hard, and that was it. The process of learning the game to me is still very invigorating. It stimulated me. Early in my freshman year, the stuff he was teaching me, I thought, "God, I wish I had known that." I don't know if you knew he was a great coach. But you knew that he knew how to coach very early.

The confidence we had, nobody else had. It was the confidence to react, make changes—the things that I know now as a coach are very important, but when you play, they're very subtle. He's a master of the psychology of the game, of team, of defense, of the energy of playing hard, of confidence—all those intangible words that coaches throw around, his team always had. Savvy, sense, mental toughness—words that nobody really has the definition of, he taught them to his team constantly.

I spent two or three days with John Wooden the year I got fired at Golden State, just watching him at a fantasy camp. Being around Coach

George Karl

Wooden, it was amazing to me how these two people—to me, the special coaches of basketball—were so much alike, yet so different. They have quiet demeanors, but their character demands respect. Their personalities are very humble. They're men of simple philosophies. But they're very strong philosophies.

As a player in the pros, Coach Smith is always there to answer questions, to motivate you. I've always respected him because he always picks difficult times to step forward. When you're doing well, and everything is positive, when it's easy to say: "Good job, George, you're doing great," he's never there. He's always there when you need him. He will share your success from a distance. He will share your depression and failure hand-to-hand. We probably talk every two or three weeks on a normal basis. When I'm struggling, we might talk every two or three days. And when everything is blossoming, when I'm doing well, we might talk once a month. And he has a lot of people he talks with. I'm amazed he can even coordinate all that.

Most of the time when you make a decision, Coach has already advised you on what to do. When I was in Albany (in 1988-89 and '90-'91, coaching in the CBA between NBA jobs), our conversations were oriented toward, "George, why don't we get you into college coaching?" I kept saying, "Well, I think I've got challenges I want to pursue in the pro game."

We as pro coaches don't complain a lot about the game. We complain about attitudes and egos and money and marketing— the psychological aspects of the game off the court. We're pretty happy with the game on the court. He didn't think you had those problems in college. You'd have control of your arena. Of course, in the '90s, players have become a little more difficult to control in college basketball.

We had talked about the Seattle situation for over a year—"This is not good for you. You cannot work under that type of management. With the way (team president) Wally (Walker) manages people, you'll never be successful." He had recommended getting out of there for a long period of time. With Golden State, that was more a resignation than a firing, but it's like he knows what is going to happen before it happens. He's very aware, and he knows a lot of people.

About ten years ago, when I was in Albany, I made some basic decisions. I was going to try to make the game fun, like it was at Carolina. I was going to try to play fast, like we did at Carolina. And I was still going to play defense, play as a team, like we did at Carolina. I took that direction because of my successes, and also because of my misfortunes. It all went back to Carolina. I've been doing that ever since. For seven or eight years, I'd do this one year, that one year. Now I'm going to try to play this way the rest of my career.

I try to go back every year, either for the golf tournament or the basketball session. The golf is very friendly. The basketball reunion is more business-oriented. I always try to get one of them in. I've probably missed that maybe once in the last six or seven years. For me, it's like an energy boost. You go all summer long, you get away from the game, and then in August or September you get together. He just lifts the game up back to that passion that is important to be successful. Not many people can be successful without spirit and passion. Seeing it in him, it just invigorates you. He's been doing it for 35 years. You're going: "I'm tired of Gary Payton. I'm tired of Shawn Kemp." And he'd be fired up, ready to go. Most of the time over the years, he was the guy who was the most motivated. And he didn't need to be.

BOBBY JONES

Jones, a forward at North Carolina from 1971-72 to 1973-74, hit 66.8 percent of his field goals as a sophomore, still the ACC single-season record. He played on the 1972 U.S. Olympic team, earned NBA All-Defensive honors eight straight years and helped the Philadelphia 76ers win the NBA title in 1983.

He is the basketball coach and athletic director at Charlotte Christian School in Charlotte, North Carolina.

I was a good high-school player in Charlotte, but Charlotte was not a large city then. There weren't that many other guys to compete against. I averaged 22 points and 20 rebounds playing against guys who were 6-foot-3, 6-foot-4. Most of what I did was block shots, go inside, go up and down the court. I didn't play much defense. I didn't have to help on defense. It was quite a change going from that to the North Carolina level of basketball. Playing every day against guys from New York, Pittsburgh, D.C., was a challenge for me.

One thing I'm really thankful for is that freshmen could not play varsity back then. I played on the J.V. team for Coach Guthridge. I was big-footed—size 16. Moving my feet laterally was something I never had to work on. All the stuff we did—learning defensive stances, doing defensive drills, learning to give weak-side help, learning to know where your man was all the time and not being afraid to give help, even if your man scored—that was tough for a lot of guys to do. A lot of guys stuck close to their own man. But they gave you the confidence to know you could go help and gamble.

They held you accountable. There were only two coaches out there, but they could see everyone's mistakes. If I wasn't in the right place to give help on the weak side, they'd blow the whistle and say: "Bobby, you need to be here." They saw so many different things out there. "I was like, 'How could they do that?'"

Coach Smith was tough. He was hard on the guys. We were sort of in fear a little bit. When I got there, he already had won three straight Eastern Regionals. We knew he was a great coach, that he had great players. The practices were very difficult, very business-like. But you felt like they were very fair. They were super-organized. The practice plan was on the board every day. You knew what you'd be doing. As a high-school kid coming in, it was a little bit intimidating.

When he would call time out, he was very organized, very clear on what he wanted to do. He didn't try to tell you too much. A lot of coaches do that. But he was good at not putting pressure on you. He'd talk in a tone that told us we were supposed to enjoy the game, that it was a challenge. He understands people very well.

I remember the two comebacks against Duke my senior year. The first one was kind of chaotic. It was a close game against a weak Duke team that hung in there. I think the score was tied. They had called timeout, I'm not sure. Dean drew up the assignments. He said: "You guard this guy, see what's available." We weren't going to let them just throw the ball in-bounds. It goes back to practice. You were rewarded for taking initiative, diving for loose balls. Because of that, you were always looking for opportunities. Probably one of the reasons I looked to get that steal was because I had the freedom to go after it (Jones dribbled the length of the floor for a layup at the buzzer, and Carolina won, 73-71).

The second game was the one where we were down eight points with 17 seconds to go. Everything had to come together just right—and it did. That was our last game as seniors at Carmichael. It was kind of a nostalgic-type thing. We were down again to a weaker Duke team. They had played very well. We had not played very well. But we had gone through these things before in practice—"You're down. What do you do?" You add it all up, it would have taken a miracle. But the scenario worked one step at a time. It was a great experience. I go back to how Dean was in the timeouts. There was no tension. He was saying: "No matter what happens, this is going to be a memorable game for us." That was transmitted to the players in a positive way. He wasn't worried about it, so why should we be? (Jones scored 24 points and Carolina won in overtime, 96-92.)

I remember my junior year, playing against Wake Forest in the ACC tournament. I had hit a shot with five seconds left to give us a lead. They throw a full-court pass and beat us. We were all dejected. Back then, only one team could go to the NCAA tournament. We're walking to the locker room, and they're tugging Coach Smith to go to the media room. There had to be a lot of things going through his mind. He pulled me aside and said: "Bobby, I want to tell you, I really appreciate the way you played. Thanks." That meant a lot, that he was thoughtful enough to say that. He was thinking about other people first instead of his own situation.

When I went to the ABA, one of the big things for me was that Denver was coached by Larry Brown—a Carolina guy. I knew how he coached. His defensive philosophy was like Coach Smith's. I just felt I'd have a better opportunity even though the offers were similar. Coach Smith didn't help me much with the decision, but my first contract, he looked over what the agent charged me. I didn't know what it should be. Let's just say that Coach added a beneficial effect for me.

Four years later, I developed epilepsy. I went to a couple of hospitals in Denver. I went to UCLA Medical Center. Coach Smith found me a doctor at Duke. That was the guy who really helped me more than any of them. He got me on medicine that was not too invasive athletically. I was already taking medicine for a heart problem. I couldn't take both drugs at the same time. I don't know what would have happened if Coach Smith hadn't recommended that doctor.

He's sort of like a second father. In the arena that you're in, which is basketball, he has a lot of influence, a lot of power. He uses it in a very positive way for the guys he's involved with. That's a very secure feeling, and it helps with recruiting. Why would you not go there with Coach Smith and Coach Guthridge? I don't think you'll find too many NBA people who will say too many negative things about Coach Smith. It's like having a second father in an environment where you really don't know what's going on.

As a coach, we try to do some of the things that Carolina does. We pressure. We try to force an up-tempo (game). We'll do some of the trapping that Carolina does. I have a greater appreciation for Coach Smith now that I'm coaching, as I try to get the kids to do the things I want them to do. You look at Carolina, they're always so disciplined and organized. He just did a great job with that.

JOHN O'DONNELL

O'Donnell grew up in New York City, attended Fordham Prep H.S. and played for North Carolina from 1972 to '74. He later served under Dean Smith as a graduate assistant, and is now an orthopedic surgeon in Baltimore.

He was way ahead of his time on so many things. I still watch a lot of college basketball. A lot of things you see, we were doing way back when. He had us doing things that nobody else was doing.

You go back to the '50s, it was more or less Hank Iba-style ball, halfcourt pressure defense. (John) Wooden came in the '60s, and he was an innovator in many ways. Full-court pressure. An emphasis on athleticism and quickness. And simplicity. If you ever heard him talk, he talked not so much about basketball as about balance. How to do simple things that would lead to complex things.

Dean Smith had a million things that he did. Probably what he was most infamous for was the four corners. That was not really a fair thing. He was an innovator in so many ways. To my knowledge, he was the first one to use the numbering system that is commonly used today—one, two, three, four, five. He had that mathematical background. He was very interested in it. You could see he was one of those people who really enjoyed numbers. We ran things that way. Things that seemed complex were actually simple.

Practice was the most organized thing I've ever seen in any situation in life. We didn't practice long. We never had two-hour practices. But it was the most efficient one hour and 40 minutes you had ever seen. There was always an emphasis of the day. It was 30 years ago, but I can still see it. There would be a practice schedule that you were expected to read beforehand. The emphasis of the day might be offensive rebounding. Boxing out. Making two passes. Denying the ball a certain way. He always had some emphasis he had gleaned from film.

He had a system that he put in, week by week. The pre-season always started October 15. In six weeks, we'd get a system, and get it down pat. We had numbers for everything. The 24 defense, I still know what that meant—full-court man-to-man. Anything in a '2' series was man-to-man. The second number was where it was on the court. The 23 was three-quarters of the court. There was a zone series—the 51 zone, they still play that. That was his innovation, too—the matchup zone. Some people have taken it and done it better. John Chaney at Temple does it better than anybody in the country. But that was the '5' series—zone defense. 54 was a full-court zone press.

Every practice we had, we'd spend at least 20 minutes, maybe 25, on last-minute situations. We'd drill and drill and drill to the point where if he called a timeout at 20 seconds, ten seconds, he wouldn't have to draw up a play. He'd say something like, "five-one-three." The five man would take it out. He'd throw it to the one man cutting to a certain spot on the court, and he'd hit the three in the corner. It would all be understood. You wouldn't have to think.

Another innovation was the run-and-jump defense. You don't see that much anymore. It was big in the '80s. It started with the concept of, "One pass away." If your man is in the corner, and the ball is on the other side, you're two passes away. In most defenses, you don't play as tight when you're two passes away—you play off the man. But when you're one pass away, your man is in danger of getting the ball.

John O'Donnell

With the run-and-jump defense, if a guy was left-handed, you'd force him right. Then the guy one pass away would run at the ball and stop in front of the ball. Your job was to continue onto his man, continue in a circle. The guy two passes away would go to the guy one pass away, and you'd go to his man. In theory, the guy you ran at would be shocked—he'd turn the ball over, and maybe you'd have a layup. It sounds like pandemonium. You had to have good players. And you had to have quickness.

Another thing was the one-four game on offense. You still see them run it. You still see it run in a lot of places. You'd get the point guard out on top of the key, two smaller guys at the foul line extended, two guys down low. The guys down low would go out to the wings, so you'd have four across the foul line. He really developed that. The offense is designed to get a backdoor layup. It worked against overplaying defenses.

The biggest thing was the passing game. He wasn't a big believer in guys going one-on-one, setting their men up. He was very much team-oriented. The basic principle was pass and go away—throw the ball right, set a screen left. Larry Brown runs it all the time—or used to, before Iverson. Iverson is his own passing game.

The foul-line huddle, he was the first one to do that, too. The purpose of that was not to tell the guy to make the shot. We always had multiple defenses. We'd all meet at the foul line, and the point guard would call the next defense. Generally, it would be some type of trap. You used it if you made the shot. Some guys in the league, you wouldn't want to trap. We had gone over all that in the strategy sessions before the game. You always had a backup defense. If we missed the foul shot, we always went back to man-to-man. It's automatic. If a North Carolina team misses a foul shot, it goes back to man-to-man halfcourt. That's just a rule. They've done that for 30 or 40 years.

The part about him stressing education was very true. Starting out as freshmen, we all had study hall. We had to go for two hours, Sunday through Thursday. If you got a 3.0 or better your freshman year, you got out of it. If you were having problems academically, he knew about it. You weren't going to play, no matter who you were. Everyone knew that, so there was no problem. There were not going to be exceptions. One of his things was that he wanted us to go to grad school. This was at a time when every fifth player went to the NBA—now it seems like half. Half the guys I knew went on to graduate work. Mitch Kupchak was a few years behind me. He got an MBA. A lot of guys went into coaching. If you're going to do that, you should get a Master's. Maybe that motivated them.

Anyway, if you were going to go to grad school, he'd try to find you a job. I became a grad assistant. It didn't pay much. But it wasn't a hard job, either. One of the things was clipping newspapers. Anybody they were recruiting, anyone they were involved with, they'd subscribe to his hometown newspaper. I'd be the grad assistant in the back room. You had 60 newspapers from towns you'd never heard of. You'd have to go through them, looking for something about North Carolina or so-and-so, and clip it out. Then it got filtered somehow. It was all part of the organization. I don't know how many he ever read.

I wasn't an NBA player. By the time I was 10 to 15 years out, there was really nothing I could do for the program. It wasn't like I was Michael Jordan. My mother's now 84. A lot of these families become avid North Carolina fans. She would, in her 60s and 70s, watch all the games. She would still write to him, long after I was gone. He would write back a two- or three-page letter once a year. I thought that was extraordinary. He was very detail-oriented like that.

You always felt better prepared. We always thought we had a good plan. It didn't always work. But we never went into a game thinking, "This team is really good. They're going to beat us." You always thought you had it figured out. I can't remember any game that we went into where we weren't confident.

DAVE HANNERS

Hanners, a guard at North Carolina from 1973-74 to 1975-76, was a graduate assistant under Smith in 1977 and '78. He worked at UNC-Wilmington, Furman, and East Tennessee State as an assistant coach before rejoining Smith's staff full-time in 1989.

Coach Smith had come to Columbus, Ohio, to recruit a former high-school teammate of mine, Ed Stahl, who was 6-foot-10, a really mobile, athletic player at the time, the mid-'70s. I just happened to play very well the night that Coach came to watch Eddie. I was a junior on the team. He came back the next year to recruit me. Thanks to Ed Stahl, I had the opportunity to get a scholarship to North Carolina.

I really didn't know much about any school but Ohio State. It's such a big state school, 49,000 students. Their games were on TV every night. When I was a young boy growing up, I was watching Havlicek, Jerry Lucas, those guys. I really was an Ohio State basketball fan until I started reading about North Carolina. The first game that I saw was with Charlie Scott against Davidson, I think in the Eastern Regionals. I just loved the way they played. They were so unselfish. They seemed to be so together. I really didn't know anything about Dean Smith at that time. I knew more about Charlie Scott and the guys on the team than I did the coaching staff. But when he did come to recruit me, I was really anxious to listen, because of what I had seen on TV.

He was very businesslike, but had a very sincere charm and wit about him. But my most enlightened moment came when we played Duke in Carmichael in '74. I was a sophomore. We were down eight with seventeen seconds to go. I really didn't know that much about Coach Smith. He's a very private person. As a sophomore, I knew he was my coach and I liked him. He always did what he said, was a very thoughtful person. But I didn't know how great a coach he was until that day, how positive he was.

When he said: "Seventeen seconds is an eternity in college basketball," I thought he was crazy. I guess I hadn't bought into the philosophy. I thought: "This guy has lost his marbles." He was always very calm and very factual at the most intense moments in our games. As a player, I remember that vividly. It was almost like tranquility would descend upon him. His clarity was much more beyond any person, his ability to see things at those moments, and see them clearly. He would outline for us what we were to do. It was very straightforward. There was no way anyone could mess up. He went: "A,B,C,D, 1,2,3,4. This is what we'll do. And this is what will happen if you do those things." And sure enough, each time we had a timeout, he told us what was going to happen next. I went from maybe being a nonbeliever to thinking he was Houdini—in 17 seconds.

By the time I was a senior, I knew the whole deal. I realized, maybe more than the other guys who were playing, how special a coach he was. I don't know if it was because I was observant, or because I didn't have anything else to do but watch Coach. I picked up on a lot of the little things that he did that made him a great coach, the way he would look at you when you needed to be looked at. The fact that I didn't get to play really helped me as a coach.

He would do things to show that he was for the team. When an official would make a bad call, he would maybe clap his hands and have a very angered look on his face. But he wouldn't do it to the official. The official never knew it. But the team knew it. And he was reaffirming his belief in the team, his loyalty to the team. Maybe no one else in the arena would know that. But we knew he was for us. We knew that he would always be on our side. That was just one little way of him showing us. But it made us believers.

Watching Coach Smith while part of his staff, I learned the only way your destiny comes true is if you really put all your energy into fulfilling that destiny. He has a lot of favorite sayings. "Nothing great can be accomplished without enthusiasm" is one. I think he lived by that motto. You can't ever attain greatness without an awful lot of hard work. I know he would stay up hours watching tape, to two or three o'clock in the morning, after practice, after games. It really was his life. The reason he maybe saw so much when he watched a segment of film was because he had done it so much. He, of course,

Dave Hanners, player

was very, very bright. But he learned what to look for, how to spend his time more efficiently by watching so much tape.

Another important thing I learned is that everything you do as a coach, you convey a message to your team. Is it the message that you want them to receive? If it's not, then don't convey that message. So many coaches act angry at the wrong times or kid around at the wrong times. He seemed to always do the right thing at the right time. I don't think it was all planned. Part of it was his innate ability as a coach. But some of it was planned. He was always careful not to say or do something that would give us an impression he didn't want us to have.

With recruiting, his philosophy is probably so simplistic, you wouldn't believe it. He's always lived by the golden rule. The first time I really had anyone talk to me about it was when I came to school here. I knew about it, but didn't really understand it. For example, he would want to be the type of coach that he would want his son to play for. If he lives his life that way, why wouldn't everyone want their son to play for him? That's really the way he

Dave Hanners, Assistant Coach

coached. That was his philosophy. He treated us all well. If he got on me, he got on Michael Jordan. If he got on Michael Jordan, he got on me—for the same things. Very few of us ever thought: "Why is he doing that to him? He didn't do that to me."

One of his big things was always consistency. That brings on such intense loyalty. That's why his recruiting has always been so good. People sense his sincerity, his genuineness, his compassion. All the things that you'd want your son, brother or best friend to be around that kind of person. When he recruits you, that comes out. It comes out because some of the kids he doesn't get still write him letters. They may have chosen another school. But when they write him, he answers as if they had come here.

It's almost like having the ultimate ace-in-the-hole. Your president of your company is better than any other president of any other company— and the whole world knows it. That gives you a very good feeling, a feeling of confidence and pride. If Phil Ford is out recruiting, and he has this sense of loyalty, this sense of pride, it's going to come across. Kids are going to pick up that message. They're going to want to be a part of that.

Phil and I as young assistants, there were many games where at half-time, because our team wasn't playing well or the outcome wasn't quite what we anticipated, we'd be angry in the locker room. We wanted to kick the trash can, and maybe grab the guys and shake 'em a little bit. Coach Smith was always so calm. He never got to that anger point because he was busy analyzing and searching for solutions. He never bothered himself with anger or frustration. He always turned that problem issue into a search for solutions so quickly.

I think that's one of the reasons he had such longevity. He never got frustrated like that. Well, he did, I'm sure. But he didn't dwell on it. So often when Phil and I wanted to strangle someone, he would say, "Everyone knows we have a problem. Give me a solution." That would bring our focus back: "Why are we frustrated? Our guys aren't executing certain things. OK, let's write these down. We'll go in there and deal with it." I've never been around another person who could zero in on the positive aspects of a problem as quickly as Dean Smith.

JOHN KUESTER

Kuester, a guard at North Carolina from 1973-74 to 1976-77, played three seasons in the NBA and later coached at Boston University and George Washington. He spent seven seasons with the Boston Celtics before joining the Philadelphia 76ers as an assistant coach under fellow Tar Heel alum Larry Brown in 1997.

The thought that comes to all of our minds is what he has done for each one of his former players individually. What has amazed me is that any time you need him, he's there for you.

I can remember as a professional player, you go through so many different experiences. Sometimes you needed a lot of guidance. He always made time for your phone calls. I thought that was something every coach did for you. Until you get into coaching, you don't understand how many different messages you get. I didn't realize that in a day's time he'd get 50 to 100 messages. You'd always feel touched that he'd get in touch with you within an hour.

As time went on, I didn't call him as much. I realized how many messages he received. I wouldn't take valuable time away from other former

John Kuester

players. He always said: "John, you call when you need me." You always felt that Coach would be there, just like a father.

I remember when he started recruiting me. I knew what kind of player I was with regard to little things, diving for loose balls, drawing charges. When you added up the kind of player and personality I was, I knew Coach Smith was the kind of person I wanted to play for. Those were the things he talked about. A lot of coaches would say: "You'll average this many or that many." That's not what Coach Smith was about. He talked about little things.

For a lot of freshmen, it's a traumatic experience to go down there and learn what it's all about. Coach Smith was a friend, but he also was a disciplinarian. He wanted to make sure that if you were supposed to do something, you did it right. Many times in high school I could dribble between my legs or pass behind my back. The first time I did that, the ball kind of stuck to my leg. He blew the whistle and made sure that I was aware that that wasn't a smart decision. I started laughing to myself. I said, "Whoa, welcome to college basketball."

I always tell people about the Duke game, when we were down eight with 17 seconds to go (March 2, 1974, at Carmichael Auditorium). I was fortunate to be in that game (as a freshman). The only reason I was in it was because Darrell Elston had fouled out. It's considered one of the best comebacks of all time. He almost predicted every play that occurred. It was very special to be in that huddle. He knew exactly what was going to happen. And I knew from that point on we were going to win a lot of big games.

Bobby Jones had hit two foul shots and I believe we stole the ball twice to get within two. He said: "They're going to get the ball in this time." I was laughing to myself, thinking: "It's about time—they're a good team." He said to foul immediately. I fouled Pete Kramer (with four seconds left). He was something like an 80 percent foul shooter. Coach Smith said: "He's going to miss the foul shot. Call timeout. We'll draw up a play."

Sure enough, he missed the front end. We called time out, and (Mitch) Kupchak threw the ball in. I set a brush pick for Walter Davis. Walter got the ball, took one dribble and banked it in (from 28 feet as time expired, sending the game into overtime; Carolina won, 96-92). After the game, Coach was quoted as saying that we had the option of hitting either Walter Davis or John Kuester. I remember thinking, "Thanks for putting my name in the paper, Coach." No way the ball was going to me. There was no shot.

I had to speak at a church at the end of that season. It was the first experience I ever had speaking in front of a group. There were 35 to 40 people. I'm telling you, my knees were shaking. I talked about playing for Carolina, what a privilege it was. Before you knew it, I had Coach Smith on a par with Jesus Christ. There were times I thought: "This guy is too smart."

NBA coaches always appreciated players who came out of the Carolina system. They played hard, they played unselfishly, they were good people to be associated with. The second year I was with Kansas City, we drafted Phil Ford number one. I always teased Phil —Cotton Fitzsimmons wanted me to teach him the plays, then he cut me. That's basically what happened. But I'll never forget being in Milwaukee for an exhibition game before I was cut. We weren't getting a lot done. Cotton Fitzsimmons brought up my name and Phil's name. He said: "Give me players from Carolina like Phil and John, guys who play hard." That's the way we were brought up.

WALTER DAVIS

Davis, a star at North Carolina from 1973-74 to 1976-77, was one of four Tar Heels to earn gold medals playing for Dean Smith in the 1976 Olympics. He went on to be named NBA Rookie of the Year in 1978 and become a five-time NBA All-Star.

My first impression of him was when I would watch him on TV. Growing up in Charlotte, I got interested in North Carolina. They had the state of North Carolina painted down the middle of the floor, in Carolina blue. I would watch his teams play. All the guys played hard. It seemed like they were having fun. When they would show him on the sidelines, he wouldn't be ranting and raving. He and his assistants would be sitting there like they were fans watching the game. I thought that was nice.

I went to South Mecklenburg H.S. in Charlotte. Initially, the reason they noticed me was because of Bobby Jones. He was two years ahead of me. He went to Carolina, and dropped a little hint to the coaches. He said: "There's a player at South you maybe should look at." They started recruiting me after we won the state tournament in March. I had never heard anything from Carolina. I didn't know they were even recruiting me. When I got a letter from them, my high-school coach called me down from English class and said: "I've got something for you." He knew I was a Carolina fan. I was wondering if they were ever going to recruit me. But they were just waiting for the state tournament to be over.

Coach Guthridge was the first one who came down to see me play, and he came down and made another visit. Then Coach Smith came to my home. I told him I wanted to come to Carolina. I was happy they were recruiting me. When I first met him in person, I thought he was a very cool guy. He was very polite to my parents, very courteous, just a wonderful person. I thought: "This is someone I'd like to play for." The rest is history.

There were five freshmen who came in. They put us all on the JV the first week. We kind of had to graduate to the varsity. We had five guys who got a lot of publicity coming out of high school —me, Tommy LaGarde,

Walter Davis

Bruce Buckley, John Kuester and James Smith. But they weren't just going to give us jobs. We had to earn them. That really made a big impression on me. You've got to work hard to get anything. They didn't promise anybody anything.

Once you got on the varsity, the freshmen had to chase all the loose balls that went out of bounds. You had to go for 'em like you really wanted 'em, really chase those suckers. I told the guys: "I'll go hard after 'em, but I'm not going to knock anybody over." I didn't want to get hurt going up in the stands. The seniors led the team. The freshmen were go-fers. At night, you had to go for pizza, do anything the seniors wanted you to do. I didn't mind. I wanted to be part of it. And I knew my senior year, the freshmen would work for me.

The game against Duke when we were down eight points with 17 seconds left? I had a pretty good game that day. Coach Smith started letting me get the basketball. We never called plays for anybody. We had the passing game. But right at the end, he called that play, not for Bobby Jones, but for me. We called our last timeout after Duke missed the front end with three seconds left. Mitch Kupchak took the ball out of bounds and went from one side to the other. He hit me at halfcourt, I took two dribbles and let it go. I never used the backboard facing the goal. But I shot it too hard. It banked in for a swish. That tied the game, and we won in overtime (96-92).

Every time we called time out, Coach Smith had time to set up, tell us what we were going to do. Every time he told us what we were going to do, it worked. Duke had beaten us early in the year in the Big Four tournament. Then Bobby Jones stole a pass to win the first game at Duke in a dramatic finish. They just outplayed us. We had to fight back. We didn't fight back enough in the first game. The last two, we were able to do it.

My freshman year, we got knocked out of the ACC tournament in the semifinals by Maryland (105-85). I watched all the ACC tournaments growing up. I saw when someone would win it, they'd cut the nets down, get the trophies. I didn't get to experience that my freshman year. But my sophomore year, we got Phil Ford. That put us over the top. We were able to win it. I had to guard David Thompson in the final. I didn't get much sleep the night before. I thought he could sit on the rim if he wanted to.

I didn't think much about scoring. I just wanted to deny, deny. He and Monte Towe had that thing with the lob passes. I figured if I just stayed in the passing lane, I'd be OK. He shot twenty-one times—but went only seven-for-twenty-one. I didn't think I had done much. But he gave me credit afterward, said I played good defense (Davis also hit twenty-two of thirty-three shots in the three games of the tournament).

I played for Coach Smith in the Olympics after my junior year. There were no NCAA rules. He could cheat then. We got all kinds of cab money, things like that. The Olympic Committee gave us money all the time. Coach Smith had inherited the North Carolina program after a probation. He promised that it would never happen again. It never did. But during the Olympics, the only thing I remember is that the Olympic Committee gave us a lot of money, man. We were down there in Chapel Hill practicing. That made it great.

My senior year, won the ACC tournament again. We beat Virginia. I broke my finger in the semifinal. I only got to play two or three minutes in the championship game. After the game was over, I had to go into surgery. Before they put me out, I remember looking up, and Coach Smith was right there in the operating room. This was very late at night. After the championship game, we had to drive back to Chapel Hill. I probably didn't get to the hospital until 12:30 or 1. But Coach Smith was right there with me. I remember seeing him, and the screws getting drilled into my finger.

Having Coach Smith around, I always felt it was like having a second dad. I told my father that. When Coach Smith came down for the recruiting visit, my dad had been very impressed. He asked me later: "Is he still the same person?" I told him, "Dad, he's even better." He was always wonderful to his players, both when they're at Carolina, and when they're gone. That's just the type of person he is.

When I went through a drug problem in the mid-1980s, Coach Smith called, wrote me letters. He's there for you when things are good. He's there for you when things are bad. That's the sign of a true friend, and Coach Smith is a true friend. He would say: "Hang in there. One day at a time. Things will get better. This too shall pass." Things like that. Just getting his letters and phone calls, that means a lot. That gives you hope.

In the last letter I got from him, he wrote: "We were young friends. Now we're old friends." What more can you say, when you have a friend like that in every sense of the word? He's not just going to be around when you're shooting the basketball. When things are bad, and you're down in the dirt, he's there, no matter what people are saying.

How important has he been to my life? Coach Smith is probably right up there with my mom and dad, right there with my kids, right there in the top five or six. He's on my first team.

MITCH KUPCHAK

Kupchak averaged double figures in both points and rebounds for North Carolina in 1974-75 and 1975-76, started at center for the gold medal-winning 1976 U.S. Olympic team and played for three NBA championship teams with the Washington Bullets and Los Angeles Lakers.

He joined the Lakers' front office in 1986 and was named general manager in 1995.

At some schools you visited during recruiting, the players were kind of separated. They didn't hang out together. One school in particular had the manager show me around, and he introduced me to the players. At North Carolina, the players all seemed to be together. They looked forward to having me visit. It was something that stuck in my mind.

Then there was Coach Smith. My first year (1972-73) was the first year of freshman eligibility. Most coaches, if they were recruiting someone

Mitch Kupchak

they wanted, would say: "You're going to start." They'd promise you that you'd start. At that time, freshmen had never even had the opportunity to play until they were sophomores.

I thought it was kind of cool, going from high school to starting at a Division I school. But when people start promising you things, somewhere down the line, you start wondering what they promised other people. I remember visiting an ACC school with another big guy from Long Island. On Sunday morning, we had our meeting with the coach. I remember sitting in the lobby after the other guy sat down with the coach. Then I went in. The coach promised me: "Mitch, you'll start immediately if you come here." Here I am walking in, and the other guy had just walked out. I was thinking: "What did he promise him?"

Dean, he didn't do that. He said: "Listen, I'm not going to promise that you're going to play, that you're going to start. If you ask me, I think you're good enough to play for us. But I can't promise. Practice starts October 15. We'll let practice determine who plays." I felt there was more substance. Nowadays in college recruiting, there's so much flash. Even 25 years ago, there was a lot of flash, and less substance. But he had that integrity.

The players that were there, even the guys who didn't play, had something very positive to say, which was very unusual. I had some schools where the players would call me up at home in New York and say: "Listen, you don't want to come here." That didn't happen at North Carolina.

I was a sophomore in the game against Duke where we were down eight points with 17 seconds left. That one tells you all you need to know about his coaching. He walked us through that like a sergeant walks a recruit through an obstacle course. People were leaving the building. Time was running out against a team we should have beaten handily at home. He had complete composure and control, walking us through what to do step by step. Each step, we'd do what he said, then call another timeout. And our confidence just grew and grew. After that game, if he had said: "Hey listen, what I want you to do now is run to Durham and back in seven minutes," we would have tried to do it.

It got to where we were down two with six seconds left. You knew you had to foul. He went through the free-throw shooters, who to foul, who not to foul. All the information was out there. But the ball went to their best free-throw shooter, and there was no choice—we had to foul him. Now there were four seconds left, down two. He called time out and brought us to the bench. The guy we fouled was Pete Kramer. The crowd was starting to wonder now. Half the crowd was gone. We all had eyeballs as big as teacup saucers. He said: "After they miss the free throw, call time out right away." Pete Kramer was their best free-throw shooter. And he missed the front end.

He always saved timeouts. It never would have been possible if he hadn't saved timeouts. We had numbered plays that we'd practice at the end of every practice, with three-digit sequences. Each player had a numbered position. The three-digit sequence determined who took the ball out of bounds, who ran interference, who was the primary receiver. It was all planned. We were completely prepared. It wasn't like you had 30 seconds left with the TV cameras on, the crowd going crazy and the coach trying to design a play. You see that on TV all the time now, the coach with the board scribbling. But we knew exactly what to do on the last sequence.

You couldn't advance the ball in college—we had to start in our own end. I inbounded the pass—he had put me back in, knowing I had been a baseball player. Walter Davis ran the route. I threw to his spot. He was supposed to do a square-out—run to midcourt, then go sharply to the right. When he turned around, the ball was going to be there, just like a football play. Thank God he ran the route. He took one dribble and hit a (28-footer) at the buzzer. It would have been a three-pointer today, and we would have won right then. But we won in overtime instead.

I had back trouble that started after my sophomore year. During my junior year I had continued problems, and missed a couple of games. After my junior year, I ended up having back surgery. I remember a game we had on a Saturday night when I was a junior. There was a procedure scheduled for early Sunday morning, like at 7 or 8 a.m. It was called an epidural block. We played the game, and I was just supposed to show up there the next morning. They did it in an operating room. They dressed me, put me in a gown, scrubbed me, got me ready for the procedure. As I'm getting ready, guess who shows up wearing a mask and a gown? It was Dean Smith.

Again, this was early on a Sunday morning, right after a game. He came in and held my arm during the procedure. Not being from that area, it wasn't possible for my family to come down on such short notice. To have someone you trust do that . . . it was a morning when he probably should have been with his family. I did not expect him to be there. Nor did he say he would be there. He just showed up on his own. It was all new to me. When you're 19 or 20 years old and all these doctors are doing things to you, it's an awkward feeling. To have someone there with that look of concern, it meant a lot.

I never saw Dean lose his cool. He would get angry. But to this day, I have yet to hear him cuss. He would stop practice when he got upset. There are certain guys, if they just raise their voice, you're petrified. If someone is yelling at you every day, getting upset, turning red, how do you know if the guy is upset or not? He was not a screamer or a yeller. He commanded such respect from the get-go. He was so organized, so in control. You just knew he knew what he was doing. He was so in control, all he had to do was raise his voice or stamp his foot. Sometimes, he'd call me by my full name—Mitchell.

I learned such organizational skills. I'll never forget our practice plans. They'd be posted at 3:30. When you walked in at a quarter to four, they were on the board. Every minute of practice was detailed. At 4:01, there was fast-break drill number one. At 4:04, there was fast-break drill number two. And don't be late. If you're late, you're saying your time is more important than somebody else's time. You learned all the team facets, how to pat people on the back, how to win, how to lose. All those things carried over to business. The integrity part, I would hope some of that rubbed off. But that's for somebody else to answer.

My senior year didn't end on a good note. We got beat in the first round by Alabama (79-64). We had an excellent season (finishing 25-4), but it didn't turn out the way I had planned. It ended so abruptly. But then I had a chance to play underneath him in the Olympic experience. The '72 U.S. team had lost the gold medal to the Soviet Union. It was a chance to win it back and take the sting off the way my college career ended. That made it a no-brainer for me.

A bunch of big guys at the time were concerned about their pro careers—Leon Douglas and Robert Parrish didn't even try out. You had been drafted, but you couldn't sign a contract until the Olympics were over. And if you got hurt in the Olympics, your pro career was doomed. I thought about that, but with all those things I mentioned, I wanted to play.

He was a little bit softer with that team than he was at North Carolina. He had recruited us. In the Olympic experience, the players were picked by a committee, and he was asked to coach them. They didn't recruit players to buy into his system for four years. The players committed to buying in for six weeks. He wasn't about to try to physically wear out All-Star college players and make points about seniority and other things that were so important at North Carolina. What he had to do, in three or four weeks, was mold an All-Star team. I do recall almost all the guys on the team saying: "How do you guys make it through practice during the year?" I looked at them thinking: "This is nothing." To them, it was very demanding. I felt he lightened up. And I think he had to.

I knew at the time I was playing for somebody special. But year after year, as the program has continued to grow, I felt more and more proud to be part of it. Looking back on it, to say I went to school and played for him, it's no different than being able to say you played for John Wooden. No different at all.

TOMMY LaGARDE

LaGarde played for Carolina from 1973-74 to 1976-77 and also was a member of Dean Smith's gold medal-winning 1976 U.S. Olympic Team. He spent six years in the NBA and now works in New York as commissioner of "Nibbles

Tommy LaGarde

and Jibbles"— the National In-Line Basketball League and the Junior In-Line Basketball League.

I was just thinking about Dean the other day. Looking back, there were times I didn't like it, but the consistency was amazing. It was a psychologically safe place.

That's probably good when you're young, when you're 18, 19, 20 years old. You knew when practice was going to be. You knew what you were going to do every game, how Dean was going to treat you. There were no surprises. And a lot of other things in college at that point were very surprising.

It was just this solid place for kids that came from very disparate backgrounds. We formed a sense of unity. We were very united. There were always kids who thought they should play more. But nobody ever caused a problem. It was just a very safe place, even when you were down by seven with a minute to go. It was like, "OK, time out, Walter Davis takes it out, we'll run this play, John Kuester will hit a jump shot, we'll call time out. If we miss, we'll foul, and they'll miss the free throw." And then we would win. There was no panic. It was methodical.

I saw Dean not long ago. He looked great. He had lost weight. When he was coaching, he has such a demanding schedule, I don't think he took care of himself. I told him he looked good. And he said that he had been working out 30 minutes a day. As a kid, you're prone to cram, stay up all night reading a book. His thing was: "Work 15 minutes a day on your jump hook, and the rest of the season will be great." That's a valuable lesson for everyone. You don't have to get things done overnight. There is some kind of progression, a method. Especially in this society, people don't realize that there are sacrifices you have to make.

I was from Detroit, a very good boy, a Catholic kid from a Catholic high school. I didn't know much about North Carolina. Frankly, I didn't know that much about Dean Smith. I remember talking to an assistant coach at Niagara, a nice guy. He said: "Look, Tom, I know you're not going to come here. But where are you going to go?" North Carolina was one place I was looking at. He said: "Do yourself a favor, go visit at least." I went down and fell in love with it. Dean was great. There seemed to be no dissension. At other schools, they wouldn't let you meet the players. But it was such a great group of guys. And being from Detroit, I loved the campus.

When I got there, I realized that Dean was bigger than life. Everyone treated him reverentially. He was like the Godfather. Back then, there was only ABC, NBC and CBS. There was no ESPN. I had only seen Carolina play on TV once or twice, and they had lost to UCLA in the NCAA final or something. I wasn't aware of what the ACC was. But I learned.

In a group situation, he was strict. He wanted to do it his way. It had to be done that way. But if you had a problem, you could always go to him. In private, there would be more give-and-take. He would be less stringent. The reason he was strict is that he would have had 16 guys going in different directions if it wasn't for him. You wanted strictness. But his door was always open. You might be too in awe to go knock on the door. But if you felt comfortable enough, you could do that. And he always had the assistants to be the buffers. Everything was fair. I can't say anything was unfair.

There's a funny story I remember. When I was a junior, we lost to Virginia in the ACC tournament final and had to go play in the Mideast Regional in Dayton against Alabama. We had to fly to Chicago and change planes. Dean would have all of us sit in first class, and he would sit in coach. He wasn't as big as us. And it was also a symbolic thing, that the players came first. Well, we got on the plane in Chicago, and all of a sudden, the Marquette team walks on the plane. The players all file into the back and sit in coach. Then Al McGuire gets on and sits in first class. I thought that was really weird.

I tore knee ligaments midway through my senior year, missed the rest of the season. Dean was there when I came out of the operating room. It was just a shock, a harsh does of reality. You're not on the practice floor. You're not in games. You feel a little distanced from your teammates, a little out of it. It was tough not to play. And then we lost to Marquette in the NCAA final. You don't know would have happened. Phil had a bad elbow. Walter had a broken finger. I didn't play at all. That was a good team.

After the season, I remember going to see several doctors all across the country. Some said I would never play again. Some said I would play in a week. Some said I would play next year. Some said I would play, but only be half-speed. I ended up getting drafted by Denver, the ninth pick of the first round. Larry Brown was there. I guess that helped me out.

When I got out of playing basketball, I didn't really know what to do. I had majored in economics. I wanted to move to New York. Dean hooked me up with Tommy Kearns, a player who was there when he was an assistant, and he got me interviews at different investment banks. Bill Harrison, now the head of Chase Manhattan Bank, talked to me. It was kind of like the "Carolina Mafia". They were very instrumental in me getting a job.

And now? Because I had bad knees, I couldn't run anymore. I was starting to feel fat. And then I saw some guys skating in Central Park. It's true—skating is low-impact exercise. I can skate for 30 minutes, but I can't run a quarter of a mile. I missed basketball. I got some guys together and said: "Let's play basketball on skates." We got some media attention, got some sponsorships.

I live on the Lower East Side. The neighborhood has changed, but it was very depressed then. There were a lot of black and Hispanic kids who saw what we were doing, and wanted to play. I couldn't afford to organize it for them. So I made it a non-profit thing. Basically, it's basketball on skates with modified rules —really fast. I think Dean is a little skeptical. But he has given me nice contributions. He's a generous man.

RANDY WIEL

Wiel, a player at North Carolina from 1975-76 to 1978-79, is the head coach at Middle Tennessee State.

I came in as a 24-year-old freshman. I was older than all the seniors. I had been working as a police officer in Aruba. Of course, I played basketball, ran track, did other things. We had an American as a basketball coach. His name was Dick DeVenzio. He was an All-American at Duke. My final two choices were Carolina and Duke. Coach Smith had always stayed in real close contact with Dick even though he played at Duke. When it came down to making my decision, Dick said: "I think you should go to Carolina." I don't know if the people at Durham appreciated that very much.

At the time, I didn't know who Coach Smith was. To me, he was an American coach who was interested in me. After spending some time with him, I realized he was something very special. I could identify with him. I was working as a police officer right out of high school. It took a lot of discipline. I had no problem adjusting to his coaching personality or style. He was a very demanding coach.

Then I found we had a very formidable team—Mitch Kupchak was a senior at the time, Tommy LaGarde, that group. I had a lot to learn about the game, mainly about the mental approach. Down in Aruba, you just played on your ability. That's how I got very interested in the coaching aspect. I spent a lot of time on our bench. I played some as a junior and senior. But I was one of the guys who had a bunch of questions all the time. Coach Smith knew that I had an interest in becoming a coach.

When I graduated, I was going to coach high school. But I got an offer to play professional basketball overseas, in the Netherlands. When I came to Carolina, I was going to major in physical education, go back to the police force in Aruba and work as an instructor. At the police academy, all the instruction was done by mostly people they hired from Holland. They wanted one of their own. That was my whole plan. But I ended up playing in Europe for six years. Through all that, Coach Smith stayed in contact with me. Every two weeks, we'd talk about the season. I'd keep up with Carolina. And every summer, I made my home in Chapel Hill. All the players were there, everyone who did play and didn't play, the managers.

Randy Wiel

I worked the basketball camps, and he would let me use his office. I sat around and watched game tape of the whole season. Remember when Ralph Sampson played at Virginia? I heard all about those games, but I never saw them. Each day, I would come in early until he came to work. Then I'd go to another office and continue. He always knew I was interested in that type of stuff. He kept me abreast of everything that was happening.

I remember talking to him in '84. I was in my mid-30s. I knew my playing career was coming to an end. I enjoyed playing the game, but your body starts to need a rest. I told him I wanted to get into coaching, but I played that season. He called at the end of the season and said that if I wanted to coach, a good way to be start would be as a grad assistant, go to grad school, get my Master's, go from there. I was going to get my Master's, anyway.

So, that's what I did. When you become a member of his staff, your relationship with him changes totally. As a player, Coach Smith is your friend, but he's not your buddy. You can't walk up and just hang out with him. But as a coach, you get to see him more as a person. Then he gets real close to you— once the players are gone, he gets real close.

We had a great staff—Eddie Fogler, Roy Williams, Coach Guthridge. It stayed like that until Eddie went to Wichita State. I was there until 1993. I spent a lot of time with him exchanging ideas about coaching. We traveled a lot. He liked to drive to certain games— the ones in Charlotte, or at Virginia. I would drive. Coach would work. He had so much work to do all the time, dictating, answering letters—he answered all his letters personally. But of course, we talked. We talked about a lot of things. Basketball, life, family, theology. It was a great, great time.

One of the things I learned was to treat everyone the way you like to be treated. As a coach, the best player should be treated the same as No. 15. From a work standpoint, I learned to be prepared for everything, leave nothing to chance. Even things you think might never happen can happen. And then you'd be ready. We'd work on something. It might have a one in a million chance of happening. But then it would. And you'd be ready.

You'd be down ten with two minutes to go, and Coach would say: "This is where we want to be, work at it and we can come back and win." It happened so often, you started believing in it. When it didn't happen, you were shocked. My senior year in '79, we didn't have any big names. Our biggest star was Dudley Bradley, and he was a defensive standout. There was nothing expected of us. We ended up winning the ACC championship, beating Duke in the final.

I remember as a sophomore, playing in the Charlotte Coliseum. My brother had driven down from New York to watch the game. He wanted to spend the weekend in Chapel Hill. He had to follow the bus. At the time, it was a three-hour drive. Now it's shorter with I-40. Coach was very strict with his rules. My brother asked if I could drive with him. I just knew it was a no-no.

We won the game. Afterward, I walked up to Coach Smith and said: "I have something to ask you. I don't know if it's possible." He said: "Well, shoot." I explained the situation. He said: "Hmmm, that's a tough one." He walked on to the bus. He said: "Well, if anybody has family they want to go with—and they're older than 24—they're welcome to go." Of course, I was the only one older than 24. I got to drive home with my brother. I don't think he bent the rules. He just made a new rule.

Now that I'm a head coach, we speak every week. Usually, we speak on Sunday or Monday night. We talk to each other from home. Otherwise, I have to take office time. He's been active for so long, he could not just stop cold turkey. He has his office. But when I visit him, he has a lot of work. It seems like nothing has changed. He's always very busy. But he takes the time to call. We keep each other updated.

Coach Smith is a very good man. I always tell him, if I didn't know who he was and heard people talk about him, I would think: "It's impossible." And I always tell him, if it wasn't for the chance he gave me, I wouldn't be here. He'd always reply: "You made the most of it." But if it wasn't for him, I would probably still be working as a police officer in the Caribbean.

MIKE O'KOREN

O'Koren, a first-team All-America at North Carolina in 1978, '79 and '80, spent eight years in the NBA and is now a broadcaster with the New Jersey Nets.

He was a freshman when Carolina lost the 1977 NCAA final to Marquette, 67-59. He was hot in the second half, took himself out, then sat kneeling at the scorer's table, trying to get back in.

Assistant coach Eddie Fogler suggested to Smith to call time out so he could reinsert O'Koren. Smith declined—Carolina had gone up a point, and was running the Four Corners.

Marquette outscored the Tar Heels in the last 12:45, 22-14.

I get mad to this day that I took myself out of that game. We were down 14, and we made a heckuva run—I scored eight points, Walter Davis scored six. I took myself out. We always did that. We raised the fist, the tired signal. Then you could put yourself back in. He didn't need to put you back in. I went to the scorer's table, and six minutes must have gone by.

We had tied the score. He wanted them to play man-to-man. He thought we had a bigger advantage that way. Al McGuire would say: "Stay back! Stay back!" Then, all of a sudden, he would say: "Come out and play them!" We would go into our man-to-man offense. McGuire would yell: "Get back in a 2-3 zone!" I'm in the middle of this thing. Smith is on one side of me, McGuire on the other. This went on for six or seven minutes. There were no points scored. It was like, one possession. If the horn had sounded, there would have been a timeout, and I could have gotten back in. I got in after a while. I did play the last six or seven minutes. But I still kick myself for taking myself out.

I can remember the first team meeting I ever attended—October 14, 1976. The season started October 15. Me and my roommate, Rich Yonakor, were supposed to wear a coat and tie. I don't even know if we had a coat and tie. Dumb as we were, we went to the meeting, not knowing we needed a coat and tie. Coach Smith was nice enough to let us enjoy our meal. He got up, put his glasses on like he was going to read something, then gently threw them back on the table.

Mike O'Koren

He said: "I forgot what I had to say. I can't believe that two freshmen are not obeying the rules of the team. We're a first-class university, a first-class athletic department, a first-class basketball team. We stay at the finest hotels, eat at the finest restaurants. Now, because of O'Koren and Yonakor, we'll have to stay at cheap hotels and cheap restaurants."

That was my first initiation. I got back to my dorm and said to Rich: "I don't need this. I'm getting out of here." A few guys talked to me, said he was just trying to make sure I went by the rules. I had to go to study hall at seven o'clock the next morning. He used to put the rules up in practice. I just missed it. The older guys could have told me. But they wanted me to pay the price.

We were in the NCAA tournament when I was a sophomore, out in Tempe, Arizona. He always closed practices. We were in practice, and the media was there. Some fans might have been there, too. He said something to Dudley Bradley—"Dudley, we need you to be over here." Dudley said: "What? Me over here?" He kind of disrespected him a little bit. I don't remember the exact words.

Coach Smith blew the whistle and said: "Everyone come in." He said: "Listen"—and he was talking a little low—"I'm talking to Dudley Bradley right now." But he was looking around, making believe he was talking to everyone. He said, "Dudley, if you ever do something like that again, you'll never again put on the North Carolina uniform." He let him have it. It only took a minute. Then he said: "C'mon, let's go." He didn't want to embarrass Dudley. But he let him know that would not be tolerated.

We always had an emphasis of the day. On offense, it might be, make five passes before a shot goes up. On defense, it might be, move in the direction of the pass. We had Jimmy Black. He was a freshman, a great guy. He would ask freshmen before practice started what the emphasis of the day was. He asked one of the freshmen for the offensive emphasis, and the guy told him. He asked Jimmy for the defensive emphasis, and Jimmy said: "Pressure on the rock."

It was pressure on the ball, obviously. Coach Smith always had the practice plan in his hand. He said to Coach Guthridge: "Bill, did I misspell on my practice plan? Didn't I have pressure on the ball?" Coach Guthridge said: "Oh yes, coach. You had pressure on the ball." Everyone went to the (end) line. We had to run a sprint or two because Jimmy said it like that.

At Duke in 1979, the halftime score was 7-0, Duke. We came out in the second half, played them even and lost, 47-40. Reporters came in after the game and said: "What about the stall?" I said something to the effect like: "I didn't want to stall. He wanted to stall." It got in the papers. And Coach Smith called me in.

He said: "Listen, I've won a lot of games here. I'm not a bad coach. I'll do the coaching. You do the playing." I had to run the stairs with the weighted vest on for like, half of practice. The next week we beat them in the ACC final (71-63). I knew I was wrong. Sometimes you get so mad, you just shouldn't talk after games. It happens everywhere. I see it now in the pros.

No matter what the score was, he was always calm. During games, he might get on an official, or get on players a little bit. We could be down late in a game, and he was always calm. That really helped us win games. Look at the picture of Jordan hitting the shot to beat Georgetown. You see the Georgetown bench standing, and John Thompson has his towel. You look at the North Carolina bench, and they're all sitting calmly. It looks they're going to a picnic, like it's the first exhibition game. He won more games instilling that confidence, that calmness. You talk about preparation. We were always prepared for anything. He had it all. He knew what he wanted to do on the first day of practice, and the last.

One thing I'll remember is the day before the NCAA final in '77. He was going to let all the seniors sit down during practice. He brought out five chairs so the seniors could sit down when they were on the sidelines. I remember thinking: "I hope we make it to the final when I'm a senior—I want to sit down." All my years there, I never sat down in practice.

He's the best. I talk to him occasionally, but I don't bother him. We get the blue book. He puts a beautiful note in there. He always asks about my family. In a way, you do get to know him better after you're gone. He always asks what I want to do, where my career is going. It's a beautiful relationship. That's why I can't understand why every athlete would not want to go there. They do it right, the way things should be done. From top to bottom, every-one has good things to say. I know it sounds corny and all that. But it's all true.

Chapter Three

THE EIGHTIES

JIMMY BLACK

Black, a point guard at North Carolina from 1979-82, is an investment broker at Morgan-Keegan in Durham, North Carolina.

I was pretty much set on going to Iona. It was basically a done deal. I would have been staying close to home. But at the last moment, my mom encouraged me to visit North Carolina. She's originally from North Carolina. She really liked the coaching staff when they came to visit. I guess mothers have an innate ability to know something good.

She said: "Go visit. Take a look. If you still want to go Iona, then you'll go to Iona." I came down, and it was over—over and done. When I came home from the visit on that Sunday, my eyes were as big as they've ever been. I said: "Mom, I'm going to North Carolina." And then I said: "Mom, can you do me a favor? Can you call Coach (Jim) Valvano for me?" She said: "No, sir. Get on the phone and tell him the decision you've made."

It was probably the toughest phone call I've ever had to make. I had gotten close with those guys (Valvano and assistant coach Pat Kennedy). Obviously, Dean was a big part of it—he was fun to be around, fun to be with. But a major part of it was the instant bonding with the players, as well as the coaching staff. That had a lot to do with it.

Dean explained the game very clearly, gave us a feel for what we were going to do that day, what we wanted to do. As a point guard, you would go out and try to execute the game plan. When I became the starter (as a sophomore), I toned my game down, didn't turn the ball over. As you're in this system a little longer, you get a better feel for what to do. As opposed to thinking, you just play on instinct.

There were tough times. Every youngster thinks he should be playing more. Every youngster thinks his game is complete prior to college. Some people resent being told: "This is not the right way to do it. Try it this way." That's the nature of being a competitor and an athlete. But once you see the person you're taking guidance from not only has succeeded previously, but knows exactly what he is talking about, there's no resistance at all.

Dean was very demanding in practice. He wanted you to work hard. Our practices were tougher than the games. They were so much more demanding, so precise. There was never a situation we hadn't seen before. You'd see the whole world in practice, then you'd condense it for a game. He wouldn't yell when he got upset, but his pitch would go up a little bit if you weren't working hard. The only time I ever heard him raise his voice is when you weren't playing up to your capabilities in practice.

It bugged him when an opponent played dirty. It bugged him when fans would say things out of the ordinary boundaries of sportsmanship. Those things bugged him. He would just rally the troops and say: "That makes us play a little harder." He took great pride in leaving opposing arenas with the fans quiet as opposed to outwardly showing them emotion. You just played harder. And in the end, when you won, you won that battle as well.

He never conveyed any frustration about not winning a national championship (prior to 1982). It became a situation where we got sick of hearing about it in the media. The media really played it up, how great a coach he was, yet never won the big one. Here we were, around him every day. We knew what kind of person he was, what kind of basketball coach he was. We couldn't figure out why that would be a measuring stick for someone so successful. It was fun to finally take that label off his back.

That was a wonderful team—not just the starters, but everyone. We were solid down to the last man on the bench, even the managers. Everything fell together nicely. We knew what we wanted to do, having lost the year before. That was our goal. Winning the ACC championship wasn't good enough. Winning the (NCAA) Regional wasn't enough. As a matter of fact, we didn't even want the nets from those two. Our goal was to win a national championship. I remember his reaction when we beat Georgetown. It was elation, mixed in with exhaustion.

When people talk about Coach Smith, they mostly talk about his basketball. But he's an innovator in so many different ways. You're talking about the civil-rights movement. You're talking about playing in people's hometowns as seniors to make sure their families get an opportunity to see them. You're talking about making sure students attend church. Little things. They never get mentioned or spoken about. He didn't want them spoken about.

To a man, we all have called at some point in our careers and our lives and said: "What do you think about this? What's the best way to do that?" You always lean on him for everything. He has the ability to make you feel better about what you're getting ready to do, or what you've decided. That's a unique quality. He's positive. He's honest. And because he's treated people fairly his whole life, his network capabilities are extensive.

I learned so many little things. Punctuality. Honesty. Treating people equally. Trying to help as many people as you can. Friendship. Quality of life. You can just go on and on. I'm disappointed for young men coming up now that will never have the opportunity to play for him. My experience was wonderful. I feel badly that some of the young kids now won't be able to share that experience.

SAM PERKINS

Perkins, one of four North Carolina players to be first-team All-America three times, is the Tar Heels' all-time leading rebounder and second-leading scorer. He has played with the Dallas Mavericks, Los Angeles Lakers, Seattle SuperSonics and Indiana Pacers.

I first met him at the Olympic Sports Festival in Colorado. They really didn't have contact with the players at the time. I was a high-school player at the time (in Latham, N.Y.) I was on the floor after a loss. He walked past me and said: "Good game." I found out who it was. I didn't know. I knew he looked familiar. I was right. It was Dean Smith. After that, I got several letters from different schools.

Of all the visits I had, that was probably the best one. James Worthy was the guy who took me around. Not only that, Dean was probably the only one who talked about schooling just as equally as basketball. It seemed like all the other coaches were just involved with basketball. They mentioned school, too. But he adamantly talked about school, getting an education. And he was warmer than everyone else.

Once I got there, it was like training camp, on and off the court. You were told what to do—"This is your tutor. These are your classes." Everything was mapped out. All you had to do was do the work. And all the freshmen were in the same boat. You were on your own in a sense. It was your first time making decisions. But he was always there to guide you. And he treated everyone the same.

I remember the NCAA championship game against Indiana my freshman year. It was the night Reagan was shot. We were aware of it. They talked about canceling the game, but decided to go on. We thought we were going to beat Indiana. Then Isiah (Thomas) just took over. We had leaders like Al Wood. But things just turned around on us, and we lost (63-50). As a freshman, I didn't know what was happening. I couldn't believe it. We had a good team.

Sam Perkins

My sophomore year, the Final Four was in New Orleans. I never went to sleep. I think I hung out all night. I remember the Superdome. They said it was a mile up, from the floor to the last seat. I didn't believe it. I still can't believe it. It was a phenomenon. There was a lot of hoopla. It was crazy.

Beating Houston, that was probably my best game of the whole tournament (Perkins hit nine of eleven shots and all seven of his free throws, finishing with 25 points and 10 rebounds). The Georgetown game was like pins and needles. Then Worthy took over. That was a collective effort, to win that one (63-62). Everyone remembers Michael's shot. It was even more memorable when Fred Brown threw the pass to Worthy. That overshadowed everything.

We had so much passion for Coach Smith, and still do to this day. We wanted him to be one of the coaches who won an NCAA championship. When we finally did it, there was so much exasperation coming off our backs. We hugged each other at the end of the game. We hugged not only because we won, but because we finally did it. It was more a hug of relief.

He was like: "Thank you." And we were thanking him. It was a hug that was felt by all of us. It was a happy-sad moment. But we were all proud of each other. From there, we never went to sleep. We had roommates, and I don't think I saw my roommate at all— it was Worthy or someone. I was out in the French Quarter, seeing a lot of things I had never seen before.

The game when I scored 36 points against Ralph Sampson my junior year? If you're the underdog, you've got nothing to lose. You go out there and play as hard as you can. Against Sampson, him being 7-foot and change, I was always the underdog. He was the one with the skills and everything. I just wanted to play well against him. I always played hard against him. We had some good matchups. He got the best of 'em. But that game, I was just ready. It was at Virginia. And it seemed that everything went in. I had a lot of opportunities. It was fun. I couldn't believe it. We always went at it. And we never said a word to each other, ever.

Coach Smith didn't treat anybody different. The twelfth guy was treated the same way as the first guy. That was the big thing with us. He kicked us out of practice a couple of times, punished us, made us run steps. I woke up late for practice one day. I ran all the way to practice, but didn't make it on time. I had to wear the weighted vest and run the steps. He treated everybody fair. If everyone was on time and you weren't, that was a problem. He taught us that lesson. He taught us to be on time. He hated if you wasted other people's time. That stuck with me. Every time I'm late, I always think of that vest.

We had a meeting after my junior year about coming out early. I think he said I would have gone eighth to Detroit. But I was enjoying college. I really wanted to get that degree. Coming out early wasn't important to me.

I just wanted to finish four years. And I ended up getting my degree in communications.

Once you're out of school, you try to keep in touch with him. He knows what you're doing, to this day. The remarkable thing with him is that he knows so many people's names. He keeps up with his players, from Charlie Scott to King Rice. He still keeps in contact, still manages to say hello. He sends you telegrams saying: "Good luck with the season." He takes the time.

There have been times during my career when I've called him. I still do. We talk all the time. Without even asking, he gives you advice. He knows the situation before you tell him. He keeps asking: "Are you married yet? Are you saving your money?" He knows your whole portfolio. He's like the FBI, a secret agent of college.

BUZZ PETERSON

Peterson, a guard at North Carolina from 1981-82 to 1984-85, is the head coach at Appalachian State University.

I went to the camp for probably nine straight years. When it came time to make my decision, Michael (Jordan) and I had become friends. We had made the decision to go to the same school. But he committed before I did. He committed in November. I committed in January.

I was leaning toward Kentucky. I got overwhelmed by the place. I had verbally committed quietly on a Sunday night to Joe B. Hall. The next day, I kind of changed, once I talked to my high-school coach. He talked me out of it a little bit. He said, "You're a young kid. You might be making a mistake. Let's talk about this." Michael had called me. He said: "What are you waiting on, Buzz? We said we were going to school together. You still haven't made up your mind."

To tell you the truth, I saw the chance to play at North Carolina quicker than at Kentucky. They had Jeff Masters. Maryland had Greg Manning. Virginia had someone. With Duke, Coach K had just gotten there. You didn't know what was going to happen. At Carolina, I only had to beat out another freshman.

I grew up in Hickory, North Carolina. I was a fan of (UNC). When Coach Smith came into my house, I could sense his honesty. He showed me who was at my position, who I had to beat out. Academics were stressed. Life skills were stressed. And when my mom prepared a meal for him—the other coaches got snacks—I knew where she wanted me to go. She was a Carolina fan.

Going to school there, discipline was the number-one factor. Good, strong discipline off the floor leads to discipline on the floor, and a good ballclub. You had so much respect for the man, you'd do anything for him—all the coaches. The players came first. The players were the program. The coaches would do anything to help you. And vice versa, you'd do everything you could for them. The loyalty was overwhelming.

I remember my freshman year—we would travel, and never see Coach Smith. He traveled separately. We could be out at practice, shooting around. I'd always look for him, and he wouldn't be there. Then, all of a sudden, practice would be about to start. You turned around, and there he was. I was amazed at how he would just pop up.

Practices were like a classroom setting. You had to think. And when he was talking to somebody else, especially at your position, you had to be listening. Anytime he would ask a question, you had better know the answer.

Buzz Peterson

I remember my sophomore year, we were playing Tulane. We had already lost to St. John's in the Tipoff Classic. We had lost to Missouri in the Checkerdome. We were 0-2 coming off a national championship, and there we were struggling, in double overtime, trying to get to triple overtime. We were down three with about two seconds to go, and they had the ball. Coach Smith got out his pen and paper. He said: "Buzz, you go right here, Michael you go here, Matt (Doherty) you go here." There were a lot of lines going everywhere. I'm thinking: "Wow, I see what I'm supposed to do, but look at all those lines."

We came out of the huddle and I looked at Matt. I said: "Do you know what you're supposed to do?" He said he did. I thought: "Well, if each of us knows what we're supposed to do, I guess we'll be OK." The only thing I remember is that I denied my area, and the ball was thrown over my head. I turned around, and there was Michael, shooting a three. Boom, we go to triple overtime (Carolina won, 70-68). Coach was always thinking three or four minutes ahead of the game.

I had an up-and-down career. Sometimes I struggled, trying to play different positions. He would help me through it. I tried to play point guard my junior year. I didn't feel comfortable. Kenny Smith ended up starting. There were some tough times, but a lot of good times. They outweighed the bad times. If I had to do it all over again, there's no hesitation about where I'd go. I'd go right back there.

Once I got my degree, I had grown up so much as a person, I felt that I could make it in the world. Before, I didn't think I could have. A lot of that came from things we did on the court. We worked so much on conditioning. I didn't think I could go that hard or that long. It was like a big hump you had to get over. But once you got over it, you felt so good about yourself, you were full of confidence.

The things you learned were amazing. You learned how to be properly interviewed on television. My first job interview was with Hyatt Hotels—to be a personnel manager in New Orleans at the hotel next to the Superdome. They didn't ask, but I knew the table setting, the proper utensils, everything. You know Coach Smith knew about that. He knew a lot of guys would have job interviews, and would need to know about table settings. It was like, "We're going to eat in nice restaurants. Let's make sure we know how to eat properly."

It was Coach Smith who recommended that I take the assistant's job at N.C. State. He thought so much of Coach (Les) Robinson. And it wasn't like I was the first one—a lot of people had gone from North Carolina to North Carolina State. The athletic director had played golf at North Carolina. The associate athletic director had played football at North Carolina. Bobby Purcell, the man who ran the Wolfpack Club, had gone to both State and Carolina. I did the best I could for N.C. State. Coach Smith completely understood. Every important decision I've made after college, except who I've married, he has plotted the course.

Wendell Murphy, a big supporter at State, bought us these red sport coats—ultra-suede, pinkish, reddish, hot terrible jackets. It was a little weird wearing it when we played Carolina. It was so hot, I'd lose at least eight pounds when I wore it. One night, Desert Storm broke out, the game was cancelled and I didn't have to wear it. But that's where my loyalties were. Wendell Murphy was a huge supporter. Whatever the athletic director said, that's what I did.

You feel like this is a family. Even now, I'm the head coach at Appalachian State, but I feel like this is my team. There's a bond with the North Carolina basketball team. I'm still tight with the basketball program. I'll never forget my first conference win here against VMI, on January 4, 1997. I remember the next day I got a phone call from Coach Smith congratulating me. To him, it was probably just a simple phone call. But that meant a lot. It meant so much to hear from him.

BRAD DAUGHERTY

Daugherty finished his college career as North Carolina's all-time leader in field-goal percentage (.620), a record since broken by Rasheed Wallace. The first pick in the 1986 NBA draft, he spent his entire career with the Cleveland Cavaliers.

The first time I met Coach Smith, I was actually a junior in high school. He was speaking at a banquet in Asheville, North Carolina, on behalf of the seniors getting ready to graduate. I happened to be going to that banquet. It was an awards banquet for high-school players. Coach Smith was talking about Eric Kenny, some of the players. He said: "I'd like to meet Brad Daugherty and talk to him some time. But obviously, I can't do it right now. It would be against NCAA rules." I just started laughing. Nobody was going to know. I made a point to say hello at the end of the night, but that was it. He's a real stickler for those kinds of things.

As a senior, I was recruited by everyone in the country. Bobby Knight, Lefty Driesell, they all came to my gym to watch me play pickup basketball. Coach Guthridge always came to my games. I never got to see Coach Smith a whole lot. The thing that sticks out in my mind is that I had so many promises made to me. I was fifteen years of age—I started school early and skipped eighth grade. I made my official visit to Carolina and went to watch a practice. He was just killing the guys. I had been to practice at all the schools where I made official visits. Nothing was even close. I played with Danny Ferry a long time in Cleveland. He told me that one reason he didn't come to Carolina is because he had watched practice, and it scared him to death.

I thought it was just phenomenal. It was 90 percent conditioning and ten percent basketball. After practice, Coach Smith talked to me, asked me some academic questions. He didn't say much about basketball. He said: "I won't promise that you'll start on my basketball team. But I promise that if you stay here four years, you'll receive a quality education." He's the only guy who said that to me. At 15, I heard a lot of things I wanted to hear. That was not one of them. That really jarred something in me. A light clicked on, and

Brad Daugherty

I made up my mind that I was going to North Carolina. I made my commitment and signed.

I came down the first time and Coach Smith welcomed me to the campus. He picked up my bag and said: "I'll carry your bag to your room. This will be the first and last time I'll carry your bag." From there on, he set the tone, being a disciplinarian. A lot of people don't understand why we love Coach Smith so much. But it's a family-type situation. He's like a second dad to all of us. He's the strictest disciplinarian I've ever been involved with in my life. But he did it in a way that was unique. No cursing, no berating, just a lot of psychological things he explained to make you realize that you screwed up, and make you agree that the punishment was just. It takes someone very smart to discipline that way.

We were playing Brown one year. We were killing Brown. We ended up beating them by 40 points. We played really good basketball. Obviously, they were outmanned. After the game, Coach Smith came in, and he was pretty upset. He told us what we did wrong, pointed out all the things we screwed up. It almost felt like we had lost the ballgame. We came back later and played Georgia Tech. Georgia Tech had beaten us twice. They ended up beating us a third time in the ACC tournament on a real controversial call. We all went into the dressing room, feeling bad. Coach Smith just smiled. He pointed out all these positive things that happened, everything we should take from the game. It was just amazing. He did that often. Whenever you let your guard down, thought you were king of the castle, he put you right back in your place, put you in check. But when your confidence was shaken, he was always right behind you.

He was extremely fair. In almost every instance, if it came down to a judgment he was going to pass down, you were going to have to work. He didn't give anything to anyone. One year, we were playing a pickup game. Michael (Jordan) got fouled, said a bad word. We're all sort of laughing. But he didn't make Michael run. He made all of us run. We all had to pay the price. That's because we were all a unit, all working toward the same goal. During conditioning, we'd do it in stages. If one guy didn't make it, the whole group continued to go, because you were only as good as your weakest unit. Those kinds of things, he was really good at implementing.

I think I improved as much as any player who has ever been through there. I came here at 16 years of age. I had a really good high-school basketball coach, but our school only had 600 or 700 kids. We played really small schools. I was so much better an athlete, I really didn't have any competition. But then I came into this environment, and the competitive level was extremely high. For me to make this adjustment, along with the social and academic adjustment being 16, was extremely difficult. But one thing that Coach Smith taught me is that confidence is of the utmost importance. People don't look at it this way, but you have to be confident when you're learning and participating, confident in your approach. And the only way to gain confidence is through extremely hard work. Our work ethic was second to none, no doubt about it.

When I was getting ready to be drafted, you hear all the nightmares players go through with agents. I only talked to two—Lee Fentress of Advantage International and Donald Dell of ProServ. Coach Smith said: "You're not talking to anyone else. These are the only people you're going to deal with." At both meetings, he was present. I ended up going with Fentress. I'm still with him. It has been 13 years now.

I talked to Coach Smith constantly while I was in the NBA. He watches all of our games, the ones his players are in. Several years in a row, we lost to Michael in the playoffs. He would always tell me: "Michael does this well, but you do this well." I'd laugh. I hurt my back at the end of my career. He was a huge source of wisdom and knowledge. I came to Chapel Hill to let the doctors here see me. Coach Smith was really concerned. I was young. I wanted to keep playing. I was having a great time. He was the one who brought to light what I had done to myself. He said if it didn't heal, it was something that could affect me the rest of my life.

I had a lot of things I wanted to do with the rest of my life. It was a tough time. I was a five-time NBA All-Star. To get hurt in the prime of my career was extremely disappointing. I had gotten my game at the NBA level to where I was in control each night—except when we played Michael. But he was a great source of wisdom. He always gave you tapes and books that would help.

A couple of small businesses I bought and sold, he gave me advice on that. He's always been there. When you play for Coach Smith, a ton of constructive criticism comes your way. He can be hard on guys at times. But when you look back years later, you stop in your tracks—"I'm glad he did that. I'm glad he taught me that." It's always a player-coach relationship when you're in school. Once you're out, he wants it to be more of a Dean-Brad relationship. I have a tough time with that. I have so much respect for him. But I do feel like he's a good friend.

Coach Smith is probably one of the three people in this world I could tell anything. He's not going to judge me on it. He knows my character. He's going to help me. There's not many people like that in your life. And we all feel that way about him. That's why we like coming back, hanging around the University of North Carolina.

STEVE HALE

Hale, a guard at North Carolina from 1982-83 to 1985-86, is a pediatrician in Essex Junction, Vermont.

The visit when I first met him was interesting. We probably spent an hour driving around Chapel Hill talking about a variety of things, not only basketball, but as is his wont to do, politics, religion, a little bit of everything. It was kind of unique. He can be a little bit obtuse sometimes. I was kind of intimidated, anyway. The conversation was a little bewildering.

He was intimidating, not that he meant to be, but obviously his reputation preceded him. He was kind of intimidating to talk to. He wasn't the sort of coach that as a player you could just kind of joke with or hang out with. He was very much an icon.

He'd come out of the blue with things. You'd feel like you've caught him in mid-thought or mid-sentence. But he always has a point he wants to make. He wanted to be gentle. He never wanted to impose his views, say this was right or wrong. He'd come at it obliquely.

I remember one time I went in to see him, I can't remember why. I supported Jesse Helms that year. I was more of a conservative. Coach Smith was more of a liberal. I'm sure it was just appalling to him. I didn't know all the history. We were talking about basketball. The next sentence was: "So, you really think Jesse's OK, huh?" Then he went back to basketball.

I was taken aback. It was out of nowhere. I said: "Yeah, I like him. These are the reasons." I started asking him about something else. And he started talking about basketball again. It just came out of left field. He would do that sometimes.

I spoke for the Fellowship of Christian Athletes in college. I went on a mission project that he helped arrange and support after my freshman year. Some of our conversations about religion; I never decided if we talked about it or argued about it. I was never quite sure. I couldn't get him to articulate his beliefs. It makes it difficult to have a conversation about religion. I'm a conservative Christian. I knew what I believed, A-B-C-D. I could never get him to pin down where he was. I'm not exactly sure what his religious views were. He'd come out of the blue and hand me a book, or a tape about Apologies. We hadn't talked in weeks. But it would just kind of show up in my locker.

He was always in control of the conversation. He was behind a big desk in a big chair. You were down lower. It was definitely a psychological thing. You always felt you were looking up. He would control it, throw something out, move on to something else. I don't know if he didn't want to make me feel uncomfortable. But when you got out of basketball, the general conversations were difficult to follow. Those conversations were always interesting. I appreciated the fact he would talk to me about it. But I could never quite figure out what the point was, whether he approved or disapproved. I never got it. Those conversations are still kind of that way.

Looking back, what stood out over the years was his wisdom in learning that each player needed to be handled differently. The system was the same, but he treated each person differently. Any successful manager of people learns that. People are different. But he learned it instinctively. Some guys, you've got to jump on and yell at to get them to perform. Other guys, you don't.

It was a part of his genius that you couldn't really appreciate watching the team play. All that was done in practice, or on trips. The rules were the same for everyone. But how he handled discipline with guys was different. It took me a while to realize why he's always picking on this guy, yet never says anything to that guy. Really, what he was doing was maximizing everyone's potential.

My senior year, I got injured against Maryland—I landed on Len Bias' knee and punctured my lung. I missed the last game against Duke, came back for the ACC tournament, and we lost in the first round. The chanting of the Duke fans? (In-hale, Ex-hale). It never bothered me. I loved playing there. I thought they were ingenious. I never minded anyone yelling at me. That's kind of what happened in the ACC. I never felt it was mean-spirited. If you were arrested for stealing pizza, they'd throw pizza boxes at you. You'd reap your reward.

I heard it bothered him. I might have read something in the paper the next few days. Most coaches—he's no different—try to protect their players. They can yell at you, but no one else can. But for the ACC, that was fairly tame.

During your playing years, he never said: "I care about you. I want you to be a responsible person." He wasn't forthright. He felt that would be intruding. He would say it in a group setting—"I want you to be responsible, good representatives of the University." But one-on-one, he was much less direct. He knew he had power. He wanted us to be successful, responsible people not because he said it and he was the coach, but because it was the right thing to do. In that respect, he was much more subtle.

He was different things to different people. I didn't need a father figure. I had good parents, a good upbringing. He didn't try to fill that role. But I could see him doing it with other players who didn't have a good upbringing, and didn't have good male role models. As we talked among ourselves, you could get a sense of what he was saying to each member of the team. Some guys really saw him as a father figure and mentor. Others didn't. They saw him as a coach.

You'd have scheduled conversations with him a couple of times a year. It involved basketball. But it also involved your summer plans, how

Steve Hale

your family was doing, how your girlfriend was doing. It wasn't until later that you really figured out how much he cared. It comes through over the years.

He still sends Christmas letters to everyone. He calls my parents even though I haven't played in years. He's still in touch with people related to me, my high-school coach, my family and so forth. You can put that on during the recruiting process, be nice to everyone. You can put it on for the few years that someone is playing for you. But to put it on for 15 to 20 years . . . and he's that way with everyone. He has an incredible memory. He knows my family members better than I do.

I was in medical school at Carolina after I graduated. I was on campus for another four years. He helped me out, gave me a job being a tutor. I ran study hall for the guys. Occasionally, when the rules allowed, I would talk to recruits if there was one similar to me. He was incredibly accessible, even after you left. If you called, they'd put you right through, or he'd call you right back. You're made to feel part of the family.

He writes more frequently than I do. He's proud of all his players. Obviously, a lot of them are in basketball, either playing or coaching. There are about six or eight of us who are physicians. It didn't really matter what you did. It was more the kind of person that you were. There are still a few who he feels probably haven't done quite what they wanted to do. It doesn't matter whether you're 22 or 52. He'll still push you.

WARREN MARTIN

Martin, a center at North Carolina from 1981-82 to 1982-83 and 1984-85 to 1985-86, is teacher and basketball coach at McDougle Middle School in Chapel Hill, North Carolina.

As a coach, pretty much everything I do is colored through Coach Smith and the Carolina program. When I was playing, two coaches I was impressed with were Lenny Wilkens and Larry Brown. A lot of the things Lenny did in Cleveland reminded me of what we did at North Carolina. Then I had Larry Brown in training camp at San Antonio. Larry just blew my mind. I knew he was a great coach —I had followed his Kansas teams when I was in school, met him a couple of times. But some of the things he did in practice, I didn't think any coach could do but Coach Smith. It's like everything is in his mind's eye. He sees the entire court. Regardless of what he's focused on, he can see the other side of the court. The only person I've ever known who could do that was Coach Smith.

When I decided to quit, Coach knew I wanted to get into coaching. We talked about my options. I knew of Coach Ken Miller at Chapel Hill High. He had heard that Coach Miller was going to get a new job, leave Chapel Hill for Lee County. He already had one assistant. I became the next member of his staff. I ended up working him with four years. That's where I started my career.

A good coach has to be tough at times. If he's not, he's not going to get the results. Coach could be really tough. He could say something simple like: "Could you get around that screen?" But the way he said it, he'd make you feel two feet tall instead of seven feet. One of his favorite phrases was, when it's time to practice, it's his time. Nothing else going on is as important.

I remember one story with Michael (Jordan). I always tell people that Michael didn't get enough credit for being a tremendous offensive

Warren Martin

rebounder—he did so many other things. One day in practice, Michael mistimed a rebound. Coach jumped all over him. He was having a great practice. But he mistimed a rebound. He came down, and the ball went right over his head. It's because he wasn't concentrating that he missed it. That was why Coach got on him.

I'm from Axton, Virginia. My whole family was excited when Coach Smith came to our home when I was in high school. He was one of the first ACC coaches that I had met. We didn't talk about basketball until the end of the visit. It was all about what I wanted to do academically. Toward the end of the visit, we talked about where I might fit in on the team. The question was, where could I possibly earn the right to play? My chances were slim. It would be a learning experience. As a freshman, I would be a backup to Sam Perkins and Jeb Barlow. They were always loaded. But I wanted to go to Carolina, anyway.

I didn't play basketball until I was in ninth grade. My coach, Hal Wilson, saw me one day and realized that if I stood up, I might be tall. He basically taught me everything I know. But I wanted to continue learning about basketball. Coach Smith has always been known as a great teacher as well as a great coach. My final list had six schools on it. It was a struggle to make the decision. I had a lot of things to deal with. There was pressure to stay instate, go to Virginia.

My whole freshman class, nobody associates any of us except for Buzz and Mike. We also had me, John Brownlee and Lynwood Robinson. We talked about red shirting my freshman year. I wanted to play. Coach Smith said OK. I played in the postseason, a minute or two every game except for the Georgetown game. Our lead was never big enough! The next year I played, but my junior year, I had arthritis and bursitis under the kneecap. We had Joe Wolf and Dave Popson coming in, and I would have missed a significant part of the season, so I red shirted. I came back as a senior and was the last line of defense, a shot-blocker and rebounder. Dave Popson started, and I came off the bench.

With our practices, you knew what was on the practice plan before you went in. There were several things you had to remember. One day, we had to practice in Woollen Gym—they were having the circus in Carmichael. But when we went on the floor, I hadn't picked up on the circus being there. At the beginning of practice, Coach Smith asked me if I'd seen the tigers. I started looking around the gym. I didn't have a clue. I remember Sam Perkins just dying. Because of all the things we had to remember, I expected Coach to ask me to tell him the thought for the day, or the offensive or defensive emphasis.

As a coach, I'm astonished by what he did. It's an amazing accomplishment. On the other hand, I'm not. You know the old phrase, "Practice like you play. Play like you practice." That's what we did. At Carolina, you did your homework before the game. You were not going to be caught by surprise by anything. The preparation was just awesome—which, I think, prompted Coach (Terry) Holland to totally change his offense days before he played us, so it wouldn't be as obvious. He knew we'd sit down and break everything down. If you did the same thing, you wouldn't have much success. During my time, we were forcing the issue. We wanted to, one, take the other team out of its offense, and two, make the other team stop us if it could.

When we talk about family, we are. I try to extend that to my players, too. You have to be able to communicate with each other, get along. There are different ways to do it. My teams at Carolina had might not have hung out much together, but when we got to the court we were together. J.R. Reid and King Rice and them, they hung together all the time.

One of the things I always liked about Carolina is that all the alumni knew who you were. They would speak to you. We had that shared experience. And it continues with Coach Guthridge and Coach Ford. One thing I wish is that we could get more guys from the NBA to come back and play pickup games, the way we did in the '80s. The nature of the game has changed. They have all these endorsement deals now. They have to try to fit it into their time.

I remember Kenny Smith coming back after he won his first championship with Houston. I was shocked. We had the Carolina camp going on. We always had a speaker. I turned around, and Kenny walked out. I had just seen him on television the night before. But he was so excited, he wanted to speak to the kids about it.

KENNY SMITH

Smith, one of ten freshmen under Dean Smith to start the first game of his career, finished his career as North Carolina's all-time assist leader. He went on to play for the Sacramento Kings and Atlanta Hawks and was the starting point guard for the Houston Rockets' world-championship teams in 1994 and '95.

He became an NBA analyst for Turner Sports in 1998.

The first time I actually sat down and met with him was the home visit. He had his Carolina colors on. He had been golfing. He had his golf pants on—plaid pants, all different colors. To a young kid from New York, it was kind of strange. I had never seen yellow, blue and green all at once. I had never seen anyone who had gone golfing.

I thought: "He's very confident to come into Queens, New York, with those pants on." But he has a presence and an aura that he brings into a room. I kind of sensed that. It was what I was looking for: "Think about all the stuff I have to offer. You'd be crazy not to take it. And if you don't take it, a lot of kids will want it." He didn't say that. But that was his aura. It was like: "Listen, I'm choosing you to take this." A lot of the coaches said: "I need you to make my program. If you don't, it's going to hurt."

I knew it was the place for me, even though the worst of all my visits was North Carolina. I had played the night before. He had come to see me play. I scored 42 points, but I had the flu. The next day, we flew down to Carolina. We were on the same plane. I was sick the whole flight, throwing up, everything. I got to Carolina and felt even worse. I just wanted to go back to my room. They had a big dinner planned. But I was just so sick. Coach said: "If you want to go walk around campus on your own, that might be a good idea." I was too sick. I laid down and fell asleep.

The dinner was at 7. At 7:45 I hear this banging on my door. I open the door, and it's Michael Jordan and Buzz Peterson asking: "What's with you? We had this dinner planned." They didn't know what had happened to me. Basically, I don't remember anything about the visit. Brad Daugherty took me to a party. We stayed like ten minutes. They thought I didn't like my visit. I had to weigh everything without actually seeing the university. And it still outweighed all the schools I was considering. It had the total package. And Coach was a big part of that.

He said one thing that really stood out. A lot of schools promised me different things—"We'll play you 25 minutes, and by your sophomore year, it will be your time." Or: "We'll play you right away." Coach Smith just said:, "I play the five best. If you're one of the five best, you'll be on the court. That's all I can promise you." That was enough. I was there. I could deal with that. That was fair to me.

I didn't want to be sitting behind a junior because he was a junior. I didn't want to sit behind someone I was more talented than because his uncle was a booster. I wanted a fair shot. I was going to give them a fair shot. I wanted it to be a clean slate. I didn't want them to owe me anything. And I didn't want to owe them anything. As a freshman, I worked my way into the lineup before we started the season. I was one of the best five. There was no doubt—I should be on the floor. That's all I asked for. And that's what he gave me. He gave me the opportunity.

I always tell him, he's the only person I know who treats every single person exactly the same. That's an unbelievable talent in itself. If you walked into our practice and you were blind—if you could only listen to what was going on—you couldn't tell from his tone of voice who were the best players and who weren't. Parents don't treat all their kids the same. My mother and

Kenny Smith

father didn't treat all my brothers and sisters the same. For him to treat every-one the same, that was amazing. How could he do that?

When I got there, Cecil Exum was a senior. Coach had this rule where the seniors kind of made the decisions. Cecil Exum was the tenth or eleventh man. But every meeting, everything that happened, he'd say: "Cecil, should we leave at 3 or 3:15?" Because Cecil was a senior. It didn't matter that he was the tenth man on the team, and Michael Jordan was the best player. Coach never asked Michael when we should leave. He wouldn't ask me or Sam Perkins. We played all the minutes, and he didn't even care. When I first got there, I couldn't understand it. Then I started to see what was going on. If you were on the team, you were on the team. That's why walk-ons got scholarships after they made it. There were no such things as walk-ons. If you made the team, you made the team.

I remember seeing something in the paper. He was asked: "How are the freshmen doing?" And he said: "I just hope that they make the team." I was like: "Make the team? What is he talking about?" But after a while, I understood. He told us our first goal should be to make the team. And he meant it.

The point guard probably had the biggest role at Carolina. You'd call the offenses, call the defenses. You had to be an extension of him on the court. You'd sit down with him before games, go over defensive strategy. He didn't want me to have to look over every minute to figure out what we were doing. We'd go over what percentages of defenses we'd play, what kind of traps. He gave me some leeway with what I wanted to call. You'd go through a game, then kind of freelance.

He'd get a kick out of it if we put up the same signal at the same time. When you do that, that's when you know that you're on the same page he is. I was fortunate. It took me only about half the season before it started happening. He mentioned that it had happened with Jimmy (Black)—"I'd put up my hand, and he'd put it up at the same time." And then it happened with me.

Differences? Everyone thinks they want to shoot more. I don't think there's a young kid anywhere who doesn't want to take more shots. That was the only thing we talked about. I felt I could score more than I was actually doing. I told him I could help the team by scoring more. He said we had a rule—we didn't want just good shots, but open shots. To me, if a guy had a hand in my face, I was still open, if it was just one guy.

He said: "I'll give you one play a game, let you do what you want." This was my senior year. It was an out-of-bounds play. I started hitting the shots. And he kept calling it. It was his way of saying: "We'll do a little bit of what you want, but what we did was working before you got here. We're not going to change."

I talk to him more meaningfully now than when I was playing. Every major decision I make, I kind of get his insight on. In college, it was a coach-player relationship. I kind of shied away. I didn't want to get too close to my coach—when he talks to you, that's when you talk to him. But once you stop playing, the relationship is different. Now I talk to him about everything. I've talked to him about being married, how much I'm spending, picking an agent, how much to ask for from the Houston Rockets, TNT. His back is probably hurting from me leaning on him.

I remember a game at Clemson my senior year. Clemson is like Duke. The fans were on you, screaming and yelling. Dick Vitale was there, going: "Oh my God," and everything. It's a crazy atmosphere. It's one of the best in the ACC when it's packed and they're doing well. We go in there, we're ranked number one, and we get down by 20 points. Coach gives us a little speech at halftime. We make a little run, cut it to about 15. And he calls timeout. He looks at us and says: "We're right where we want to be."

I'm like: "We're down fifteen, the crowd is going crazy, Dick Vitale is going crazy. We're not right where we want to be." But he had prepared us so much, we won the game by nine in regulation (108-99). We had drills in practice—you're down 15 with eight minutes to go, you're down three with 30 seconds to go. We always used to argue about it—why are we doing this thing when we're down 15? We understood doing it, but doing it every day?

Well, we all knew what to do at Clemson. He never said a word. We went into running our plays, running our defenses. We did everything we had done in practice. He never called a play. He never called a timeout. And that's the way I think about being prepared in life today. If I prepare myself, I can be down 15, and still come out on top. Or, I can be up 15, doing well in life, but be like Clemson, not really prepared, then lose. I go through my life because of what happened in that game. If anything happens, at least I'm prepared.

RANZINO SMITH

Smith, a guard at North Carolina from 1985 to '88, works as a processing assistant for the State Bureau of Investigation in Raleigh, North Carolina.

I was born and raised in Chapel Hill. Back in the 1940s and '50s, my father was a big-time college-basketball fan. The University of North Carolina was his favorite team, of course. But there was a player in college basketball at that time who turned out to be a three-time All-American at North Carolina State. His name was Sammy Ranzino. And that was my dad's favorite college basketball player.

My dad fell in love with him from Day One, when Mr. Ranzino was a freshman in college. His last name just stuck with my dad. When I was born, my mom told me that the nurses brought her a list of boys' names to consider. My dad had a piece of paper in his pocket. He pulled it out and told the nurses that he already had a name. And the piece of paper had the name "Ranzino" on it.

I was named for a player from N.C. State. But it was destiny that I would go to North Carolina.

My first experience going to a college basketball game was the game in which Carolina came from eight points down with 17 seconds left to beat Duke. I was eight or nine years old. I was hanging out with somebody four or five years older than me — I don't remember his name. The first half, I stood in front of Carmichael right outside the door, next to a security guard. He and I both were standing there, listening to the game on the radio. At half-time he felt sorry for me, and told me to go in.

I went in, stood by the court and watched the rest of the game. After the game, of course, everyone ran on the floor. I was excited. I waited for the players to come out. The first player I met face-to-face was Mitch Kupchak. Mitch was real nice. The thing that really impressed me was that he didn't just give me his autograph. He asked me questions—How was I doing? Did I enjoy the game? Mitch Kupchak was definitely my favorite player at the University of North Carolina—the first player I ever met, before I started really playing.

When I was in seventh grade, I met James Worthy. It was the summer before his freshman year. He was swimming in a pool. I was going to the pool. He was standing up. I knew he looked familiar. My dad had shown me pictures of the incoming players. I went over and told him that my dad knew who he was. He was really nice. He shook my hand. He talked to me for a few minutes.

The first time I met Coach Smith was at his basketball camp the summer before seventh grade. He had heard I was a good free-throw shooter. There was a clinic going on at camp. He called me up to demonstrate how to shoot free throws. I think I shot 25 or 30. John Lotz, the assistant athletic director at the time, bet that I would make all of the free throws. And I did. He put the pressure on me. And I made like 30 in a row. That really impressed Coach Smith, doing that in front of a lot of people. I think that really stuck with him.

It was a dream come true when Coach Smith recruited me. Actually, I recruited them. That's where I always wanted to go to school. My mom and dad and I had a conference in Coach Smith's office at Carmichael. Coach Guthridge and Coach Williams were there. So were my junior-high coach, my high-school coach and my high-school principal. Coach Smith came out and said he wanted to me be part of the basketball program. He offered me a scholarship. I was very stunned, very shocked, very excited.

It was truly a dream come true. Ever since I was six or seven years old, I had dreamed of playing for Coach Smith. More than anything, I was very excited and happy for my parents, for the job they did raising me. They had wanted this to work out for me. They knew I wanted to go to Carolina. When I got the opportunity, I was just so happy—more happy for them than I was for myself.

My father had told me about when Coach Smith had recruited Charlie Scott. It showed me the kind of man and the kind of coach that the University of North Carolina had. You can only imagine the pressure he had to deal with by recruiting Charlie Scott. It just showed his character, that he accepted that challenge and stayed focused without letting it bother him. I'm sure there was a lot heat on him.

You just know after you meet him the first time that Coach Smith is not a racist. Coach Smith is a very religious man. He doesn't see color—it doesn't exist to him. To him, every human being is equal. He deals with people in different ways. But everyone is equal. You knew that from the jump.

One of the things I respected about Coach Smith, more than anything, was that he was straight-up and honest. He basically said I wasn't going to get a lot of playing time my first year. He didn't know how much playing time I would get after that. He said if I worked hard and gradually improved, I would see some playing time. I accepted the challenge. I wanted to be part of the program. I wanted to work hard. I went in with an open mind and focused on

Ranzino Smith

improving. At the end of my senior year, he and the assistant coaches told me they were very impressed. They didn't think I would have as wonderful a career as I did.

He was a man who truly believed in the good Lord. He cared about his players genuinely, from the heart. You had so much confidence in him, he was like another father to you. If you were stressed out academically, if you had questions, felt like you were struggling, he was always there to listen, lift your spirits up.

Right before my freshman year, I didn't know how well I would perform on that level, especially playing at Carolina. I was a 6-foot swing man. I was nervous as a freshman, playing against 6-4 and 6-5 players at my position. He looked at me and said: "We watched you in high school. You can definitely play on this level. One of the rare pleasures you'll get out of life is accomplishing what people say you will never accomplish. With your ability and skill, you'll accomplish a lot, prove your doubters wrong."

My freshman year, I was just glad to be part of the team. I made two free throws to help us beat Auburn in the Sweet Sixteen (62-56). It was great to be in that situation, to be able to hit two crucial free throws in a big-time game with 18,000 people screaming at you—the game was in Birmingham, Alabama. Before I walked up to the line, I remembered the time I hit 30 free throws in a row at camp. I also thought to myself: "This is the easiest shot in basketball." I looked forward to shooting free throws. You didn't have a defender on you. I said: "I'm supposed to make them."

I got a lot of pleasure out of 18,000 Auburn fans screaming, just knowing the freshman was going to miss. It tickled me. I knew these people had no idea that I was going to make the free throws. They didn't know what kind of free-throw shooter I was. I just knew I was going to quiet them down.

Another game that stands out was against Loyola Marymount in the second round of the NCAA tournament my senior year (Smith scored 27 points in a 123-97 Carolina victory). That was the most fun I had in a game. That was my style of play, up and down. I like to run. And I knew before the game that I would play a lot. Coach Smith had said to me that it would be my type of game. You didn't have to play defense for more than two seconds. It was a lot of fun, just to go up and down, playing ball.

We never got to the Final Four when I was in school, never won a national championship. As I look back, winning a national championship is everyone's ultimate goal and dream. But just the experience of college life, being able to play for the best college basketball school in the country, that was all I had ever dreamed of. I saw it truly as a blessing.

He gave me an opportunity to fulfill my dream and my parents' dream. He was also a father figure to me. That's something I'll always cherish and carry with me throughout my life. He's truly a legend as a coach, and as a man.

DAVID MAY

May, a walk-on at North Carolina in 1987-88 and 1988-89, is a gastrologist at the University of North Carolina Hospitals in Chapel Hill.

I didn't start playing basketball until eleventh grade. I had gotten cut my sophomore and junior years at Page H.S. I switched to Greensboro Day, and ended up playing half my junior year and my senior year. I didn't have any expectations of playing college basketball. I didn't even know they had JV basketball at Carolina until a couple of days before the tryouts.

I tried out freshman year and made the team. I ended up playing two years, first under Roy Williams, then under Randy Wiel. I figured my college career was over, until I got a call on October 13 of my junior year. It was Roy Williams saying they needed someone to help out at practice, which I was happy to do. I ended up trying out and making the team. So, I went from not thinking I was going to play high-school basketball to being on Carolina's team. It was quite a change.

Under the Carolina system, a walk-on gets treated just like any other player. I guess that's hard for some people to fathom. But you can't find any instance where a walk-on is treated any differently than anybody else, from the respect from the coaches right down to who gets to drink water during breaks. That's important. As someone who didn't play a lot as a walk-on, you realize that the coaches understand that your role is important. They show you that respect. There's that old saying: "You're only as good as you practice." You realize that if you don't push your teammates hard, they're not going to be ready.

I ended up playing more than I ever thought. My first game was the Tipoff Classic in Springfield, Massachusetts, my junior year. I think we were number one and Syracuse was number two. I ended up playing six or seven minutes— J.R. Reid and Steve Bucknall were suspended. I had graded out well defensively. They told me I'd have to play a lot. I went from not thinking I was going to play to being on national TV, number one versus number two. I just had to do what I had to do. It was more like a dream. It wasn't like I expected it. Everyone else on the team was ranked in the top twenty coming out of high school. They knew they'd be there. I thought I'd be up with the students cheering.

David May

A couple of times, I came in with the game still on the line. Most of the time I came in after the game was decided, which was probably appropriate. I got a start against Duke my last game as a senior—that's the tradition. I won the screener's award. I was only in there two-and-a-half minutes. But I remember screening anyone in my way—my own teammates, the referees. I set, like, 13 screens in two-and-a-half minutes. I had to break the record for number of screens. If I had played the whole game, I probably would have set, like, 200 screens.

I always realized I was a role player. Defensively, I always went out and played the best defense I could. When it came to offense, I just wanted to have no turnovers and set screens. They would grade you on every game. I wasn't going out to win the screener's award. But I don't think anyone in the history of North Carolina basketball has set more screens per minute.

You hear so many good things about Coach Smith. To find out what you hear is true, I think it's very rare nowadays to have that. Not only did he provide me with a chance to play for Carolina for two years, but as a walk-on, he always made me feel like I was part of the Carolina family. He always writes Christmas letters. He sent a gift and a note when I got married. When you have children, he sends you a note. You feel like he's interested in what's going on, not only when you're there, but after you're finished.

He impressed as a person first, and as a coach second. His honesty, his integrity—all those things people say about him, it's true.

SCOTT WILLIAMS

Williams, a center at North Carolina from 1986-87 to 1989-90, won three NBA titles with the Chicago Bulls before joining the Philadelphia 76ers in 1994.

He remembers the comfort that Dean Smith offered him in 1987, when he lost both his parents in a murder-suicide.

It happened after my freshman year. I was just getting ready for my sophomore season. I remember being in my dormitory, getting ready for an early class. It was an eight o'clock class. God only knows why I took that class—I'm not a morning person. But I remember being up early that day. I normally had to hustle, throw on a pair of sweats. But I got ready to leave on time. I got dressed, had breakfast, the whole nine yards.

There was a knock on the door. It was Coach Smith. I'm going: "My God, what did we do? What is he doing here at a quarter to eight in the morning?" I thought we were really in deep water. Lo and behold, he sat down. He asked my roommate to step out. He told me what happened. I didn't even react at the time. I remember shedding a few tears, but not really reacting. I was in a state of shock. But the sorrow and the comfort that he showed . . . it would be very hard for me to tell someone that. But he was very comforting. He helped me through it. He helped me through a very difficult moment in my life. He helped me tremendously.

This wasn't one of those things where a week after the funeral, it was over, you tried to put your life together. I struggled with this for a number of years. I really had some problems. The biggest thing Coach Smith did for me at the time was realizing that this was something I would need professional help with. I always thought that only crazy people sought psychiatric counseling. He really convinced me that I needed to talk to somebody about this, not try to keep it inside. And I'm glad I did.

It really helped me, being able to discuss it. I wasn't a very talkative person. Talking to somebody I didn't know wasn't easy at first. But I realized it was an opportunity to share what I was feeling. My older brother, Albert, relocated from California to North Carolina, and that was a tremendous help as well. It was just the two of us. We were able to share things when we had bad days, and we were there to help each other on good days. He's actually getting his degree from the University of North Carolina right now.

Some people said: "Take a year off." Basketball, for me, was therapy in itself. Being out on the floor, busting my butt in practice, being with my teammates, being with the coaching staff, that was probably some of the best therapy. For that two hours, being out there banging and running and dying in practice, I forgot about everything else. It was a great escape. I'm glad I continued playing.

I was one of their first recruits in California. Originally, I was contacted by Eddie Fogler. He told me a little bit about the program at North Carolina and Coach Smith. When he talked about Coach Smith, he didn't brag on his accomplishments. Yet, you could tell that he was really impressed with the man. When he spoke about Coach Smith, you got a sense that this was somebody you had to meet. That really captured my attention.

I didn't know a whole lot about North Carolina basketball. I had grown up outside Los Angeles, a big UCLA fan, the Coach Wooden teams, all the great players that they had. I always wanted to go to UCLA. The only thing I really knew about North Carolina basketball is that they beat my Georgetown Hoyas in the '82 championship game. I was pulling for Georgetown. I didn't really follow much basketball outside of the Lakers and Bruins.

Listening to Coach Smith talk about his program, his philosophy on basketball and life, it really connected with me. It wasn't like some of the other coaches who came in and sat down with a hard sell on their program, why this was a school for you, what they could do for you. He just basically

Scott Williams

sat down and talked about himself and the program. It was a sense of comfort speaking with him. This guy was a straight shooter. He's not sitting here—not to put down other coaches—like a used-car salesman. They would come in to visit you in a short period of time and try to sell you everything.

He was the only coach to extend an invitation to my mother to come with me on my recruiting visit. I had taken visits to DePaul, Georgia Tech and Villanova. None of the other coaches had extended invitations to my mother. She was obviously impressed with that right away. He didn't promise me a starting position, a certain amount of shots or minutes. It was straightforward—"Here's what we have to offer the Williams family." They didn't pay for my mother's trip. But they extended the opportunity for her to come with me. At the end of the three-day visit, I remember sitting in Coach Smith's office—it was still in Carmichael—and her wanting me to tell Coach Smith then and there that I was coming. I was like: "Ma, let's go back home and think about this for a while." She was sold right from the very beginning.

He coached different generations of players. He was able to adjust. When we came in, we were the guys dunking, swinging on the rim, growling when we got rebounds, whooping it up a lot on the court. We weren't the Fab Five, with all the noise they made. But we definitely had a different personality from some of the North Carolina teams in the past. We liked to get in your face, challenge people. He adjusted to that. He toned us down a little bit, but he didn't take away our individuality. He allowed us to be the players that we were, but he molded us into the players he wanted us to be.

He wasn't a tyrant. He ran the program, there was no doubt about that. But he didn't wield his power in a way where you felt it was overbearing. He didn't keep his thumb on top of you the entire time you were there, either. He watched out for you as a father influence. But he allowed you to grow as young men, trying to fit into society, becoming a team.

One time, we had a party back at the dormitory. It was one of those late-night parties. We made a lot of noise. Administrators were called to quiet us down. Of course, word got back to Coach Smith. He found out about everything. Well, we always ran sprints at the end of practice. The next day, he said: "Everybody that was at the party last night have a seat." Everybody was honest about it with Coach Smith. He was one man you did not want to try to fool. Then he said: "Everybody who wasn't at the party, on the end line."

He went off about how we were a team, teams try to stay together, play together. He let the guys have it in a negative way. He told them to run six crossings—down, back, down, back, down, back, the length of the floor. He gave them pretty tough times to meet. I was thinking: "Boy, those guys really got it." They ran. They barely made their times. They were out of breath. Then he said: "Everybody who was at the party, on the line."

He ran us until guys just started dropping, puking, everything else. He said there was no reason for all the complaints he got from the administrative staff. He put 100 points on the scoreboard. Every time you ran down and back, he would take off two points. If we didn't make our times, no points came off the board. It was something I'll never forget my entire life, how hard we worked that night. I remember Marty Hensley just rolling off to the side of the court. He couldn't make it up and down. Coach Smith told Bill Guthridge: "Just take him over there and run him 'til he drops."

I remember that he quit smoking while I was in school. When I first got there, he would have a couple of cigarettes—and I mean a couple at one time. We'd have a two-minute break for the seniors, 1:30 for the juniors, 1:15 for the sophomores. He never smoked in front of his players. He would go off into a back area and close a curtain. All you would hear was the whistle blow. You knew it was the next class's turn to get water.

What we didn't realize until after we'd been there for a while is that he'd be back there sometimes with two or three cigarettes lit at the same time. You'd go back there after practice and see little cigarette butts. That was the thing with Coach Smith. He didn't try to make you think he was perfect. He was a man like all of us. We sometimes thought he was perfect. He just tried to be a good example. Smoking is something I don't do to this day. But it was something he wouldn't want us to do. It was a problem he struggled with. And he dealt with it.

The fundamentals that he taught me, they've kept me in this league. I'm not the quickest guy. I'm not the strongest guy. And I'm not the tallest guy. But I've played nine seasons. That doesn't happen very often. The fundamentals I learned at North Carolina have really been a bonus for my career. Look around at a lot of the Carolina guys—J.R., Joe Wolf. We don't have the physical skills that a lot of kids have nowadays, but we have the edge because we were taught all the fundamentals, taught how to play basketball right.

When I was with Chicago my first year in the league, I was really playing well in practice, and I wasn't getting any playing time. I'd get four or five DNP-CDs—Did Not Play, Coach's Decision—in a row. That was very difficult for me. Whatever level I had played in any sport, I was always out there. I wasn't always the best player, but I competed as hard as anyone. It was difficult for me to sit there and have to watch, not be a contributing part of the team.

He was there for me, to calm me, to comfort me, to encourage me to continue to work hard in practice, that my time would come. Sure enough, Bill Cartwright, one of the players I was sitting behind, got injured. There was an opportunity for me to pick up a few more minutes per game. By the playoffs, I found myself out there playing against Magic Johnson, James Worthy, Byron Scott and A.C. Green in the championship series against the Lakers, on the Forum court, the court I had been to many times growing up, to see the teams that I idolized. Winning a championship on that floor was the most satisfying thrill that I think I've gotten in professional sports.

But the biggest thing I learned about Coach Smith is that he didn't care if you played in the NBA. He cared about your development as a person, no matter if you went to grad school, the NBA or right to work. Talk to anybody who went there—he knows if you're married, single, kids' names, how your parents are doing. That's not because he tries. It's because he loves the people who played for him.

We're all family. I see Joe Wolf, and we talk like we're still back in school together. It's like we never left. It's like that with all the guys who have played there. It was not necessary for us to join fraternities. Carolina basketball, that was our frat. We realized we all played for the same man. We all ran the hill. We all ran the Finley Golf Course. We all did things that you were required to do to be part of that family. No one got a shortcut. No one got a break, whether it was a star player out of high school, or a guy from the junior-varsity team called up to the varsity. Everyone was treated the same.

He gives all the credit back to his players. He's never taken credit for any of his victories. But what I do like is that he takes credit for all the losses. You don't find that with every coach. He'll always say: "I didn't do a good job preparing the team." We all know that's not always true. But with the media scrutiny that comes at a high-level program like North Carolina, all the players do appreciate it.

I grew tremendously as a man at North Carolina. When I got there, I was a very young 18 years old. I grew up in a suburban community outside Los Angeles, a well-to-do area. My parents weren't well-to-do, but they saved every dime to afford me a better education, a nicer home. I was very naive, very young. I left North Carolina not only with my college degree, but my life degree. I became a man at that University. A lot of that is due to Coach Smith. Probably most of it is due to Coach Smith.

It's funny, I still get sweaty palms, even when I sit down with him today.

J.R. REID

Reid, one of the most heralded high school players in the nation when he chose North Carolina, was the 1987 ACC Rookie of the Year, a consensus All-American as a sophomore and the ACC Tournament MVP as a junior. In 1989, he became the fourth Carolina player to enter the NBA draft with college eligibility remaining, and was the fifth pick overall by the Charlotte Hornets. He also has played for the San Antonio Spurs, New York Knicks and Los Angeles Lakers.

I went to the camp from the sixth grade until the tenth grade. I knew the staff for years. Eddie Fogler, Roy Williams, they had been recruiting me since I was 11 or 12 years old. And as I got older, I realized that no one else could offer me what Carolina offered. I wanted to go into communications, and they had the best communications program. They had the best coaches in the league. And they had the best returning team—Kenny Smith, Joe Wolf, those guys. I would be playing close to home, just three hours away, so my mom could get down and see me. That was important, too.

As a freshman, I was willing to listen and learn. Coming in, we had great seniors. They helped teach me the offense. I learned the defensive rotation. After the first couple of games, I started feeling more comfortable. But Coach Smith stayed on me. At the time, only a few freshmen had started at Carolina. I took it as an honor. I tried to bust my tail. I played hard. I might have talked a lot of stuff, but I still respected everyone. I wanted to be treated like the other guys.

I was just a talker. That was just the way I played. Carolina had the reputation of being a bunch of nice guys. Myself, Steve Bucknall, Scott Williams, we were a little temperamental. We played with a lot of emotion. For a Carolina team, it was kind of a different perspective. I used to get into it with players on the court. But he would never let you get a technical. You couldn't get a technical. I played physical, but I was never dirty. And as long as I worked hard in practice, Coach Smith and I never had a problem.

He was upset when I was on the cover of *Sports Illustrated* as a freshman, just because of the way the Carolina tradition is. You go through, work hard, pay your dues. When you're a senior, it gets a little easier at practice. We had players like Kenny Smith and Joe Wolf. Coach Smith thought they should get the publicity, and rightly so. But I came in with the hairstyle. I just seemed to get a lot of attention. Everyone was good about it. We played unselfishly. It wasn't my fault they put me on the cover. If they wanted to do that, that was on them. I came in and did what I had to do.

The sign they held up at Cameron, saying, "J.R. can't Reid?" That was Duke. They didn't have anything else to say. They knew my SATs. They knew Scott Williams was a good student. They knew what kind of students Danny Ferry and Christian Laettner were— they went to school with them. I got my degree. Scott went back and got his. As long as we could go in and beat up on them, we didn't care. But Coach Smith didn't like it. He thought there might have been a little racial element to it. He really stood up for us. That's the type of man he is. That's why you never hear any players say anything negative about him. He's a genuine person. He always treated everyone the same.

He was upset when Steve Bucknall and I got into that bar fight (near the North Carolina State campus in the summer of 1987). It was part of college life. Things like that happen. A couple of State guys were messing

J.R. Reid

with us, and we got into it. He suspended us for a game, and that was it. We went on.

We sat down after my junior year, when I was thinking about leaving school. He came to me. Teams had been calling. We talked, and my parents were there. He said: "If it were my son, I would tell him it was time to go." I had an opportunity to do great things. I was only twelve hours short of graduating after my junior year. He said to make sure the team put a bonus in my contract for graduating. He handled everything for me, sat in when all the agents came in. He went all out for us.

I probably could have gone to Maryland and averaged a lot more. But I knew that when I went to Carolina. I knew they had a system. When I was choosing schools, I knew it was the best place for me. Just look at all the names of the people who went there. And it worked out great. I was looking down the line. I knew I could have been dropping 30 (points) and 15 (rebounds) somewhere else. But I wanted to go where I would become a better player, and maintain it in the next league.

I still talk to him. With all this trade talk (in early 1999) about me going to the Lakers, he was the first person I called. Coach Smith knows everyone. Everyone knows him. The GMs in the league call him to get information. Everyone likes to talk to Coach Smith. He's in the know.

I still call and chat. I had a blast playing for Coach Smith. Even now, I wouldn't go anywhere else. I had a ball.

RICK FOX

Fox, a forward at North Carolina from 1987-88 to 1990-91, has played for the Boston Celtics and Los Angeles Lakers.

We had more incidents when I was a senior than when I was an underclassman. I really looked forward to becoming a senior. I knew what it meant. I knew it meant that it was my team, along with King (Rice) and Pete (Chilcutt). It was finally my time to show Coach Smith I was a leader. We were going to get it done at all costs.

Sometimes I got a little too confident. I remember a few times he pulled me back to let me know: "You're the team leader, but I'm still the coach." I remember one time when we were practicing. I was working really hard. I kind of leaned over, and pulled on my shorts with my hands. Coach Smith stopped practice. He said: "Rick, are you tired?" I stopped for a second to think about it. In my mind, I was quite obviously tired. I said: "Yes, I'm tired."

He said: "What?" He couldn't believe I had said that. He said: "What do you mean you're tired? I'll ask you one more time: 'Are you tired?'" I knew I had already said yes, so there was no way out of it. I said yes again. He said: "Coach Ford, take him over on the sidelines and run him to death."

He put 100 points on the board, so we could count down. I just remember running and running. He asked Coach Ford if I was working hard. Coach Ford said: "He's working, Coach." And Coach Smith said: "Get him back over here." He asked: "Are you tired?" By now, I knew what to say. I said: "Nah, I'm OK."

I was constantly trying to work on my game in practice. Sometimes that might have aggravated Coach Smith. I was always trying something new. I started trying to be a passer, create for other people. I felt I needed to penetrate more. During practice, I'd penetrate, leave my feet and throw a pass. But the young guys, they wouldn't catch it, and the ball would go out of bounds.

After three possessions like this, Coach said: "Look, Rick, you're a scorer. Put the ball in the hole." A few minutes later, I went up in the air and somebody was wide open underneath. I threw it to him, and it went out of bounds. Coach stopped practice. Now he's mad. And I'm mad—the guys weren't catching the ball.

**Rick Fox (Photo
by Jim Hawkins)**

He said: "Rick, don't you listen to me? Do I have to tell you to throw it out of bounds to get you to shoot? Next time, just throw it out of bounds." We ran a play—and King, to this day, is guilty of this, he wanted to see what I would do. I came off a screen, caught it, stopped and threw the ball up in the stands. It was like this eerie silence came over practice. Coach finally said: "At least you listened to me." I wasn't doing it out of disrespect. He was trying to make a point—"Do I have to tell you to do the opposite to get you to do something?" Everyone who knows Coach or who has been to one of our practices knows that is one of the craziest things I could have done.

It wasn't until I actually met Coach Smith on the home visit that I knew I wanted to be a part of the program. Not only did he want me to be a part, he also challenged me. He told me he admired my ability and potential as a basketball player. He thought I would enjoy my experience at North Carolina, get an education, learn a lot. But at the end of that, he said: "I have to tell you, we're going to win with or without you." I always remembered that. It stuck with me.

It wasn't arrogance. It was just confidence. He knew the program would provide certain opportunities for kids. He wanted to see me be one of those kids. But when he said: "We're going to win with or without you," I thought: "Shoot, you've proven that." I didn't want to be a fool and lose somewhere else. I visited four other schools, but just to play hooky. All along after he said that, I knew I wanted to be there. I accepted the opportunity to be part of that.

The biggest adjustment was being on my own, away from a family environment. When you leave home, you're used to certain things, having that support, parents who nurture you, direct you in a certain path. In college, you're in an atmosphere where you're technically on your own. More or less, you suffer the consequences of your choices you make, good or bad. At Carolina, you're out there on your own. But at the same time, I felt like I walked out of my immediate family into another family.

There's so much emphasis on the fact that we are a family. We look out for each other. Coach Smith is like a father figure. The people who work under him are like your uncles. The secretaries are like your mothers and sisters. There's a complete feeling of warmth. You're able to still feel loved by that group of people. When your four years are over, you've gained maturity, grown into manhood.

I was new and young to the game. I still needed to learn how to play. Coach Smith, to my mind, after playing for him, is the best teacher of the game. I learned to play under him. The game became easier and easier. You have your ups and downs. You struggle at first. But he's always there in such an instructive way, a fatherly way. You couldn't help but turn to him. He was in it for more than just basketball. You knew he stood on your side.

As a freshman, I didn't really enjoy seeing Coach Guthridge. I thought he was a dictator. Every time you saw him, nothing good came out of it. He was the arm of the law for Coach Smith. He was the guy who laid down all the discipline, all the academic and team rules. But when you get your diploma, graduate and look back, you realize you wouldn't have made it without him. He and Coach Smith worked as a team, good cop, bad cop.

My first year, most of my contact with Coach Smith was in film sessions and meetings. At that point of my career, he had more of a God-fearing presence than when I was a senior. Going from your freshman year to your senior year, he gives you more responsibility, challenges you more. He challenges you to step to another level, and he gets it out of you.

Some people have to be handled differently. He's a master of knowing what strings to pull with certain individuals, when he needs to back off. I was always an individual who wanted more and more instructions, to be challenged. He knew that. He pushed me in many ways. By the time I became a senior, I definitely felt as if we were working together on the same page. I knew what needed to be done.

At times, the egos get out of hand. Guys think they should be playing more. He would always bring us back to reality. People would say to me: "You're from Indiana. Why didn't you play for Coach Knight? Were you afraid you couldn't handle his screaming?" What people didn't understand was that he was no different from Coach Knight. Yes, Coach Knight swore, and Coach Smith never swore. But Coach Smith has an ability to make you feel as small as Coach Knight does without swearing.

He knew how to get his point across. He knew how to kick your ego out from under you, so you know that team was the most important thing. Carolina basketball is all about team. Individual success comes after team success. That's a lesson you learn. He teaches that through humbling you. Many times, he would make you well aware that there was no "I" in team. He'd say: "You're not back in Warsaw, Indiana. This isn't some All-Star team."

Losing to Kansas in the Final Four my senior year was probably the most disappointing thing I can remember. I hate to even bring up something negative. It's something I'll never be able to go back and do again. That's what hurt the most. To me, that's what going to Carolina was all about, winning a national championship. To go from getting to the Final Four one week—something that Carolina hadn't done in nine years—to losing the next week, I always put a lot of that on myself. I kind of felt I let Coach Smith down. Winning an NCAA championship was something that I always dreamed about. Getting there wasn't good enough. If I had another year to go back, I would have been fine. But I knew I'd never return.

Was I surprised Coach Smith got thrown out of that game? Nothing about that game surprises me anymore. It was such an uncharacteristic game for us. I was playing in Indiana, where I started my basketball career. All I can remember about that day is leaving my heart in that locker room, pouring out my emotions. It really hurt. To say I was crying would be an understatement. I never cried like that in my life.

Today, my relationship with Coach Smith continues to grow. I talk to Coach more now than I did in college. A lot of kids don't get that out of their school—it's: "Thanks for four years. See you later." He leaves me messages. He keeps up with how I'm doing. He went from a mentor and father figure to a friend and confidant. It just stays that way. The longer you're out of school, the more you get to see a side you didn't see in college.

I can remember the camps in the summer. There would always be parties for the coaching staff and counselors. They'd get together and go have a beer at the end of each session. My first couple of years out of college, I worked the camp, but couldn't have a beer. There was a five-year waiting period—you had to be out of Carolina five years. I still haven't had that beer yet. I worked the camp my first four years out of school, but haven't been back since.

I just want to have a beer with him. Someday, I will.

HUBERT DAVIS

Davis, the nephew of former Carolina great Walter Davis, scored 35 points in his last regular-season game at Duke and 25 points in the 1991 national semifinal against Kansas. The 20th overall selection by the New York Knicks in the 1992 NBA draft, he now plays for the Dallas Mavericks.

I wasn't highly recruited. In fact, he told me on his visit that he didn't think I was good enough to play at North Carolina. I had known him since I was three years old because of my uncle. I went to his basketball camp for eight or nine years. But he thought I would get guaranteed playing time at a lower Division I school. He couldn't promise that I'd be anything more than a practice player at Carolina. He said that he would still give me a scholarship if I wanted to come. And he said he'd call me in three weeks, let me decide.

He called the next night. He asked: "Do you want to come or not?" He said he was going to recruit someone else, but he wanted to give me a last shot at it, if I wanted to go. I said I would. He didn't think I could play there. But I thought I could help the team.

I was talking to high Division I schools—all the other ACC schools were recruiting me, plus Indiana. North Carolina was a little different than the high Division I's. Coach Smith thought at someplace like Richmond I'd start all four years. But my dream was to go to North Carolina. I had been a fan since birth. I said: "If I ever get the opportunity to go to North Carolina, I'll do it. If it doesn't work out basketball-wise, I'd still be going to a great university and be part of great teams." It wasn't even a hard choice for me.

How soon did Coach change his mind? The first day of practice, he said: "You might have something here." And I played a little bit my freshman year. Jeff Lebo got hurt. I was in the rotation, playing OK. But it took until the beginning of my junior year for him to finally say: "OK, you're going to start." It took two years to break through what Coach Smith had thought, to become the starter every night.

I absolutely loved it. He could have done anything. I don't think people understand—I was a North Carolina fan. I was just so excited to be in the program. I couldn't believe I was playing with Jeff Lebo, Steve Bucknall, J.R. Reid, and Coach Smith was telling me what to do. To dream about that since I was three years old, then to actually live it each day at practice, it was awesome.

Of course, it didn't always go smoothly. The beginning of my junior year, we were playing South Carolina in the Diet Pepsi Tournament of Champions in Charlotte. We were up by one in the final minute. South Carolina missed, and I got the rebound. For some reason, I didn't hold the ball. I dribbled all the way down the court, shot a 20-footer and bricked it. They got the rebound, came back, scored and won (76-74).

Coach Smith was on the sidelines, going: "Hold it! Hold it!" As I kept dribbling down the court, he kept increasingly jumping higher. I was in the doghouse for a while. I couldn't do anything right. They always teased me about that shot. It's very rare when Carolina doesn't win that tournament. And when we lost in the '90-'91 season, it was definitely my fault.

He didn't usually talk to you after games. We'd talk about it the next day. He was really good about that. After a game, your emotions are running high, you might do something or say something that you wouldn't the next day. He likes to let it rest for a day, then talk about it when it's still fresh in your mind. He's very firm in his voice. But when he talks, he never makes you feel small. The great thing about Carolina is that there's no cursing. They treat you with respect. But they are hard on you.

My junior year, when I was in that doghouse, I also was in a little slump. I went to him and said: "Coach, I can do a lot more to help the team." I said: "Coach, it seems like you don't even like me." He said: "What? I love you! I love you!" We started talking. He said: "How did you play in high school?" I said I played free. I just played ball. Nothing mattered. He said: "Do that in practice, and after practice we'll talk about your game." I had a good practice. I felt real loose and free.

The next game at North Carolina State, we went in at halftime and I had zero points. I hadn't made a shot. He said: "Hubert, come here. Didn't I tell you to play like you did in high school?" I went out and had 17 points in the second half, and was the leading scorer the rest of the year. We went to the Final Four. And my senior year was everything that I expected.

Getting to the Final Four in 1991 (at Indianapolis) was a great opportunity. North Carolina hadn't been to one since '82. It was incredible to see 35,000 at practice at the (RCA) Dome. It was unbelievable. But I still remember the game. It's still a nightmare. I think the world of Coach Roy Williams and the Kansas Jayhawks. They were a tremendous team. I just firmly believe that we had the better team.

Maybe we took them a little bit too lightly. A lot of us were off with our shooting. It just wasn't our night. That happens. But it was sad. I really felt like we had an opportunity to win. And if we had won, we would have

Hubert Davis (Photo by Keith Worrell, UNC)

played Duke—a team we had beaten by 22 points in the ACC championship game three weeks earlier. Not to say we would have beaten them, but we felt pretty good about our chances.

That was also the game that Coach Smith got thrown out of. I can't remember him getting the first technical. But I remember him trying to put Kenny Harris in. He was asking: "How much time do I have?" Mr. (Pete) Pavia called the technical, just on that. And the films show it. He was asking, "How much time, Pete? How much time?" It was really weird. Coach Smith didn't do anything that would warrant getting thrown out. It was the Final Four. There was a lot of emotion. It was just a very ugly situation. I didn't think it needed to be handled in that way.

My senior year, I felt like we had a really good team. But we were young. George Lynch was a junior. Everyone else was just starting to play. Eric Montross, Brian Reese, Derrick Phelps—they were all first-year starters. Donald Williams was a freshman who had never played. But I thought we had a really good year. We didn't have enough maturity to get there. But then next year, they were ready to go, and they wound up winning the national championship.

I never thought I would get drafted, that I'd be in the NBA after my four years. I thought I could help the team, but professional basketball, that was not even a dream. Maybe that's why I went to Carolina. I was going to get a good education. I always wanted to be a coach. I thought I would be a really solid player for the team. But I don't think anyone thought I would be here today, not even my father. It was so farfetched, I didn't even dream about it.

I've known Coach Smith so long, it's just really good as an adult to have a relationship with him. We're able to communicate a little bit more freely now. It's just incredible having him as a friend. Not just him, but the entire coaching staff. They call every week. And not just me, but walk-ons, too. They don't care about basketball. They care about you as a person.

When I got drafted, Coach Smith was like: "Oh my gosh, I'm sorry. I'm no judge of talent." I'd say: "Coach, you told me not to come here. What's up with you?" He would always start laughing. He said: "In your case, I made a mistake."

MICHAEL JORDAN

Michael Jordan declined to be interviewed for this book without a formal request from Dean Smith. The following combines Jordan's remarks from interviews with reporters after Smith's retirement on October 9, 1997, a speech he gave at a black-tie dinner honoring Smith in Chapel Hill on November 12, 1998, and an appearance with CNN's Larry King on June 14, 1999.

He is like a second father to me. I mean, at the time I was going to the university, I had never really left home before. My father and my mother (had) the confidence in him to take me to another level away from the game of basketball, in terms of making sure I got an education.

It's not the basketball talent, but the people that you are that he takes an interest in and tries to enhance with your time at the university. With that approach, he extends far beyond the university. He always has been really genuine with his players, and the education that he has given us was more as a person, and not so much as a basketball player.

My parents have always taught me that your first appearance sometimes dictates the personality that you carry and the way people view you. And that was, I guess, advanced even further with Coach Smith in his approach, how he felt athletes or college athletes should be presented in our travels. But you would be surprised in the way that he approaches fashion. He's not known for it,

Michael Jordan

Michael Jordan

you know, because he doesn't promote it. But yet, I think he has a certain style and certain eloquence about the way he dresses.

He advised me to (leave school). He thought that my skill level was ready for the pros. He felt that I needed a bigger challenge and he advised me to go . . . . His knowledge of the business surrounding basketball and certain things it takes to operate in front of the cameras or publicly have been a big help.

These are things I was taught at the University of North Carolina, and I carry these lessons with me every time I step in front of the media or in public life . . . I'd think: "Don't be a Charles Barkley. Don't just run out there and say something." Charles Barkley is one of my best friends, but he should have gone to Coach Smith!

I guess the memory that stands out is 1982, when he gave me the opportunity to make the basket. He had confidence in me when I didn't have confidence in myself. But by him doing that, it gave me the confidence that, "Hey, I have those skills." From that point forward, in making that shot and the confidence he showed in me, it propelled my career. I've always said that and believe that to this day. Without that shot, I don't know where I would be today.

It's sad that my kids are not going to have the opportunity to play for him, but I'm happy that he chose to leave at his own time, that he was able to make the decision for himself. He's left a legacy that we can all reminisce about, have memories of and carry forward.

Chapter Four

THE NINETIES

GEORGE LYNCH

Lynch helped Dean Smith win his second national championship, in 1993, and finished his career as one of only two players in ACC history to compile at least 1,500 points, 1,000 rebounds, 200 steals and 200 assists.

He was the Los Angeles Lakers' first-round pick in 1993 and later moved on to the Vancouver Grizzlies and Philadelphia 76ers.

My sophomore year, we lost to Kansas in the Final Four (79-73). Coach Smith believed in the seniors. The three seniors (Pete Chilcutt, Rick Fox and King Rice) were supposed to lead us. It just so happened, that night, they shot terribly. We were in that game, but we lost the game. The seniors had a bad ending to their career. That was one of the things I wanted to remember when it came my time to be a senior. I wanted to have one of my best games in my final game.

My junior year, we knew we had a young team. Hubert Davis was our only senior. Everyone else was a sophomore or junior. Ohio State, the team we lost to in the Sweet Sixteen, was a more experienced team. We played them in Lexington. We knew that we had a better chance of going to the Final Four the next year. But it was still disappointing. At Carolina, you expected to go to the Final Four every year.

The pressure was mounting up. Duke had just won back-to-back national titles. Whatever Duke does, Carolina expects to do better. There was a lot of pressure as far as going back to the Final Four and winning a national championship for Coach Smith. It had been ten years at that point. All of us wanted to get Coach Smith back in position to win a national championship.

He downplayed a lot of it. He told us it was more important for us to become men than winning a national championship. That kind of put things in perspective.

When you go to Carolina, you go because you have an opportunity to graduate, and an opportunity to win national championships. I always watched Carolina when they had Michael, James and Sam Perkins. My stepfather was a big North Carolina fan, a big supporter of Dean Smith. I knew I wanted to play in the ACC. I didn't know where.

Maryland was one of the schools. Virginia was one of the schools. And North Carolina. Being a young kid, I hadn't been on the campus of either Maryland or Virginia. Once I got more involved in the recruiting process—looked into the academics, saw what each school had to offer—it all kind of fell into place.

I didn't want to go to Maryland because of the Len Bias situation. Virginia and North Carolina both offered great academics. It came down to North Carolina being the better basketball program, Coach Smith being a future Hall of Famer, one of the greatest coaches ever. And it was one of my dreams to play in the NBA. Coach Smith did a great job preparing guys to get the opportunity to play in the NBA.

My freshman year was real tough. You always said: "If he gets on you, then he cares about you." I was one of those players he saw a lot of potential in. He rode me pretty hard. I expected it. All my high-school coaches (at Flint Hill Academy in Virginia) were tough. But he demanded a lot. Freshman year was by far the toughest year. He always saw the little things— boxing out, being in the right spot, running the play, being on time to class. He always knew about it. There was no room for freshmen to make mistakes.

I contributed right away. My high-school system was pretty much taken from Carolina's. My high-school coach, Stu Vetter, went to all the Carolina clinics. We tried to do everything exactly like Carolina—the practices, the pre-game meals, the game preparations. It wasn't a big adjustment. The competition—the quality of the players—was the biggest adjustment.

By my senior year, he knew the work ethic that I had, knew that I was going to be a leader for that team, do everything in my power to prepare the team, prepare myself. He let the seniors make a lot of decisions. It was like, if you're going to be a senior captain, you have to help us get there. I led by example. I lifted weights every day. I got there early and tried to be the last to leave.

We played Florida State in late January and trailed by twenty-one points in the second half. Coach Smith prepared us for that type of situation in practice. He would put the second team up by ten, give us a minute or two minutes to come back, just to teach us what to expect, how to come back. You can't get it all on one play. You've got to make each possession count.

He said: "Wouldn't it be great if we could get the lead under ten with two minutes left?" That was an attainable goal. We knew we could do it. Then, once we got it under ten, he said: "Wouldn't it be great if we could win the game?" He was loosening guys up. He said: "What do you think Florida State is thinking right now?"

Coach Smith (in that game) didn't really expect me to do things I couldn't do. I knew if I did what I could, did it within a team concept, I wouldn't be out of character. I wanted to get rebounds, stick-backs, play defense. Those are the things I did. I didn't try to shoot a lot of threes. I played within myself, and things worked out (Lynch stole a crosscourt pass by Charlie Ward and dunked to give Carolina the lead with under two minutes left, and the Tar Heels wound up outscoring Florida State, 28-4, over the last nine minutes to win, 82-77).

It was nice to talk about winning a national championship. But Coach Smith had put a picture of the Superdome in our lockers the first day of practice. The scoreboard said: "1993 NCAA Champions North Carolina." If you saw where the Final Four was going to be that year, that made it a little more attainable. It was one of those things where if you found yourself slipping, it reminded you of your goal.

We wanted to win the ACC tournament bad. Unfortunately, Derrick Phelps went out with an injury. Derrick talked to us after we lost in the ACC final to Georgia Tech (77-75). He said: "We're not going to lose any more games from here on out." That was great. He was hurt, but we knew he would work hard to get back in there. And he did a great job coming back and being our floor leader. It gave everyone else inspiration to play hard.

Knowing Coach Smith hadn't won one since 1982, we wanted to do it for him. There was a lot of talk that year about going back to New Orleans, déja vu with what happened in '82. We knew if we could get back there, Coach Smith would put us in a situation to win the game. And that's what happened.

A lot of people say Chris Webber's timeout cost Michigan the game. But we had a foul to give. Coach Smith instructed us to foul. Webber traveled after getting the ball inbounds. A lot of things might have happened. But if he hadn't called time out, we would have fouled. You never know. A lot of things happened before the timeout. The timeout was just the icing on the cake.

Before we went back on the court, our coaching staff said: "Michigan doesn't have any timeouts. Apply pressure." We picked them up fullcourt. He traveled. He got on the side of the court, and had nowhere to go. He called a timeout. That was their coach's fault. They should have been more prepared.

Coach Smith and I still talk. We talked more when he was still coaching—I could get hold of him in his office. Now that his schedule is a little different, he's tougher to get in touch with. But he makes an effort to return my phone calls. As a matter of fact, when I was deciding which team to go to as a free agent, I called Coach Smith. And things worked out for me. Of course I knew that Larry (Brown) had played at Carolina. But Coach Smith said I couldn't go wrong with Milwaukee—George Karl had played at Carolina, too. We sat down and talked about it. And I made the decision to come to Philadelphia.

He has meant a lot. I was the first in my family to make it out of high school, go on to college, graduate and make it to the NBA. He has helped me in a lot of professional decisions, as far as choosing an agent, choosing a financial adviser. As a free agent, it was very important to go to the right team, get my career jump-started again. I didn't call my mother or father. I called Coach Smith and asked him for advice. He has helped me make a lot of decisions in my life that helped me become the person I am.

Eric Montross

Montross, the starting center for North Carolina's 1993 NCAA championship team, was selected ninth by the Boston Celtics in the 1994 NBA draft. He later played for Dallas, New Jersey, Philadelphia and Detroit.

It's hard to put a measure on how much I improved. It's kind of a stepping-stone process. Going from high school to college is an incredible step. Going from college to the NBA is an incredible step. You're the best player on your high-school team, maybe the best in the state. All of a sudden you get to college, and you become teammates with those same types of players, and you're playing against them at Clemson, Duke, Wake Forest.

Especially as a post player, you have to learn how to control your body better. In high school, nobody was stronger than I was. I was always stronger, and most of the time I was bigger. Now, all of a sudden, you're going up against guys your size and your strength. It's almost a whole new learning process. I remember going up against guys like Kevin Salvadori and Matt Wenstrom. There were days I just remember thinking to myself: "I know I should be able to score on these players." It was very frustrating. Here I am, playing against guys my size, and they're bothering me, pushing me off-balance. I think I improved drastically.

Coach Guthridge would work with the post players, Coach Smith more with the perimeter players. But Coach Smith floated around. He was involved in all facets of the game. Just when you didn't want him to notice something, he'd come over and say: "You ought to be doing this." You'd think

Eric Montross

you could get it by him. But he noticed, and you got better. He had a real eye for little things.

I'm from Indianapolis. Dean and Bob Knight were, and are, fairly good friends. They kind of had an agreement that they wouldn't go into each other's backyard and recruit. But my high-school coach, Jack Keeler, had been at Coach Smith's camps for many years. He said: "Have you ever thought about going to North Carolina?" At that point, I really hadn't. I was in Big Ten country.

That summer, Coach Smith came to one of our open gyms and watched me play. That was one of the first times I had much interaction with him. He was under one of the baskets on a side court just watching us play. It was pretty exciting for me as a high school kid, and of course, for the other kids on our team.

I remember him coming to my home for the home visit and just being floored by him. I was impressed with him. He was so straightforward, so honest. He didn't make promises to me as a player. You know how it can be. Coaches would call on Mother's Day. I'd answer the phone. They'd ask: "Is your mother home? I just wanted to wish her a Happy Mother's Day." I'm sure Coach Smith would have said: "Happy Mother's Day," too. But he wasn't going to use those tactics.

He never promised me playing time. He never promised me a starting position. Those things were in front of me from other schools. I was looking forward to having a great college career. But I knew enough about the game of basketball to recognize that I had to go through a learning process. It got down to Indiana, Michigan and Carolina. I had family ties to the University of Michigan (the alma mater of both Montross' father and grandfather). I had local ties to Indiana. I grew up going to Indiana games. I thought it was going to be a very close decision, a very tough decision. I tried to put it off in my mind. But it was actually one of the easiest decisions I've ever made.

I guess other people would say this about their recruiting class, but I couldn't have picked a better group to be a part of. There were guys from all walks of life. College was a great learning experience for all of us. We were dedicated to winning, dedicated to working hard. We all had one common desire to play. Pat (Sullivan) was pretty funny (during the recruiting period). He'd call me, we'd talk about North Carolina, call Brian Reese, talk to him. Pat was sort of networking, as I look back on it. He was the one with a lot of spunk going into it.

Freshman year was a crash course in Dean Smith basketball. It took me a while to get adjusted. I thought of myself as a pretty smart player. I realized pretty quickly there was a lot more I needed to know. I tried to do everything perfectly, as most players would, to impress the coaches. I ended up making mistakes, fumbling around. It was a learning experience.

I didn't start. Looking back, that was probably one of the best things for me. I wasn't frustrated that I didn't start. There were times I was frustrated with myself for not being able to get the plays right. But there was never a frustration level with the coach on our team. The relationship we had with Coach Smith was great. You knew exactly where you stood on everything. Everything was right in front of you.

My freshman year, we went to the Final Four and lost to Kansas. It was a tough loss, but I was just along for the ride. I really didn't know what college basketball was all about. We were having a great time. The ACC battles were incredible. But I didn't fall head over heels for college basketball. Sophomore year is when I started to feel more comfortable. I was starting to play more. I was totally enveloped by it.

That year, we lost to Ohio State in the Sweet Sixteen (80-73). That was a terrible loss. We thought we were better than that. But that summer, players started blossoming. Brian Reese really came forward. Derrick Phelps was a great point guard his entire four years, but he really grew into being the leader of the team. Pat was going to give us great minutes—he was a very smart player. The group of guys I came in with resolved that we were going to win. Not just win the ACC or the conference tournament. We were going to win the Big Dance.

Coach Smith challenged us to get better and better. When you lose, some coaches will say: "It's only one loss, don't worry about it, just keep going." Coach always broke down tape. He was very positive in the film sessions. But it was very much a learning experience when we lost. Our losses improved us more than our wins did. Late in the year, our losses made us a better team.

We beat Duke (83-69) right at the end of the year. That was a big win for us. It was something that stuck out in my mind, kind of a rallying point. Anytime you play Duke and win, it's a huge, huge win. But the game that really stood out was in the NCAAs against Arkansas in the Sweet Sixteen. Coach designed a backdoor play in a game that was right down to the wire—a backdoor to Brian Reese to basically win the game. A lot of coaches understand how the other team plays you. But that play worked so flawlessly, in one of the biggest, toughest games we had been in. We all kind of looked at each other and said: "That's incredible. The play worked perfectly."

The championship game against Michigan, a game like that has so much scrutiny. When someone makes a mistake—like Chris Webber calling a timeout when his team didn't have any—it's going to be highlighted for years to come. But the fact of the matter is, we had a foul to give. In our minds, we were in control.

Every day in practice, we worked on last-minute situations —up one, down one, up five, down five. We knew exactly what we needed to do as a team. And the team we had on the court was so focused. We felt very confident in that situation. I don't think it would have made any difference if he hadn't called time out. All it did was ice it for us. When Donald Williams made those free throws, that was it.

I can't remember exactly what Coach Smith said at the end. Obviously, he was thrilled. There was so much emotion running through the whole game. He was just so happy for the team to have succeeded, met the challenge that he had given us. It was the culmination of all the trials and tribulations of the season. We only lost four games. But you always have highs and lows, dips to the season. To finally come through and be the best, that's like Mecca for a college team and a college coach.

After we won, I had my end-of-season meeting with Coach Smith. He very plainly told me: "You've done an incredible amount for this team, this university. I want you to do what you want to do. If that's to go to the NBA, I want it to be your decision." He thought at the time that I probably would be picked number eight with an outside chance that I would go one or two places higher.

I looked at him and said: "Coach, I'm having too much fun. I'm enjoying college. I want to be on the team next year." And that was the truth. As much as basketball was part of our lives, going to school and getting a degree was as big a part of the experience. I wasn't just looking at it as trying to win a national championship. I wanted to stay at Carolina. And I did.

PAT SULLIVAN

Sullivan, one of eight players to be a part of three Final Four teams at North Carolina (1991, '93, '95), is an assistant coach at North Carolina under Bill Guthridge.

My father left my home when I was 14 or 15. I remember talking to Mike O'Koren when I was in high school. He knew I was interested in Carolina. He saw that I might be good enough to go down there and play. He talked to me about what kind of place it was, the feeling of family that I'd get. I could tell he was really sincere. It meant a lot to me coming from another Jersey guy. I figured he wasn't going to steer me wrong.

The coaches came to my home in September of my senior year—Coach Smith, Coach Guthridge and Coach Ford. Coach Smith was this legend that everyone knew about. They pulled up in a white Lincoln. There were a bunch of kids around. All the kids ran up to him and asked him for an autograph. It was a pretty big deal to have Coach Smith come to your high school, then sit in your home. It was overwhelming. But the coaches were so down to earth, really laid-back. I remember at one point, my mom was doing something, and I was talking to Coach Guthridge and Coach Ford. The doorbell rang. And he got up to get the door. He wasn't too good to do something like that.

That great recruiting class we had—Eric Montross, Brian Reese, Derrick Phelps, Clifford Rozier—I didn't really consider myself like that. I knew Brian and Derrick pretty well—they were from the New York area. I had never seen Clifford play, and the only time I had seen Montross was at a Nike All-America camp. At the time, he was the top center in the country, maybe the top player. The recruiting class, I didn't really think about it too much. I knew who Eric was. I knew Brian and Derrick were going to be good. Everyone hyped up how good the class was going to be, but Eric didn't commit until after his senior season.

I called him fairly often. I had taken my visit to Carolina and fallen in love with the place. I got to spend time with Coach Smith. I knew he was very genuine, very sincere. I could tell he was a father figure. I could tell the team was close-knit. I called Montross to let him know often that it was a great place. We had visited together and formed a friendship.

My freshman year was pretty tough. With all the hype we got, it seemed like there were five of us, and ten other guys. Coach Smith did an unbelievable job bringing us down to earth. You're obviously going to have an ego when you go into a program like that, and with all the attention we were getting. Coach Smith brought us down to earth quickly. At times, I didn't think he knew what my name was. He called each of us "Freshman." Sometimes, I felt like I wanted to reintroduce myself to him—"I'm Pat Sullivan."

One of the first or second days of practice, I was dribbling down the baseline. Rick Fox was this big, strong kid, a senior. I thought he pushed me out of bounds. The coaches didn't see it that way. Coach Smith called me out and said: "Freshman, don't they have lines on the court in New Jersey?" Right away, I thought: "This guy is not fooling around."

Coach Smith would have the five of us play together against the starting group. Those guys took it to us at times. We held our own in the preseason. But when he was out there coaching them, he would whisper something in their ears. Next thing you know, we'd be losing in the drill like 20-2. He did it in front of a lot of people, too, at a coach's clinic one day. There was a passing drill we did. We couldn't stop the other team. They made like 90 straight passes against us. He whispered something like: "Let's play the motion offense." And the next thing I know, we couldn't do anything. This was in front of 600 or 700 coaches. That was sort of an ego buster.

My freshman year was a little bit of a wakeup call, but it was great. It was a dream come true to come out of high school and play in the Final Four—and I actually got to play, too. My sophomore year, I got to play more. But I lost some confidence. I wasn't shooting the ball well. I didn't feel like I wanted to shoot the ball. But that was the year that turned me around. Coach Smith had confidence in me. He'd be yelling at me to shoot the ball. The other guys would say: "You've got it made." They wished they had that problem. Some of them were getting the red light.

But I had lost confidence. I didn't think I belonged. After the season, he helped me more than anybody by instilling in me that confidence. He said he didn't know what came first—confidence or success, success or confidence. He told me that was something I

Pat Sullivan

would have to figure out on my own. But he told me I was a really good player, that I would be able to play my junior year if I worked hard. He liked me as a player and as a person. That's when I knew he really cared about me, wanted what was best for me. I worked as hard as I could that summer. All the members of the team did, wanting to get back to the Final Four—we had lost to Ohio State in the Sweet Sixteen. Coach Smith challenged us at our team banquet to be better.

There was a lot of talk after my sophomore year, people saying the game had passed him by. We did get some mail that we weren't any good, and he wasn't any good. I remember him coming back real intense. He challenged us to be really intense. It was just an unbelievable year, and it started the summer before. The team was really close. We went to the movies together. We were in a softball league together. We did everything together, mainly because of one guy—George Lynch. He was the senior leader. He wanted to win for Coach Smith more than for the team. He said: "We've got to do this for Coach Smith." Coach Smith never made us feel that way. We never heard individual goals from him. He wanted what was best for the team. We had incredible team defense. Coach Smith spent a lot of time making it that way.

In the championship game against Michigan, I was the one who missed the foul shot near the end. I got fouled. We were up one. I hit one to put us up two. I thought the second one would be easier, but I shot it long. (Chris) Webber got the rebound—traveled, in fact, but they didn't call it. I remember going back on defense, mad about missing the foul shot. He came downcourt, and Derrick and George got him in a pretty good trap. He called time out, and they didn't have any. One of the reasons why is because Lynch and Phelps did a pretty good job in the second half forcing them to use a timeout.

I was still upset. I didn't know they didn't have any timeouts. The guys on the bench knew. I'll always remember Scott Cherry jumping up and down. I remember him being so happy. I didn't know what was going on. I was still pretty mad about missing. But once that happened, and I saw Donald Williams going to the line, I knew we were going to win. It was like a dream come true, especially to win it for Coach Smith. The first thing I did, me and Henrik Rodl, we ran to hug him. I remember grabbing him and thanking him, and then acting like little kids.

What Webber did, that wouldn't have happened with us. Coach Smith had a rule—he was the only who could call time out. All of us knew that if we couldn't get the ball in, or if we were trapped, we couldn't call time out. It's either your fault you're getting trapped, or someone else's fault. Those were things we practiced. We knew to be in certain spots in certain situations. One thing Coach Smith preached to us was that he wanted to make practice harder than the games. During the games, he just wanted to sit and watch.

Going into my fourth year, we had Montross, (Jerry) Stackhouse, (Rasheed) Wallace, (Kevin) Salvadori—a bunch of guys at the 3-4-5 positions. There was going to be a big logjam for playing time. There was no telling how much playing time any of us would get. I remember him calling me in and asking if I wanted to sit out (as a redshirt). He said I could be playing anywhere from five minutes to 35 minutes per game. He said that I definitely had a chance to play a lot more in my fifth year, depending on how well I played.

It's funny. Everyone thought about what an unselfish thing that was on my part. I thought it was more unselfish on his part. He didn't need to do that. If other guys weren't playing well, he might have needed me for five, ten minutes, and could have used me. It seemed to me that was really special. It said a lot about Coach Smith. He had my best interests at heart, and not his own.

There were times I felt guilty about doing it. I remember losing to UMass early on, getting on the bus and Coach Smith saying: "We could have used you tonight." He was just trying to say something nice, make me feel better. Those were my guys— Montross, Reese, Phelps. I had to leave those guys. I consulted with them before I made my decision, asked if they didn't mind. They thought it was good for me. They were happy for me. But we had been through so much together. I didn't want to leave them high and dry. We're all still good friends, to this day.

My last year, I had trouble with my back. We had a great team, but I wasn't a part of it. I had surgery on my back early, and missed something like 23 games. I never remember Coach Smith being at a loss for words. He always had something positive or insightful to say. But I remember telling him I had to have surgery. He just sort of sat back in his chair and almost broke down. I knew that he felt so bad for me. He knew how hard I had worked.

I had the surgery, and I remember him coming over with a bunch of VHS tapes, things I could watch, practices and games. He did anything he could for me. With things like that, you can't describe what he means, For me, without a father in the house for a long time, he has been that father figure for me.

I got into coaching because of all the time I spent watching him as a redshirt and during my last year. It was so interesting to watch him, what a master he was. Not only could he tell us what to do, but he could tell us what the other team was going to do, too. It was like choreographing a dance, almost. It was pretty to watch the team when it was playing well.

He knew I wanted to get into coaching. There was nothing open here. He called a high school in Raleigh that needed a varsity basketball coach. The next thing I know, he called me in and said: "You're the new coach at Hale H.S." It was amazing. And I was working part-time here, doing a lot of administrative stuff around the office. My second year out, I helped the video guy and with the administrative stuff. Then, in the fall of '97, Coach Smith decided to retire.

I remember him calling us into his office, all of the coaches and secretaries. I thought he was mad at all of us. But he told us he was going to retire. He said Bill was going to be the coach, Dave was going to move up and Phil was going to be his top assistant. And he said: "Pat, by a three-to-two vote, you're going to be on the staff, too."

SCOTT CHERRY

Cherry, a guard at North Carolina from 1989-90 to 1992-93, is the assistant women's basketball coach at Middle Tennessee State.

It was every kid's dream, being able to step out on the floor and play in a national championship game in front of 80,000 people and countless others watching the game on TV. I got a minute. It was probably one of the best minutes of my life.

It was an unbelievable experience. It goes by so fast, you don't realize what's happening at the time until you sit down later. I played 45 seconds. I got the ball and ran the shot clock all the way down to zero. It was at a point in time where we were down one point to Michigan. He brought five people into the game, three of them hardly ever played. We weren't really in there to score. He brought us in because the starters had played eight minutes straight —we had gone through a TV timeout without stopping. They were exhausted.

It was a calculated risk, bringing us in. Billy Packer mentioned it on TV. He said he didn't know if it was a good idea. But it paid off. Michigan took a four-point lead, but our starters came back fresh. Coach Smith had confidence in everyone. He didn't just put people in the game because he felt sorry that they only played a couple of minutes. He put you in feeling confident you could do your job.

You kind of accepted your role. You didn't accept it by saying: "I'm not going to get playing time, so I'll just forget it, ride out the scholarship." You worked as hard as you could. Our starting point guard, Derrick Phelps, got hurt a lot in his senior year. I filled in, got to play 15, 20 minutes against Virginia Tech—Derrick was hurt, and Donald Williams was injured. As a senior, it was nice to have a mix, to have role players. George Lynch was our senior leader. But it was good to have guys in the second group and third group to carry that over.

Some of the young guys were frustrated that they weren't playing. I knew my role. I knew I wasn't going to start games, play a lot of minutes. But I knew in practice that I had to work. If I didn't push them, how would they perform in games? I kind of liked it—in Coach Smith's system, he asks for a lot of input from the seniors. Some people agree with it. Some people disagree with it. But you have to earn everything you get.

I wasn't heavily recruited coming out of high school. I was from a small town in upstate New York. Iona, Fairleigh Dickinson, Holy Cross, Army, schools like that were going for me, nothing on the level of the ACC or Big East. I happened to get lucky late in my senior season. It must have been February. North Carolina never actually saw me play. A local sportscaster had recommended Sam Perkins and Dick Grubar. He saw me play, put me on the area All-Star team, sent a tape down recommending me. It took off from there.

Coach Smith would always put the focus on his players. He didn't want to take a lot of credit. There was one ACC tournament game I played against Maryland in my senior year. I came in late in the first half, played pretty well, knocked down a few shots. It was only a couple of minutes of the game, but he singled me out in his press conference afterward as one of the people who helped us out. What I did was so minor to me and probably a lot of people who watched the game. But it was something he noticed and mentioned.

I spent a year overseas playing for a club team in Cypress. I decided the money wasn't there for me, then came back and worked three years for a forklift company, selling forklifts. In those three years, I found out that I needed to get back in the game of basketball. I knew a lot about it. I understood it. I thought I could

Scott Cherry

teach it. The following year, I coached high school in Winston-Salem (North Carolina). Coach (Randy) Wiel helped me get this job. I tried to get a job with a men's team all summer. I didn't come up with anything. Coach Wiel called and asked if I'd be interested in a position with the women's team. Seeing as how I didn't have any experience with men or women, I thought it would be a good idea.

When I was deciding to stop selling forklifts, I really wasn't happy with what I was doing. I thought coaching would be the easiest thing to do next. Coach Smith sat down and really questioned me. Would I be willing to pick up and go anywhere on a moment's notice? Would I be willing to work basically for nothing for several years, putting in time until I could get in a better position financially? He walked me through everything to make sure that I was sure about coaching.

It's something not a lot of people would do. A lot of people would just say: "I'll see what I can do," and six months later, you'd hate coaching, want to do something else. He walks you through, makes sure you're serious about it. He asked all these questions. And as soon as we got done, he said: "It sounds like that's really what you want to do. I'll do everything I can to help you." I spent four years with him. And I'll spend the rest of my life doing something because of the way he walked me through.

My time at Carolina was probably the best four years of my life. It was just a family atmosphere. He treated me the same way he treated any superstar. It doesn't matter who you are. He expected a lot. He demanded a lot. He treated you fairly. If you performed well in practice, did the things required of you, you earned playing time. He gave me my fair shake. I wouldn't have traded it for the world.

PEARCE LANDRY

Landry, a walk-on at North Carolina in 1993-94 and 1994-95, is an associate for First Union-Capital Partners in Charlotte, North Carolina.

I grew up in North Carolina, a big Carolina fan. All I wanted to do was play for Coach Smith.

As a high school player, I was all-state in North Carolina, averaging 23 points per game. But 6-foot-4 white guys playing shooting guard, we're a dime a dozen. I attracted the attention of mid-Division I schools—Davidson, the College of Charleston, UNC-Wilmington, those types of places. My high school coach was very good friends with Coach Guthridge. He had worked at the UNC basketball camp a long time.

Coach Guthridge came to see me play, but the main reason he did that was that I was up for an award called the Morehead Scholarship. He knew if I ended up getting that award, I was probably going to come to North Carolina. The award is given to 50 incoming freshmen from all over the United States, Canada and Britain. There are four criteria—excellence in academics, sports, leadership and community service. The typical winner is a student-body president who played all sports, excelled at 'em, did community service and was a good student.

I planned to accept the scholarship if I got it. It was a full ride at North Carolina, plus spending money—actually better than an athletic scholarship. It also allowed me to continue my dream of one day playing for the University of North Carolina. They couldn't recruit me—I would have been a scholarship player, and I wasn't good enough, anyway. Coach Guthridge just came to see who I was because they knew I might be coming to Chapel Hill. And I did end up getting the scholarship and going to UNC.

My high-school coach, Mac Morris, told me to go see Coach Guthridge when I got there. I went to the Smith Center, if not my first day on campus, then my second. He was very polite. And the long and short of what he told me was that J.V. tryouts were on October 15. That wasn't surprising to me. I knew he wasn't going to say: "Congratulations! You've shown up! Here's a jersey!" But he was at least kind enough to say: "We'd love to have you play on J.V."

The University of North Carolina is one of the few schools that still has a J.V. program. It's something that Coach Smith continued to believe in after its usefulness went away. He felt it was a great way for the student body to get in on men's basketball. You had a locker at the Smith Center. You played at the Smith Center before the varsity. You got great seats for the games. And the advantage of being part of the program was that once a year, usually someone moved up to the varsity. Sometimes, it was none. Sometimes, it was two. But it was something all J.V. players dreamed about.

I played J.V. my freshman year. A couple of times, Coach had me practice with the varsity. He was always thinking ahead. He was more prepared than anyone I've ever met, certainly more prepared than the opponent. Whether he wanted someone to come work his butt off, or whether he wanted to keep his eye on me, I wasn't sure. I did well on J.V. I was always in double digits. He continued to stay abreast of what I was doing.

After my freshman season ended, he sat down with me and said: "You had a great year. I heard some great things about you from Coach (Randy) Wiel. We'd love for you to try out for the varsity next year." I spent that spring and all summer working out with the team. It was George Lynch, Eric Montross, Brian Reese, Kevin Salvadori—the team that ended up winning the national championship. I was the last player cut. An interesting thing had come up—the ACC had a rule that a Morehead scholarship was an athletic scholarship. And Carolina was at its maximum number of scholarships.

The rule was made with good intentions. The Morehead Foundation is separate from the University. It's not associated with it, other than that the scholarship is only for students who attend the University of North Carolina. The rule was put in place so a school like North Carolina couldn't set up a separate foundation to get a Jerry Stackhouse in without giving him a scholarship. Anyway, I ended up not being able to play in ACC games.

I went back to J.V., ended up averaging something like 25 points per games, scoring 40 on some nights—at least that's how I remember it. I was a pretty good player at that level. But I was more or less disillusioned with being there. I was hoping that the next year I'd get another chance. You're only allowed to play J.V. two years. I knew the next chance would be my last. And Coach Smith continued to have me practice with the varsity now and then.

In February, the varsity was playing Notre Dame at home. The J.V. was playing a military academy. I played in the game, and it went into overtime. I think I played all 45 minutes. I was kind of exhausted at the end. But Coach Wiel came up to me and said: "Pearce, if the varsity game ends up being a blowout, Coach Smith is going to put you in." Here I was in a coat and tie, ready to watch the game. I thought: "Wow. That sounds pretty cool." Notre Dame wasn't in the ACC. It was OK by the rules. Coach Smith wanted to give me a piece of the action, give me incentive.

Sure enough, I sat in the stands in the first half in my coat and tie. Carolina was ranked like, number three in the nation. Notre Dame, it wasn't a good year for those guys. But at the end of the first half, we were only up by a couple of points. I was like: "What's going on?" This was going to be my moment in the sun. Well, we came out in the second half and started pouring it on, got up by 20. With ten minutes left, Coach Wiel pointed to me in the stands and said: "Go get dressed."

I sprinted back through the tunnel, into the varsity locker room. The equipment manager was waiting with a jersey—number 15, with no name on the back. I got dressed, put on my ankle braces, put on my shoes. I got to the bench with four minutes left. I sat on the end, and one by one, all the varsity players looked down and said: "What are you doing?" They had no idea what I was doing. They were happy for me—I had worked out with them before —but bewildered that I was on the bench.

At the four-minute mark, Coach Smith started putting in all the bench players. There I was—three minutes, two-and-a-half, two—still sitting down there. With 1:30 left, he went down and asked George Lynch, our senior captain, if it was OK to put me in. George said: "Fine." So, with 1:30 left, I ended up at the scorer's table. The action just continued—no fouls, no turnovers, no anything. With 55 seconds left, Coach Smith called timeout just to put me into the game.

Before I went in, I was nervous as hell. There were 21,000 people there, a television audience. I didn't know the defensive calls, the offensive calls. But as soon as I got in the game, all that was over, and I just played basketball. No one in the stands even knew who I was. I don't know if the PA announcer even announced me. I ended up with one rebound, one assist, one missed shot, one steal and one foul—I was in every category except points. But it was kind of my day in the sun. I was just a sophomore, a regular student. It was as if he plucked me out of chemistry class. I was on Cloud Nine. I got interviewed by the *Daily Tar Heel*. I thought it was the best thing ever.

I ended up going back to the J.V., and that varsity team went on to win the national championship. I remember celebrating on Franklin Street when they won in New Orleans. And I still remember *Sports Illustrated* calling me a computer blip on the final stat sheet for the year. But after the season, Coach Smith again sat down with me. He said: "We'd love for you to try out again. We think you can make a contribution." That was all I needed to hear. I had tasted the success, the energy, of being part of the varsity program.

I stayed in Chapel Hill that summer working with the team again. I was more or less treated as part of the team. They had gotten the rule about the Morehead scholarship changed. John Swofford, then the athletic director at North Carolina, had worked it out with the ACC commissioner. They agreed it was not right. It was an easy move. They got rid of the rule. And I was able to play the next season.

I made the team my junior year and sat at the end of the bench, probably on the other side of the managers. We were pretty good. I got in 18 games, all except for one when we were up by 20 or down by 20. One game—and this was Coach Smith again giving me a flavor—was against LSU in the Superdome on national TV. I played late in the first half—the only action I saw in the first half all year. It was a close game, but he put me in for the rest of the first half. It felt like he was giving me a test, seeing how I would do. For the rest of the year, I was one of the last men off the bench, if not the last.

It was all I ever dreamed about—being part of the team, contributing in practice, traveling. I was as proud as I could be. We had lost to Boston College in the round of 32 the year before, but we had a lot of talent coming back—Jerry Stackhouse, Rasheed Wallace, Donald Williams. The big hole was, no one knew who would come off the bench. Larry Davis ended up transferring to the University of South Carolina. He could have been a guy off the bench. Pat Sullivan could play the front-court positions. But we really had no one at guard. I kind of emerged as the one guy who might get minutes here and there.

I continued to work through that summer. Coach Smith continued to tell me what to work on. But through practice, the pre-season, the Blue-White Game, it really hadn't hit me. I wasn't sure how much I would actually get in ballgames. Then Pat Sullivan threw out his back, and ended up needing back surgery a week before the first game. Suddenly, I was the first person to come off the bench. The first game came around, and I ended up playing twelve or thirteen minutes. I couldn't believe it. I was just a guy who walked out of the library.

It ended up being a storybook season. I was the sixth man, averaging 15 minutes per game. I hit a big shot late in a game at Georgia Tech, made a big defensive play late at Wake Forest, hit a three late and knocked down four free throws at Cameron. I ended up getting quality minutes, more than I ever thought. And I ended up playing in the Final Four—God only knows how I did that.

Most coaches don't bother with just anyone who walks onto campus. Most don't even have J.V. programs to nurture that type of player. Coach

Smith recognized early on that I probably was not someone who was going to make a meaningful contribution on the court, but maybe I could in the locker room, in practice. He kept me interested, gave me tastes along the way.

The guy can go out and recruit anyone he wants. But he didn't need another scorer my senior year, another player getting ten rebounds per game. He needed someone to pass the ball, set screens, play good defense. I always ended up defending the toughest guards—Randolph Childress, Allen Iverson, Harold Deane. Guys who made me look slow—and I'm pretty slow. Coach Smith was able to fill a void. Most coaches would never have thought about me. Most would not have even given me the first chance.

He was always so positive. Before each year, he gave us something to visualize a national championship, our ultimate goal. In '93-'94, he passed out a picture from the upper deck at the Charlotte Coliseum, where they were going to play the Final Four. You could see people playing on the court, fans in the stands. The scoreboard said: "The University of North Carolina Tar Heels—1994 national champions." It was Tar Heels 78, Opponent 62, with one minute left on the clock. He went through the effort of having that made. He wanted us to visualize that.

The next year was even better. We had lost to Boston College the year before in the NCAAs. In the summer letter he sent out to all the players, he made a copy of the *Sports Illustrated* cover that said: "Take That, Tar Heels." He used that to motivate us. We got to the pre-season, and a couple of days after Media Day, he had us go out to the Smith Center, cut down the nets and put them around the seniors' necks.

He got the national championship trophy from two years before and said: "Let's celebrate a national championship." We started hooting and hollering. He said: "Let's take a picture." And we took a picture with the national championship trophy, and the nets around our necks. He made copies of that picture, with the inscription: "Take that, *Sports Illustrated*, 1995 National Champions."

JERRY STACKHOUSE

Stackhouse, a forward at North Carolina in 1993-94 and 1994-95, was selected third by the Philadelphia 76ers in the 1995 draft. He joined the Detroit Pistons in December 1997.

He came to one of my high-school games in Kinston, freshman or sophomore year. It was a big thing. Dean Smith was in the stands. It was the talk of the newspapers for the next couple of days. From the first time we

Jerry Stackhouse

talked, it was always about improving, trying to become the best player you could be. I thought Carolina would give me the opportunity to do that.

Everyone said: "You'll never get the chance to be a star in Dean Smith's system." I wondered about that during the recruiting process. Why was everyone telling me not to go to Carolina? They'd say: "You go there, you're not going to play. You'll have to pass the ball a certain number of times before you shoot."

I just said: "If everyone is talking against it, there must be something good about it." I just stuck with it. They were always there in the back of my mind. I took one visit to Virginia. I came to Carolina after that. I had three other visits scheduled. I didn't take any of them.

I just took it as a challenge. He didn't play freshmen much. Not many freshmen had started there. I felt I would be the exception. I felt there was no way he wouldn't play me, no matter who he had coming back. I wanted to prove that not only to other people and my teammates, but also to myself.

Being a freshman at North Carolina, you're looked at as just a freshman. You're not even really part of the team. You're in another group by yourself. It was great I had two other guys come in with me and share the experience—Rasheed Wallace and Jeff McInnis. It's really not something you want to go through alone. It tears you down. It humbles you. But then you build yourself back up.

It was frustrating. At practice, I would play well, but all of a sudden you'd get into a game, and it was decided that I would play 16 to 18 minutes, no matter how the game went. It was hard to get adjusted at first. But that's sometimes how it is in the NBA. I'm fortunate—I've always been a 30-plus minutes guy. But a lot of guys get only limited minutes, and they have to adjust. Coming from a program like that, it's a little easier to do. I was humbled. It served me well.

I had seniors ahead of me. It didn't matter to me if I started. But when I came in, the media said I was the one freshman who would have a chance to actually start. And the first game of the season, I was the last freshman to get into the game. Coach Smith knew what everyone was saying. He felt I might have been reading it. I understood it later. I could see it happening. My family was very supportive. They knew I wasn't thrilled about how I was being used.

The ACC tournament my freshman year (in 1994) was one of my most memorable experiences. We had a pretty good regular season coming into the tournament. I looked at that as my time to shine. I remember leaving school early when I was young to see the ACC tournament. To finally be a part of it was great. I came off the bench and played more than I had in any regular-season game in the first game. Then we played Wake Forest and beat them (86-84) in overtime. I had the game-winning shot. We went on to win the tournament, and I was Most Outstanding Player.

That was probably one of my most gratifying moments, after what I had been though the whole season, feeling that I wasn't playing as much as I could have. All of a sudden, when the time was right, he put me in to flourish. I can look back and say it was all for a reason, all the times I said: "I can't take this any more." I don't think there has ever been a freshman at Carolina who hasn't thought about transferring. But looking back, I wouldn't trade it for anything else. After that first year, it's the best place to be.

My sophomore year, I was slotted to be a wing player. But our team had other guys who were wing players. Coach looked at our team and said that with my rebounding ability, I was best suited to play the "4" (power forward), so we could put our best team on the court. I was happy to finally be able to contribute the way I would like, play as many minutes as I would like. I went from trying to get minutes to not even coming out of games. I would give the tired signal, and they would look the other way. I played against some of the top forwards. I see some of the same guys now that I did in college. Who knows? If I gained 25 pounds, maybe I could play power forward in the NBA.

I thought we had a great year. We were able to go to the Final Four, but then we had some freak things happen. I had a deep thigh bruise at the start of the game. We had an opportunity to win, and came up short (Stackhouse scored 18 points in Carolina's 75-68 loss to Arkansas). After that season, I was *Sports Illustrated* Player of the Year and everything. Other than graduating, I had accomplished the goals I had set coming into college.

I wanted to win a championship, but Rasheed had decided to leave early, and I didn't know about the young guys coming in, Antawn Jamison and Vince Carter. I didn't know what kind of effect they would have. Rasheed was leaving, Donald Williams was leaving. I felt the realistic goal of winning a national championship had kind of went away. Also, with my mother getting sick during that year, I decided to leave early. That was the toughest decision I've ever made.

I don't regret it. But I miss that I wasn't able to spend another two years at college. I came back. I graduated in the summer of '99. It took me four (additional) years, but I can say I've done it. Still, there were things I missed. I made a lot of new relationships at Carolina. I knew my friends were still there, not having to worry about going from city to city, things like that. Even when I'm sitting in a hotel now, I look back and say: "Maybe if I stayed, I'd be at a keg party right now." I had a great time.

I lost one sister (to diabetes) while I was there. My other sister, I just lost recently. It was tough. But Coach was great. He helped me, let me know that these things happen; sometimes it's not the best situation, but you have to make the most of it. He was just being encouraging. At times like that, there's not always a right thing to say. It's just nice knowing that he was thoughtful enough to call. The same thing with the ladies in the basketball office. Everyone is like: "How are you doing? We hope everything is fine."

He has a great relationship with my mom and dad. When he came for my home visit, he came on the same day as Steve Fisher, the coach at Michigan. Steve Fisher came over in the morning, then Coach Smith. For Steve Fisher, my mother served donuts and coffee. By the time Coach Smith came in, she had pork chops, cabbage, corn, everything. I knew which way she was leaning without her saying a word.

She gets a call from him every once in a while. They go up to games and see him. When I'm in town and there's a function, I take them by and they see everyone. That's the best thing for them, and everyone in the office, too. They love to see my parents.

I call back up there now, and he's still around. I call and try to get input on the guys. (Secretary) Angela (Lee), she's like the liaison between all the former players and what's going on at Carolina. Coach Smith offers me pointers. He keeps up, knows exactly what is going on. I can call right now, and he would tell me: "You had a pretty good night," or: "You didn't get any rebounds."

As time goes on, I realize even more how much he meant to me. At first, I was kind of in awe, but not so much of him as a person—talking to him is like talking to anybody on the street. I was in awe of all the things he had accomplished, all the players I saw come through there. The greatest player there is, and maybe ever will be, came through the same program, did the same things I did.

I have more fans from going to Carolina than I do from playing in the NBA—by far. Carolina fans are everywhere. And everyone wants to know how Coach Smith is doing. No matter where I go, if someone asks about Carolina, it's not: "What do you think about Vince Carter or Antawn Jamison?" It's about Dean Smith.

VINCE CARTER

Carter helped lead North Carolina to consecutive ACC championships and Final Four appearances in 1996-97 and 1997-98. He left Carolina after his junior season, and was the fifth pick of the 1998 NBA draft.

As soon as I got there, after the Blue-White Game, I heard a lot of talk about how I might be the next Michael Jordan. I remember Coach Smith bringing me into his office. He said: "Well, how are you handling that? Technically, I don't think you're the next Michael Jordan. But don't even worry about things like that. It's not fair to compare. Nobody can be Michael Jordan." He broke down my game from Day One, which made me the player I am today.

The thing I remember most is probably a game we played against Clemson at our place. He always would put the roster of who was going to play on the board. He would put our starting five next to their starting five, start at center and work his way down. As he was writing the names down, he put my name next to (point guard) Terrell McIntyre instead of (shooting guard) Greg Buckner.

I raised my hand and said: "Coach, I think you put my name by the wrong person." He said: "No, I know what I'm doing." He had the confidence in me to go out and play the point guard. That was my breakthrough on defense. The knock on me was that I wasn't a great defender. He said that for a long time. It was always in the papers. Then, all of a sudden, he gives me the opportunity to play Terrell McIntyre. I did well. From then on, my confidence in my defense began to rise. I began guarding the best player on the other team.

The day he retired, it was a shock, a major blow to our program. I remember we had just finished the mile run. After that, he called a meeting. Usually when he called a meeting, he did it a day in advance. He said: "Everyone meet in the locker room immediately."

We got there, and everyone was sitting around, wondering what was going on. We were joking, laughing. He walks in and starts pacing up and down, hands in his pocket. That's not Coach Smith. Usually when he walks in, he's already starting to talk. Not this time. He looked a little nervous, like he was about to break out in a cold sweat.

He started telling a story—I can't remember what it was about, I think it was about Scott Williams. I was like, where is he coming from? Then his voice started to crack a little bit. I remember that he had said he would retire when he started thinking about golf in the morning instead of basketball. He kept talking and talking. And nobody could understand what he was saying. Then he stopped and said: "I've made the decision to retire." It was out of the blue.

It was just silent in there for like, 15 minutes. He said: "I know it's shocking to you, but I'm still going to be here." I took it hard. I had learned so much from Coach. I had been there two years with him, and I was excited about next year, ready to learn, have a great season. The good thing about it was, we kept it in the family as far as who was going to be the next coach. The hardest thing about it was that we had to keep it a secret. The press conference was the next day.

I still saw him every day. He was in the offices all the time, still dressed up in his suit, dressed up normally. He tried to stay out of the way of

Coach Guthridge. When Coach Guthridge asked for help, that's when he would help. He would still pull me in, ask about my family. It's amazing how he remembers the names of your relatives, all the people he meets from your family.

He came to me first when I was thinking about turning pro, asked what I was thinking, how I felt. I was like: "Well, that's the question I wanted to ask you." We just compared notes, laid it on the table. Coach Smith knows everyone in the world, it seems. He went to his contacts, then came back and said: "OK, here's how it is." I made the decision from there, and it worked out for me.

He ran plays for me to dunk all the time. He never had a problem with it. Michael Jordan has said that Coach Smith gave him the knowledge to score 30 points per game, even if he didn't do it at Carolina. That's very true. You don't get to exploit your scoring ability as much when you're there. But

Vince Carter

he's preparing you for the next level. It's tough to realize that at first, tough to understand it. Maybe it's tough for other people in the world to see. But when you get to the NBA, it comes so naturally. You know how to score, how to play the game. All the guys who played under him realize that. I'm starting to realize it so much. It's like, "Wow."

ANTAWN JAMISON

Jamison, a native of Charlotte, left North Carolina for the NBA after his junior season, when he was the unanimous choice as national college player of the year. He vividly recalls the day Smith told the team of his plans to retire.

It was kind of hard for him to speak. He started talking, and tears started rolling down his face. It was hard. It was like a bombshell. You weren't expecting it at all. You thought the guy would coach for another 20 years.

We had just finished the mile run. Coach said that we were going to have a meeting back in the locker room. We thought he was going to come in and say: "You're having a successful pre-season. Everything is going well. We're looking forward to having a good season."

It kind of hit everyone hard. We were surprised. We were upset. This was like our father. You trusted everything he said. He could do no wrong. He worried about you, watched out for you, made sure you didn't go in the wrong direction. But it was a good thing. I didn't feel cheated. I can honestly say I had the privilege to play for Coach Smith for two years. All the stories you hear about him are true.

He made my transition from high school a lot easier than it would have been at other programs. He was always positive. If I made a mistake, he would help me out. Coach Smith is one of those guys who is always nice. He's always trying to help you. He spent a lot of time not just with me, but all the freshmen. It really showed how much he cared about making us successful.

He has this thing about freshmen having to do this, having to do that. He pretty much rides you as a freshman. The system is really hard. You have to stay focused the whole time. One time, me and Vince (Carter) were talking about what to do. He blew the whistle and said: "Do y'all want to come and run practice?" We were freshmen. Everyone was watching us. We were like: "No." Everyone was supposed to be quiet, focused on the coach.

Coming from high school, being a freshman, of course you're intimidated. He's one of the guys where if he's talking, everyone should be quiet, all eyes on him. That's one reason the program is so successful. He really puts a lot on listening and being focused and carrying it over to the basketball program.

That first year, we lost to Texas Tech in the second round of the NCAAs (92-73). It was very disappointing. The year before, we had lost Jerry Stackhouse, Rasheed Wallace and Donald Williams. As a freshman, you wanted to come in and keep the tradition going. We started the year off 16-4, then had one stretch in the ACC where we kind of struggled (losing three straight). It was frustrating. We knew we could play better.

You'd hear a lot of speculation: Coach Smith is getting too old. He's over the hill. Can he still coach? A lot of that speculation was going on during my freshman year. We took it to heart. We knew he could still coach. We knew that he knew exactly what he was talking about.

My sophomore year, we started 0-3 in the ACC. Again, the talk started about Coach Smith: What was going on? We all relied on each other. Coach Smith always stayed positive. He wasn't worried at all. He just came in and said everything would be fine. Once you've got someone like that staying so positive—someone with that kind of tradition, who had been through the thick and thin— it lifts your hopes a whole lot. We won sixteen in a row (after starting 3-5 in the ACC). That showed you what he was really capable of doing.

Against Arizona in the Final Four, we played our worst game at the wrong point of the season (and lost 66-58). It was hard for us. We had been through so much, a lot of ups and downs. For us to play our worst game, I felt really down. I felt like I let Coach Smith down a little bit. It was one of those things where you had to tip your hat to Arizona. We just didn't play our best game.

In the locker room, he said: "Keep your head up. It's not the end of the world. We just have to start over." He had just lost his chance to win a national championship, and he was still staying positive. A lot of coaches would have their heads down, tears about to come out. But Coach Smith always found a reason to stay positive.

All during my sophomore year, he was talking to a lot of GMs about my NBA chances. They said I could go anywhere between five and 13 in the draft. I wasn't considering leaving that strongly. I was enjoying college. I wasn't ready to leave. And his whole thing was, I had a lot of room to improve. He said: "Ask yourself: Do you enjoy college. Do you want to stay?" My answer was yes. He educated me about leaving early. And when you've got someone like that in your corner, he hasn't made too many mistakes. I kind of put everything on his shoulders. I asked: "Do you think it is a wise decision for me to leave?" And he said: "No, I don't."

The next year, after Coach Guthridge took over, he was still around the offices if you needed to talk to him; he just wasn't at practice. But you could always get in contact with him. He would always call you into the office to make sure everything was fine. He still found time to interact with the players. He was still calling my mom and dad to make sure they were OK. You won't find too many coaches who keep in touch like that after they retire.

After my junior year, Coach Smith and I both knew it was time to make the (NBA) decision. I told him that I felt I was ready. I had been to two Final Fours, been National Player of the Year. He always said, "Anytime a player has a chance to be in the top five of the draft, that's a chance you don't want to pass up." He said it was a good opportunity. He didn't want me to risk the chance of getting hurt and having my stock fall. He just wanted to make sure I was feeling the same way. So, I decided to leave. (Jamison was taken by the Toronto Raptors with the fourth pick of the 1998 draft and traded to the Golden State Warriors for former Carolina teammate Vince Carter.)

I still talk to him. It's still the same. When I'm struggling, he tells me to keep my head up, everyone didn't start off on a great note. I'm playing a different position in a different system. But he said that he still sees a player who is going to be successful in the NBA. He's still very much in my life, and my parents' life, also.

Honestly, I don't think I would be where I'm at right now if it wasn't for Coach Smith. I signed going into my junior year of high school. Coming out of high school, my stock had dropped a little bit. A lot of coaches wrote me off because I didn't go to a whole lot of camps. Coach saw something a lot of coaches didn't see.

When I first came in, I didn't know what to expect, and he didn't know what to expect. He said that I kind of surprised him. It was something very special. I was a young kid coming out of Charlotte. He had all the trust in me in the world. He really helped me out a whole lot.

Antawn Jamison

Chapter Five

THE MANAGERS

LAURA JOHNSON

Johnson, a varsity manager at North Carolina in 1991-92 and 1992-93, is guest-services coordinator at the North Carolina Arboretum in Asheville.

I probably was always a little bit nervous around Coach Smith. I was in awe a lot of the time. I just had incredible respect for him. We all knew that his expectations were really high. That kind of added to our nervousness sometimes. We didn't want to mess up. He could make you feel like you were about two inches tall. I wonder if the players had the same kind of feeling.

I kept the shot clock in practice. I'd be darned if he didn't notice that thing every once in a while. Keeping stats during a game was a little bit nerve-wracking. You had a couple of minutes to tally them up at the end of a half or a game. It needed to happen pretty quickly—you'd get the stats done, then hand them to Coach before he talked to the team. I remember being nervous about that.

We were a pretty high-strung group. I don't think that necessarily described any of us individually. It was just expected things would run like they were supposed to. They had enough staff, managers, and support people for it to run that way. Probably a lot of the pressure we felt was from Coach Guthridge, not Coach Smith. Coach Guthridge was kind of in charge of the managers. I don't ever remember Coach Smith yelling at a manager. I can remember him saying: "Bill, what are they doing?"

I became a manager by luck. One of the people who lived in the same dorm that I did was a JV manager. I thought she was the coolest thing. She said: "You could do it, too." I said: "Are you kidding?" There was actually an interview process. They took most people that applied to be a JV manager.

You'd go down, get real nervous. Then they'd let you work JV practices and games. You'd work the camps. Then you'd work varsity games.

We worked every practice, pre-season, post-season. We ended up spending four hours a day in the gym. Periodically, I'd see Coach Smith. You could imagine his schedule. He didn't exactly hang out. I'd talk with him maybe once a week. He'd check in, say, "How are you doing?"

I think he is brilliant. I also think he's incredibly generous. I worked in the office when I was in school to make some extra money. I was just overwhelmed by the requests, the letters, the phone calls, the way he responded to them.

Laura Johnson

That was really nice of him. All of the players were encouraged to go to hospitals. The requests were incredible. I just thought: "How can you expect this man to do all that?" He was so busy. He had a million things going on in his head. But if there was a sick kid he knew of, a player would try to visit him.

When I graduated, I followed Randy Wiel to the UNCA (the University of North Carolina at Asheville). I got a job in the athletic department. I worked there three-and-a-half years before I took this job. In a way, I was still pretty connected. I was able to keep in touch, figure out what was going on. I didn't make too big an effort to keep in touch. I know how busy they are. But I think that if I needed something, I wouldn't hesitate to call. If you put some work into it, you can keep the relationship alive, and it will stay that way. Some managers do that, I'm sure.

I got to do a lot of traveling that I certainly would not have been able to do otherwise. As a female, I learned a lot about working within a male-dominated athletic arena. I got my first job that way. There are some relationships that I made that I'll keep forever, memories of winning the national championship. I have a big fat ring, too. I took all kinds of things with me.

You know what I have that's really special to me? A basketball signed by the national championship team—players, coaches, managers, trainers. It was just for us, the people in the program. It was one of the times I felt most a part of the team.

AMANDA BAKER

Baker, a varsity manager in 1996-97 and 1997-98, was a junior in Dean Smith's final season and a senior during Bill Guthridge's first as head coach. She recalls the night Smith told the team of his plans to retire.

I was stunned when I found out. He told the team the night before the press conference. The other head manager and I were in there. We were kind of like: "Where's this coming from?" We had just taken the team picture. It was like: "Whoa!" A couple of the players started to cry. Coach Ford was real emotional. I don't think anyone expected it. It was hard to take at first. But he really deserved a break, to see his last couple of kids grow up and go off to college. It was sad, but we were also very happy for him, that he would be able to spend time with his family, relax for once. He was always one of the last few people to leave the Smith Center after practice.

It was kind of neat to be part of history, but that night was hard. You had to hold a lot of things back. It was all over the news. My parents called, frantic. I had to lie and say that I didn't know anything about it. My roommates and friends were asking. We were getting all kinds of phone calls. Even to my parents, I had to say: "I don't know. I'm just as clueless as you." It was hard for me to do that. After a while, I told my dad that Coach Smith told us the day before. He was really proud that I hadn't told him anything. He said: "I know it was hard for you not to tell me. But I'm glad you didn't."

It was sad to see Coach Smith go, but the transition wasn't too difficult. Coach Guthridge's style of coaching was very similar. He had been around. He knew exactly how things were, the best way to keep it going. It was weird not to see him on the bench the first couple of practices, the first couple of games, for Coach Guthridge to be in charge, not Coach Smith.

I've always liked Carolina basketball. My dad went to Carolina. I was born and raised a Tar Heel. People just suggested I become a manager since I loved it so much. I went down my freshman year and told them I was interested. With the manager program, you start out with the JV team, you have to work your way up. My sophomore year, I was one of the head JV managers. I didn't have a whole lot of interaction with Coach Smith until my junior year, working with the varsity team. I was at practice every day, all the home games, most of the away games. It was the best experience in my life so far. I grew up watching him. It was really neat to watch him in practice.

You don't want to make mistakes. Through the years, they expected so much from the managers, which is fine. You were kind of always on the edge of your seat, waiting to get something done for him or one of the players. Coach Guthridge, his motto was: "Hurry up and wait." Get everything done as fast as possible in case something came up. Coach Smith was the same. He didn't understand why you would not do something right away if it needed to be done.

Amanda Baker

My first couple of years, I was sort of intimidated. I was just kind of in awe to be working with the team. By your junior year, you just kind of get used to it. It's still a neat experience. You see the players day in and day out, deal with the coaches. You see the good sides and bad sides of everybody. It becomes less intimidating.

Home games and away games are so different as far as stress. With away games, there were either three of us or six of us. Away games were a little more hectic. We always came fully prepared. If we had an empty locker room, we could provide everything. That was Coach Smith's thing. We should be prepared in the event we didn't have soap or towels, whatever.

Home games are a little easier. You have the JV managers. Their job is to do the locker-room setup. Things got done right away. It looks like we're not doing anything. But really, we're just making sure everything goes smoothly. The first thing people always asked when they found out I was a manager was: "Do you get to go on trips?" Yeah, but trips aren't always the fun part. It's great to go all over the country, but you'd be up till 3 a.m. doing laundry. That's fine. That's our job. Hey, I got a free trip to Alaska out of it.

I felt lucky to be part of two Final Four teams and two ACC championships. It was great because none of the coaches ever forgot about the managers. If we were cutting down nets, the coaches and players always looked out for the managers, so we could cut down our part. They always made us feel like we were part of the team, even though no one else would look at us. We got a lot of the same things the players got. We would go to the team dinners. They were very respectful toward all the managers. It helps with the players—they treat us the same way.

One of the neat things I remember was in my sophomore year. One of the recruits was in—Vasco Evtimov. Right before he came, I just happened to be in the office. Coach Smith introduced him to everyone. I hadn't had much interaction with Coach Smith to that point. I had just worked with the JV team. But he introduced him to me. He knew my name. He knew what I did. It was kind of a special moment. It was the first time I had been introduced to anyone by him. You knew you weren't being overlooked. You knew he did take interest in the managers.

I work for an advertising agency in Durham. I'm interested in continuing in sports. I wouldn't hesitate to sit down with him if I thought he could help me or give me advice. I know a lot of former managers sat down with him, talked with him. He gave them advice. It's a great feeling—they really try to look out for their managers. It's kind of like a full-time job that we do in college. There's not much else on your résumé.

CHUCK LISENBEE

Lisenbee, a former varsity manager and 1995 graduate of North Carolina, works as a special agent in the Bureau of Diplomatic Security for the U.S. Department of State.

For a while, every time I'd see Coach Smith, he'd say: "Chuck, have you shot anybody?" Then one time he said it, and Coach Ford just looked at him. Now he asks: "Chuck, have you shot your gun?" He's weird. But he's so focused. Think of all the people he knows, all the managers who came before. He knows exactly what everyone is doing. We'd go to University Hall in Virginia. He'd talk to the maintenance guy. He knows everyone's name. We'd be like: "How do you know all this?"

You've got to be on your toes to work for him. He's a perfectionist. He knows every detail. One of the jobs of the managers during warm-ups was to stand under the basket and write down the names of any players who missed layups in the layup lines. The team had to run the next day at practice if anyone missed. He'd tell a player: "I saw you miss that layup." He'd be watching the other team warm up, but he'd watch our guys, too. Who in their right mind would pay attention to that? But he did.

The managers always synchronized their watches with Coach Guthridge's watch. It was referred to as "Coach Gut" time. He was the number-two man in the day-to-day operation. Coach Smith sort of saw the big picture. Yet, he knew Coach Guthridge was taking care of all these things. Coach Guthridge would say: "Tomorrow's schedule says the bus leaves at 5:03." It would never be 5:00 or 5:15. And we all knew that at 5:03, the bus would leave.

I remember in New York, right before the East Regional final. The hotel parking lane was packed, the elevators were as slow as they could be. Pat Sullivan and Scott Cherry were like two minutes late. The bus left at some weird time. They didn't make it and had to flag down a ride. For every minute you were late, that was a minute of playing time. It was some kind of logarithmic calculation that Coach Smith came up with. But there definitely was a penalty. I'll never forget Ed Geth coming out of the Watergate hotel one time banging on the door. Coach Guthridge said: "Don't let him on the bus! Don't let him on the bus!"

The managers at halftime had to hand two stats to Coach Smith before he went and spoke to the team—points per possession and percent loss of ball, the number of turnovers per total possessions. One manager keeps those two stats, and the other manager keeps assist-to-turnover ratio. The ultimate goals were 1.0 point per possession offensively, 0.75 defensively and 0.15 percent loss of ball. You'd calculate the total number of points divided by the number of possessions. On more than one occasion, he would be within hundredths of that figure, off the top of his head. Before you would even give him the stats, he would know. He and Coach Guthridge were both math majors. He's just a whiz with numbers. One time, he handed it back to me and said: "No, this can't be right." I went back and checked my calculations. I was two-tenths off. And he knew that wasn't right.

The point system, Coach Smith came up with that a long time ago. Each game was graded. The assistant coaches spent four to six hours after each game grading film. There were different categories—defensive play, savvy play, offensive rebounds, assist-to-turnover ratio, steals. You go into the locker room, and all that is on the board. The players would get plus points, and they could trade them to get out of running. The seniors could will their plus points to underclassmen. You know how hard it is to keep track of all that?

It's mind-boggling. His focus is unbelievably acute. Somebody once said, life is a late-game situation. So much of what we did in practice was late-game situations. He would tell the manager: "Put 1.8 seconds on the clock." Then he would bring it down— 1.8 . . . 1.7 . . . 1.3 —showing, specifically, everything you could do in that short amount of time. That's something I use today, the utilization of time, acting under pressure. How much can you do in three seconds?

Look at how a team mimics its coach's personality in late-game situations. Look at Wake Forest and Dave Odom. He's always jumping up and down, bouncing out of his seat. And look at how his team usually performs in that last minute of critical time. Look at Bobby Cremins. He's up and down, all over the place, putting his hands through his hair, grabbing players by their jerseys. It's not calculated. I think Dave Odom and Bobby Cremins are great coaches, but look at Coach Smith. He was very calm, very business-like, especially when his team was down in the last three to five seconds. He would revert back to everything he had worked on in practice. I think that's why Carolina had so many comebacks in late-game situations. It was just routine.

One of the things that made it so great to work for him as a manager—maybe because he didn't get much playing time back at Kansas—is that he made sure managers got everything the players got. It sounds like a small thing, but one thing I'll always remember happened during my sophomore year. There were five managers. We went to the Big East-ACC Challenge. Whenever the team went to tournaments, the players got gifts. There were enough gifts at that tournament for everyone but the bottom two managers. Everyone got VCRs except me and Bobby Dawson, one of the other managers.

The next day we came back, and there were two VCRs sitting there. The equipment manager, Ken Crowder, said: "Coach Smith and Coach Guthridge wanted you guys to have these VCRs." And we were freaking managers. A lot of it's Coach Guthridge. He handled all the details. Something like that, he might say to Coach Smith: "Two of our guys didn't get VCRs." I know it's just a VCR. I know Coach Smith has a lot of money. But you remember something like that for the rest of your life. That's why we're so loyal—seeing how classy he is, day in and day out. He paid attention to all the details. Not only did he pay attention, everyone was important to him.

Everyone has their favorite "thought for the day." I've heard players refer to them since then. It would be something that pulls you out of basketball for a while, enables you to look at the bigger picture. Every year, the day before the ACC tournament begins, we would go to either Butner Federal Penitentiary or North Carolina Central Prison. We would go out to visit all the guys on Death Row. A lot of times, the guys would be getting ready to be executed soon.

I remember how the inmates would slide pieces of paper out from under their doors. Coach Smith would sign autographs and slide them back under. That created such an image, our guys seeing Coach Smith do that. The number-one fans for North Carolina were on Death Row. Guys would take him into their cells and show him all their pictures. And this would be the day before the ACC tournament. I remember the thought for the day from that day in '93—"Whatever you do unto the least of my brethren you've done unto me."

I earned a biology and African-American studies degree. I knew his sister, Joan Smith Ewing. She lived in Cary, where I was a police officer for a little over a year after I got out of school. She told me a lot about the FBI. Her daughter and son-in-law were foreign-service officers. Coach Smith asked me what I was interested in doing. I learned a little bit about the foreign service. And I applied. An agent had to come down and talk to him. It was the summer of '97—the summer he was making his huge, monumental decision to retire. I listed Coach Guthridge and Coach Smith as my supervisors. Coach Smith took 30 minutes to talk to the agent who did my background check for top-secret clearance. The agent was like: "I can't believe it's Dean Smith!" I'd hate to know what kind of questions he asked Coach Smith. I hope they were relevant.

Chapter Six

OPPOSING
COACHES

VIC BUBAS

Bubas compiled a 213-67 record at Duke from 1959-60 to 1968-69 and took the Blue Devils to three Final Fours.

It's funny. Out in the public and in making speeches and all, he never appeared to me to crave high visibility. He just got it, because his teams performed and did a good job. I always got the impression he'd be perfectly happy to just coach and let the rest of the world do what it wanted.

I remember when he was hung in effigy. My first year at Duke, it didn't happen to me, but it was damn close. I wasn't exactly a fair-haired boy two-thirds of the way through my first year. I was this guy from N.C. State who came over and was supposed to do something. I was batting around .500, but we got hot in the ACC tournament and won the whole thing, then made it to the Elite Eight.

When you're in a high-visibility profession, your following tends to be volatile. There are three areas of life today where it's: "What have you done for me lately?" —the athletic arena, the political arena and the entertainment arena. You're not much better than what you did last week. But he rode that out well. He stuck to what he wanted to do.

It started to change with Larry Miller and Rusty Clark and all those guys. For Miller, it was between Duke and Carolina. It was very close. He happened to choose Carolina. I never knew the exact reason. You win some, you lose some. He went there, and I believe he gave them the kind of toughness they needed at that time. He was a great competitor. I used to tease him a lot in warm-ups. I'd say: "Damn, you're tough."

I could see then that their recruiting program had changed. All the people today can coach pretty well. You look around, there aren't many bad coaches. Most guys know what to do. It's a question of whether you can get the players. I guess you could see Carolina coming. You have to wait for it to happen. You need several good teams in a row—three or four, before you could say: "Yes, it was coming."

One game I remember is my last game coaching, in the finals of the ACC tournament. I had decided that I was going to leave coaching early in the year. I made the announcement. I really wanted to go out with an ACC championship. We got into the championship game. And that's when Charlie Scott had 40 points, just went crazy. We were doing everything in the world to try to keep him from getting the ball. He was shooting from half-court, falling out of bounds. We were up at half by nine, but lost by eleven (85-74). He put them on his shoulders and rode them in. That was disappointing to me, mainly because I wanted to go out a winner.

I'm surprised that anyone could last that long in the kind of atmosphere that we have today. It's really intense. You've got to love it more than anything in the world. I think he did love coaching. He said to me many times: "How could you just leave? Don't you miss it?" I said: "Yeah, some parts I miss, some parts I don't. His first love and real love was coaching. That's why he stayed in it. Of course, when you're successful, it's easier to stay in it. But I never saw myself from Day One coaching up to age 65.

CHUCK DALY

Daly led the Detroit Pistons to back-to-back titles in 1989 and '90 and the Dream Team to an Olympic gold medal in '92. He was the head coach at Penn from '71 to '77 and Boston College from '69 to '71, and an assistant at Duke under Vic Bubas from '63 to '69. He chuckled when asked to recall the recruiting battle over Larry Miller.

It was Duke or North Carolina. I was outside Allentown in that little town (Catasauqua) about six or seven straight weeks. We helped arrange for Vic to speak at his high-school banquet. But he ended up going to Carolina, for some reasons I won't disclose. It wasn't money. It wasn't cheating. But there were other reasons— maybe the girls were a little prettier.

Billy (Cunningham) helped Carolina recruit him. When I became Billy Cunningham's assistant in Philadelphia, I learned more about it. Let's just leave it at that. But no question, at that point, they were on the move. I

Chuck Daly

was involved in the Charlie Scott situation, too. Some we got, some they got. But they started to get some very key guys.

When I first got to Duke, Dean was struggling. I remember hearing they had hung him in effigy, and Billy had torn down the dummy. Then I started to watch a little more closely what was going on in Chapel Hill, for a lot of reasons.

What I saw was a guy who brought something to the table that maybe had been there, but not to that level. And that was the team approach. If a guy was late, he would take a seat and watch the other guys run. If he was late and the other guys were eating a meal, he would have to eat in front of them while they waited.

Everything in the program was about team—eating, playing basketball, traveling. It was never about the individual. You'd hear the kidding about how the only person who could hold Michael Jordan down was Dean Smith.

But in reality, that's what we all wanted to do in terms of coaching, making the team better. If one guy is scoring 28 every game, a lot of players aren't touching the ball enough. Everything—his offense, his defense—was oriented, 100 percent, around the team. Everyone knew that was the way it should be, recognized it. But he had a way of getting it done. He became a study for all coaches.

I went to see a practice when I was the head coach at Penn—my coaches and I, we each went to see two teams to learn what we could. That's when I saw everything up close. In wind-sprint drills, guys would dive across the line to get there on time. I saw the commitment they were willing to give. And we're not talking about ordinary players. We're talking about great players. That further reinforced to me what a great coach he was.

Through Billy, I went to Pinehurst for the first time in 1984, to be in Dean's annual golf outing. It's a group of guys, mostly Carolina guys, in the middle of summer, invitation only. We play those courses, 18 holes in the morning, 18 in the afternoon. We play for a little bit of cash. I got to play with him, got to know him a little better, realized what a class guy he was. I'm looking at the picture from last year right now—Dean Smith, Kevin Loughery, me, Bill Raftery, Doug Moe, John Calipari, George Karl, Larry Brown, Garfield Heard, Michael Jordan, Billy Cunningham, Roy Williams.

One of the things I always noticed is that he competed to the "nth" degree in everything he did, even in conversation. I saw what a great putter he was, how he could force the ball in the hole. Certain guys who are great competitors can force the ball in the hole, even on bad putts. I saw what a competitor he was, why he was able to instill that in his teams.

I once said that it's a cult at Carolina, but a good cult. I've never heard one of his players say something negative about him. If he wants them back there, they're there. If he wants them to make a call, they do it. The word is "unconditional"—it's unconditional loyalty to Carolina, and to Dean. And, of course, he's at the top of the cult. He should have been an evangelist.

JOHN WOODEN

John Wooden, the UCLA coach from 1948-49 to 1974-75, won ten national championships—including a 78-55 victory over North Carolina in the 1968 NCAA final.

We won the game very handily. I remember speaking with Dean afterward. It was a good feeling. He sort of thanked me for the fact that we didn't beat them worse. I always thought of Dean as a gentleman. Coaches, when

John Wooden

they lose, sometimes make remarks that aren't very kind. He was never that way. Dean took winning and losing in stride.

I would see him on occasion. I had tremendous respect for him always. He was one of the great teachers that the game has had. It always amazed me that he was able to teach his teams to do so many things well. A lot of coaches have their teams do a lot of things, different offenses, different defenses. But the teams don't all do all of those things well. I never felt I could do it, teach my teams to do as many things well as he did. And many of his assistants who have gone into coaching have done well. I was impressed from the very start with Roy Williams at Kansas. His teams play tremendous team basketball.

One of the things he is given credit for is the Four Corners, which he used very successfully. He was the first coach that I know to do that. And he used it so very well. I was also impressed with his great ability to substitute as much as he did, use so many players. I never felt I was able to do that. I felt that to give the team continuity, I had to rely primarily on three backcourt players and four frontcourt players, maybe five. I felt that I had to have a certain group playing together, working together in practice. He seemed to do far more substituting and still have the same continuity, both offensively and defensively. That always impressed me. He did things that I know I couldn't have done.

I think our ideas were similar. People talk about me, they talk about ten national championships. I would prefer they talk about the fact that practically all my players graduated, that practically all have done well in the professions they've chosen. I think Dean felt the same way. He really and truly cared about what was going to happen to his players after they left North Carolina.

BUCKY WATERS

Waters compiled a 63-45 record at Duke from 1969-70 to 1972-73. He has been a television analyst for various networks since 1973.

I was a player at North Carolina State in 1958. He was not on the scene then. I coached one year in high school, then came back to Duke in 1960. I was the freshman coach for Vic Bubas. There was an immediate controversy because of Art Heyman—he had committed to Carolina and Frank McGuire, then changed his mind and decided to come to Duke. This was before they had all the ironclad rules with commitments. But neither Dean nor I had anything to do with that.

I remember him coming as an assistant to Frank from the Air Force Academy. He was a very pleasant guy. McGuire had a kind of aura. Nobody knew or cared who his assistants were. He toiled pretty much in obscurity while Frank was there. There was a good deal of attention paid to Buck Freeman, the relationship that he and Frank had. But it was clear Frank needed younger legs. People kind of wondered: "Who was this guy from Kansas and the Air Force Academy?" He was absolutely innocuous, never controversial. He was just sort of there.

Where Dean got high marks from me early is when the trouble hit at North Carolina after Frank left. He stepped into a situation that was really decompressed—no scholarships outside the state. The University of North Carolina hasn't been tainted much. But it was then, with the gambling and all that. He stepped in, and Carolina fans gave him no quarter. When Frank came back to play the first time he was at South Carolina, he got a standing ovation, and Dean was booed.

Through it all, he was a tough competitor. It didn't endear him to a lot of people externally. But internally, when you see how the players basically stay in the family — there's that quality of unselfishness that always was him. Things like having the big guys sit in first class, and he would sit in the back. Little things that he did so well for so long. The success he enjoyed over the long haul, I never felt any animosity or jealousy toward him. He really had to dig it out. His task—the lack of resources, taking over for McGuire—was just enormous.

We were both coaches in the late '60s and early '70s. Those were really difficult times. You'd go to have practice, and your players would be protesting in the president's office. The deans would say: "Well, you have to let young people make decisions." I said that if they didn't practice, they couldn't play in the game. They said if you do that, they'll burn the campus down. I said: "You don't understand athletics. Eight or nine guys made a decision. Their decision was to practice. In our world, those are the guys who should play."

It was a really hard time. But Dean coped with that really well. I didn't. I kept coaching like I was coaching, more old school. It didn't serve me well. There was a lot of frustration. Dean was much more adaptable. He let his hair grow a little bit. The way he dressed, it went with the times. He got through it much better. He was smart enough to see that in that climate, the players wanted more cooperation. At that time, the kids were pretty much adversarial. They thought that was the way they were supposed to be toward the establishment. But he adapted.

Charlie Scott was a good example. He was very demonstrative. I remember playing at Carmichael. He drew his fifth foul, and threw a bounce pass the length of the court to me. He wasn't a bad person. Being the first

African-American in the conference, it was hard on him. And he was a terrific player.

One year, we were both in the NIT, and we were somehow able to scrimmage against each other. It was just to break up looking at ourselves for another practice. Our kids were talking about how disrespectful Charlie was. Dean would make a comment, tell him to change from offense to defense, and there was always some sort of negative response. He was just a guy Dean looked like he was having problems with. But he adjusted. He adapted. He took a softer approach. McGuire was a tough guy. It's hard to go from being the good guy to the head guy. It's a tough transition. But he did it.

I didn't have the antagonistic relationship with him that some of the other coaches did. I remember one time when Clemson's Tates Locke was president of the ACC coaches, and I was vice-president. Carl Tacy was attending his first meeting as the new coach at Wake Forest. We put his place card between Norm Sloan's and Dean's, and just waited for the fireworks. Those two always would snipe at each other. But this exceeded our fondest expectations.

Just before we started the meeting, the commissioner came in. He said the NCAA office had gotten reports about some of our basketball camps, and told us to be very careful that we don't run afoul of any of the recruiting rules. With that, Norm turned to Dean and got all over him. Carl Tacy is in the middle. The meeting hasn't even started yet, and they're chirping, bitching—Norm was just yelling at him. All Tacy could do was just get lower and lower in his chair. Tates and I were on the floor.

I don't know of anyone who was more outspoken in his dislike than Norm. In that business, winning does that. The relationship among the coaches now is much better. I attribute a lot of that to the fact that it's no longer one-and-done in the ACC tournament. That made everyone a loser. Now, you hear them really pulling for ACC teams, pulling for North Carolina when they play out of conference. It's a whole different mentality. Most of the animosity was traced to the recruiting battles more so than on the court. When you lost a kid, not only did you not have him, you had to look at him for three or four years, two or three times a year. A lot of the bad blood simply resulted from the recruiting battles.

When I first started broadcasting, there was a polite coolness. As I went on—and I must have done 50 Carolina games over the years, or more—there was less of that. On a few occasions he said to me: "It's nice to have a coach in there." He has a thing about that. "You see it as a coach. You report it fairly. I appreciate that." I tried to be analytical with the understanding of how hard it is to get players to execute under pressure.

There were times from the media side where you wished he would do more, be a little more available. But it just wasn't him. He didn't want to do it. He didn't like to do it. But for post-game interviews, the guys in the production truck felt that if I asked him, I had a chance. I was not really media. I felt that way about it myself when I was coaching. Some guy who had never gotten a rebound in his life was judging me? That could make you a little testy.

It's ridiculous when people talk about him not winning more national championships. Look at all the guys who went out early, then put them back in their slots on those teams. Mike Krzyzewski's record is incredible. But he had that continuity. No question, if you've got seniors, it helps you going into the NCAA tournament. But somehow, it never seemed to bother Dean. He stuck to his guns about what was best for the kid. I didn't know the circumstances. Maybe he looks good, because the kid would have been academically ineligible. But he was not selfish. He tried to be the best friend his players had.

It's absolutely phenomenal what he's done. I can't imagine it ever being done again. That's a big statement. But the nature of the college game now, the way people move around, it's hard to imagine. I remember a few years back when they started 0-3. People were not saying kind things about him. They were saying that time had passed him by. Then he turned around, won the ACC tournament and went to the Final Four. It was amazing how much basketball he remembered in a few short weeks. There's just little patience now. It's win, baby, win.

The most impressive thing is what he's done in the league. I look back over the years, think of Jack McCloskey, Norm Sloan, Lefty Driesell, Mike Krzyzewski, Jim Valvano. A whole lot of gunfighters came through there, and they did good jobs. But he was Mt. Rushmore when it was all over. Mike outlasted him. But will he want to go until he's 65? I'd be surprised if he does.

NORM SLOAN

Sloan, a 1949 graduate of North Carolina State, compiled a 266-127 record as the head coach at State from 1966-67 to 1979-80 and won the national championship in 1974.

I went to North Carolina State. I played against North Carolina. I was well aware of the rivalry. It wasn't something that had to grow on me. Having played basketball, football, track, I was aware of the Big Four, how important it was, and how Carolina was the number-one competition—what our people wanted to talk about all the time.

Our program was in pretty bad shape when I got the job. We struggled so hard against everyone. You're not a traditional rival until you're a threat. We weren't a threat. We weren't that good. But in 1970, we upset South Carolina in double overtime for the ACC championship (42-39). Then we started getting better.

You could tell the difference. The difference starts showing up in recruiting. All of a sudden, the opponent mentions you, why kids shouldn't go there. Sometimes, it's very subtle. Sometimes, it's overt. When television came, people like Dean who had prominent programs got a lot of television exposure. And that became part of recruiting.

When we started to become a challenge (to Carolina), then we were going after the same players. For a while, we couldn't compete against North Carolina for the top players. The first player we were ever able to get that Carolina really wanted was Tom Burleson. From that point on, when we got involved with a kid that Carolina was involved with, it was really tough recruiting.

Dean was like John Wooden at UCLA. I don't think either one got the credit they deserved for the great recruiting program that they had. They were always called the "Cadillac of coaches," all that stuff Vitale and those guys come up with. They were outstanding coaches. They knew what they were doing. But they had the best talent. Carolina, year in and year out, had the best talent in the league. The same could be said of UCLA when John was there.

They had tremendous organization, great recruiting programs. Their assistant

Norm Sloan

coaches were personable. They knew how to sell the program. And Carolina had a great school to sell, a beautiful campus. I became painfully aware of all that after we became a threat. We had a railroad going through campus. That difference was pointed out in recruiting. It bothered me tremendously. Frank McGuire was very good at this, too. When they built a new coliseum, all of a sudden we had a shabby building, and they were state-of-the-art. It bothered you, but you couldn't do anything about it. You'd do your best to offset it.

My earliest memories of competing against Dean were recruiting. Then we got Tommy and David (Thompson). They were number one on several people's lists. The important thing to me is that they were number one on Carolina's list. With David, John Lotz was the guy at Carolina in charge of recruiting. Eddie Biedenbach had the responsibility for us. You could have unlimited contact at that time. I bet you that in David's senior year in high school, he ate breakfast with Eddie more than he ate with his mother. Eddie would be there to take him to breakfast, then take him to school. That afternoon John Lotz would come by. Both knew where the other was. It was a matter of staying in contact, staying there all the time.

When we got both those guys, we became a very strong basketball team. Then the competition on the court became prevalent. All of a sudden, the four corners became a factor. They were very good at it. You had to prepare for a lot of things against him. Most of the things you could solve only with recruiting. For example, their defense has always been excellent. I remember the run-and-jump. It became popular all over the country. It started with Dean.

It wasn't a factor with us until we lost Monte (Towe). Monte handled that. I didn't teach him to handle it. He knew how to handle it. He could sense it coming. He could back away from the pressure almost as fast as it came at him. It wasn't anything I did. I didn't have a special plan for the run-and-jump. I just had a player who could contend with it.

The most important thing in major college basketball is recruiting. I was talking to a coach in the league recently about Kris Lang, the kid from Gastonia, (North Carolina). This coach said: "We didn't bother to go after that kid. We couldn't compete with Carolina." Duke now has that going for them. But Carolina had it from the day I can remember. And it just got tougher when so many of their players went to pro ball, and then coaching in the pros. Now all of a sudden, they'd have these banquets on campus, and all these guys would come back when one of their top prospects just happened to be visiting. He didn't miss a lick. I'm not being critical. This was all positive. He had a great recruiting organization. And he took advantage of every bit of it.

I didn't think there was any real animosity between him and me. We were fierce competitors. After we won the national championship (in 1974), we had a Big Four meeting in Charlotte. We were addressing the sports club there. I remember Dean saying—and I know he meant it—that he flew to that particular meeting because he was tired of driving and seeing those bumper stickers about North Carolina State winning the national championship. You couldn't call that animosity. Those were true things.

I go back to North Carolina State once in a while, and people will say:0 "He was the greatest North Carolina hater of all—and we loved him for it." I wasn't a Carolina hater. I realized they were our number-one competition. I realized how important the games were. And something like I just mentioned—how Dean flew to that meeting in Charlotte—I'd use it, because people loved to hear it. But there was no hatred involved. Not as far as Dean was concerned, and not as far as I was concerned.

There was some envy on my part. He did a tremendous job, on and off the floor. It hurts more to lose than it feels good to win in a rivalry like that. You tend to take winning in stride. But boy, does a loss hurt. It really hurts. And in this area, with Wake Forest, Carolina, Duke and N.C. State, it's probably more intense than it is anywhere in the country. People are neighbors. They're leaning over the fence. They're hanging things on their neighbors' doors when they win. You live with it. You can't get away from it.

I remember sitting at a conference meeting one time with Lefty Driesell—I liked Lefty. Lefty said: "The NCAA needs to invite every Division I team in the country to the NCAA tournament. I'm so sick and tired of hearing how many times Dean has been there." These are the things that came up. Some writer covering Lefty might have written that Dean had gone so many years, whatever it was. That's where it gets under your skin. You get tired of hearing about it, getting reminded about it. He has had the dominant program in this league ever since I can remember.

One of the most memorable games we played against Carolina was played at Carolina. They had Phil (Ford). We had this kid named Al Green. They got ahead a couple of times in the second half, and Dean went four corners. We would overcome it, get a lead and they'd open it up and play again. At the end of the game, the score was tied, and we were defending the four corners. I can almost see the play. Al Green drew a charge. And he shot free throws after the clock was out that won the game for us. We overcame a tactic that he was famous for. It was a memorable win for me.

We never played golf together. We never did anything social together. The only time I saw Dean was at some official function, a conference meeting or a game. We weren't close. I don't think you could be close. When you had that kind of competition, with so much at stake—more for me than for him—I don't know how you could be close. I tried to explain to people that there wasn't anything I disliked about him. We just weren't close because the competition was so fierce. He might not remember it that way, but it was fierce for me.

I belonged to a little golf club—Mountain Glen in Newlend, North Carolina. I still chuckle about it. When Dean was coming, they would start buzzing. They would come up to me and say: "Guess who is going to be here today?" I'd say: "Who?" They'd say: "Dean." I'd say: "Dean who?" It was like that on my own golf course! We'd see each other across the fairway, shake hands. Dean is unbelievable when it comes to his memory. He remembers all three of my children, and always asks about them. I admire a lot of things about him, but that's right there at the top.

LEFTY DRIESELL

Driesell was Smith's rival at Davidson from 1959-60 to 1968-69, and then at Maryland from 1969-70 to 1985-86. He has since coached at James Madison and Georgia State, with a career record of 716-360 through the 1998-99 season.

It was competitive. We got into a few misunderstandings. Dean was a tough competitor. Everywhere else you went to play, they'd yell when you shot free throws. At North Carolina, everyone was real quiet. That was more distracting than all the noise. He was great at projecting a great image for the University and himself. His record speaks for itself.

We were competitive with them. They never blew us out. In my 17 years in the league, we won more games than anybody but them. We were right there with them. But they would win the (ACC) tournament. Back when I was coaching, you had to win the tournament to get to the NCAAs. They had the tournament right there in Greensboro. That made it tough for people on the outside to win. But Norm (Sloan) won a national championship before Dean did. It wasn't like they were rolling over the rest of the league.

We go way back. He was a great recruiter as well as a great coach. But his first couple of years, they were on his butt—there was even stuff in the papers about me going to North Carolina. We played against him when I was at Davidson. He kept us out of the Final Four two years in a row (in 1968 and '69) with Charlie Scott.

I had recruited Charlie. He had always wanted to come to Davidson. That's what he told me. He called me up his junior year. I didn't know who he was. Then I saw him play. Davidson, at that time, had an early admission plan. If you were a good student, you could apply in September of your senior year. He got accepted. He had his picture in the paper that he was coming to Davidson. It was a big thing. But at the last minute, he changed his mind.

Lefty Driesell

I was very upset about it. You would be, too. I was real mad. But that's the way recruiting goes. That's why now they've got those national letters of intent. Back then, recruiting was a lot more cutthroat than it is now. You didn't sign anything. You could change your mind right up until when school started.

Charlie was a great player. He would have been the first black to ever play at Davidson. But when he signed with me, he did help me a lot. I was recruiting Mike Maloy also. Charlie kind of sold Mike on Davidson. If I had had those two, I would have been in good shape. When Charlie changed his mind, the first person I called was Mike. I was afraid that Mike might not come. But he said: "I'm looking forward to playing against him, let's go."

Dean did his best coaching playing a lot of people, keeping 'em all happy. That's probably why he was more successful at the end of the year than I was. I never played more than six, seven or eight guys. But his team was rested at the end of the season. He had more depth than the rest of the league. But he did a better job using his bench. A lot of people do that now. He was doing it way back then. I never had the courage to do that. If I'd get four points down, I'd get nervous, put my best team out there.

I remember the game (in 1984) when Jordan blocked my son (Chuck's) shot. I still think Jordan went up through the net and knocked it out of there. If you look at the film, it looked like his hand went through the rim and knocked it out.

Dean kind of irritated you sometimes with little cutting remarks. He said: "I was surprised Lefty put his son in the game." Well, he got a wide-open shot. And if they hadn't had Michael Jordan, it would have been an easy layup. The reason that I put him in is that we had worked on that play in practice, and he was knocking it down. I said: "Get in there, boy." Dean probably wasn't thinking when he said that. But usually, he thought before he said anything. That kind of hurt Chuck's feelings. But I'm sure Dean didn't mean anything by it.

Years after that, I saw Michael's dad on TV. They asked him what was his biggest memory of Michael in college. He said: "Up by one, Lefty put his son in the game, and Michael blocked his shot." That kind of surprised me. I figured he would say the shot that beat Georgetown. I've got a tape of it. We had time on the clock even after he blocked the shot and knocked it out of bounds, one second or something. But the timekeeper let it go off, said he couldn't see over the Carolina bench.

Dean usually showed up late for the coaches' meetings. We would talk about him a little bit, tease about him. It was not any vendetta. We weren't out to get him. But whoever the top dog is, people kind of talk about him. I remember one year, I was talking at a sports club, and I said: "Dean got so-and-so because he gave him more money than me." It was just a joke. But he got all upset. That's him. That's his image—Clean Dean. My son, Chuck, is a coach. I told him: "If you want to emulate someone, emulate Dean Smith." He always got along with the press. He never said anything controversial. Me, I was always opening my mouth, saying controversial things, getting into trouble.

He works on that image, I think. I don't know where we were one year, but we were at dinner, I think maybe in Chapel Hill or Myrtle Beach. He ordered a scotch in a coffee cup—I think that's what it was. I'm not exactly sure. Whatever, I don't drink. But if it was me, I would have said: "Just bring me a scotch and water," and people would have said: "Look at Lefty, he's a drunk." But he was very concerned about his image. I don't say that in a negative way, I say it in a positive way. He would get technicals. He would say that he never used profanity. That's fine, but they do give technicals for something. Maybe he didn't curse, I don't know. But I think that was a great trait that he had, projecting such a good image. That's why I told my son to be like him. My son doesn't curse.

Norm and I used to talk about him a little bit. He was the top dog. We were trying to chase him off the top of the mountain. Norm respected him, but he was right there in the same state. Fortunately, I was a couple of states away. It's tough to be competing in the same state. He's perfect. Norm's kind of like me. He would say things to me that I kind of shook off—I'd say: "C'mon, Norm." But being 20 miles away from him, it was hard. Ever heard anyone say anything bad about Dean Smith?

The time I wouldn't shake his hand (in 1983), it was just a competi-tive thing. I don't remember what it was, but whatever it was, it wasn't that big. I shook his hand after that. That was just one time in 17. I was upset about something. I stormed off. He would never do that. He would have shaken his worst enemy's hand. But that's not me. He's great at image control. I'm hotheaded.

I don't want to get Dean mad at me. He and I are friends. We've been competitors. When you compete with somebody, you're not exactly friends during games, during recruiting. You respect him. I always respected Dean. When I got let loose at Maryland, he was the first guy to call me and tell me that I got a raw deal. He called me even when I left James Madison. We're good friends. Back then, we were just competitors. In fact, I was just writing him a letter to congratulate him for an award he just won.

I was surprised that he left. He had it going. He had great teams. They went to the Final Four without him the first year he was gone. I wouldn't have quit if I was him. I'm going to quit when I start getting my butt beat. But he wasn't about to get his butt beat anytime soon.

TERRY HOLLAND

> *Holland compiled a 326-173 record at Virginia from 1974-75 to 1989-90. After the 1977 ACC tournament final in which Virginia's Marc Iavaroni said he was shoved by Smith at halftime, Holland said: "There's such a gap between the man and the image the man tries to project."*
> *He became athletic director at Virginia in 1995.*

In 1977, North Carolina and Virginia had already fought some great battles, on and off the court. We would fight many more memorable ones as the years went on. The game was a rematch of the previous year, when we had risen from a sixth-place (out of seven) finish to win the 1976 ACC championship. In 1977, after an injury-plagued year and a dismal 2-10 ACC regular season, here the Cavaliers were, back in the championship against the Tar Heels.

The game was more competitive than anyone expected. We led until the seven-minute mark. Then North Carolina inserted an injured Walter Davis, who provided an inspirational lift similar to Willis Reed's appearance in the NBA championship. North Carolina rallied to win the championship and advanced to the NCAA Finals before losing to Al McGuire's Marquette team in the championship game.

I did not learn about the halftime incident with Marc Iavaroni until we had returned to Charlottesville. At first, I did not believe the accounts from fans who saw it happen. Our players were on spring break, and I do not think Marc would have said anything about it. But as media and others continued to ask about the details, it gradually came out. As a 34-year-old, third-year ACC coach, I was extremely agitated by this particular incident. However, after 16 years of coaching in the ACC and another nine years observing coaches as an athletic director, it is easier to understand in the context of expectations for ACC coaches.

Dean Smith got out of bed each day with expectations that the rest of us could not even imagine, much less hope to meet. The normal expectations of alumni and fans actually paled beside the expectations that he placed on himself. Those high standards became the expectation level for the rest of the league as well. While it is possible to point out gaps (or flaws) in Dean's ability to meet those high standards 24 hours a day, seven days a week, 365 days a year, the fact is that he did meet those expectations 99.9 percent of the time.

The final scorecard tells us that he met them so well that he won more games than anyone in the history of college basketball—and along the way, he won the respect of even those he had to beat regularly to get all those wins. As you can imagine, that respect did not come easily from fellow ACC coaches.

In the quote, I am referring to Dean's effort to promote an image of good sportsmanship versus his actions in this particular incident. After many years of watching and associating with Dean Smith, I am convinced that he was truly well intentioned in the area of good sportsmanship, but his efforts often were misinterpreted by his opponents. One of the things that bugged the other ACC coaches most about Dean was his tendency to give what we all referred to as "Left-Handed Compliments" (an apt description, since the old left-hander was often on the receiving end). None of us were immune, and the sportswriters couldn't wait to tell us about them.

After the 1977 ACC Championship game, before I learned of the Iavaroni halftime incident, a sportswriter told me that Dean had said: "Virginia did a great job in the tournament again this year—maybe their alumni should expect them to finish higher than sixth in the regular season." That was classic Dean—a compliment followed by the qualifier, or the "hook," as the other coaches called it.

Invariably, Dean would comment on Virginia's physical style of play after first seeming to compliment us. He would say: "Virginia's rebounding was the key to tonight's game" and then qualify it by adding, "They did a great job of checking out, but I didn't know you were allowed to check out that way. We need to check with the conference office to see if that is legal."

Of course, we all did the same thing to varying degrees, and all of us were particularly testy after an upset loss. It is important to remember that Dean's teams were always expected to win, so 99 percent of the time when he addressed the media after a loss, he was speaking about an upset. The toughest thing for any coach to do after an upset loss is to be totally gracious. We should give Dean credit for at least trying. Most of the time, the rest of us did not even try.

One of Dean's greatest strengths is his competitiveness, but as with all of us, your greatest strength at times can be your greatest weakness. Dean really tried to be a good sportsman after a loss, but his competitive nature would not let him go too far, particularly with other ACC coaches. As a result, Dean was totally bewildered by the reaction to his "compliments." He really was trying to be gracious and a good sportsman. Even when Lefty or Norm showed him the clippings of what he had said, he did not understand why they were so upset.

Dean really did believe in good sportsmanship and worked hard at it. He was the only coach I have ever seen who would go out on the floor to try to stop the Carolina fans from waving their arms to distract the free-throw shooter. For a long time, he was successful. Carolina fans would sit without moving while opponents attempted free throws, unlike fans anywhere else in the country.

That brings us back to the Iavaroni incident, which is again a case of a man's greatest strength becoming his greatest weakness in certain situations. Dean's support of his players is legendary. His attempts to "protect" them during games led to face-to-face confrontations with opposing players and with opposing coaches on a number of occasions. Because the Iavaroni incident occurred on the way to the locker room and at halftime, I felt this was a different and more dangerous situation for all involved than the "popping off" that happens to all of us during the heat of battle. I made the statement out of frustration. Dean was obviously trying to project good sportsmanship, but did not seem to understand the seriousness that this particular incident held from my viewpoint.

One of the hardest things for all of us was having to live up to the image that we were trying to project. It just created another whole set of impossible expectations. I think the fact that Dean was not perfect (just closer than the rest of us) only makes him "human." I wish that we all could have taken ourselves a little less seriously and really laughed out loud at some of the things we did and said.

One great example of the inability to laugh when we should was the "dog named Dean." The Hollands actually did have a golden retriever named Dean, named after a neighbor who taught at our Judge Advocate General's School, Dean Dort. But you can imagine the reaction of everyone who learned the dog's name. It was like having a photograph on display for everyone to write their own caption: "Oh, I see why you named it Dean—look at that nose!" or: "It must have whined all night—that is why you named it Dean!"

My wife, Ann, got it right when Dean's wife, Linnea, indicated that she did not understand why we named our dog Dean. Ann just said: "Linnea, you and Dean have two goldens. Why don't you just name them Terry and

Ann and this thing will be over?" Living in the ACC fishbowl can distort almost anything. Have you ever said a familiar word over and over until it becomes almost unrecognizable? That is what happens when every word is analyzed and repeated with a different spin in every telling, depending on who the teller cheered for.

The media attention and fan interest in ACC country sometimes got things a little distorted, but the real action was always in the arenas, and the competition there was spectacular and inspiring. The rivalry on the court was the best part for me. Playing North Carolina always brought out the best in everyone. Two of our games in the early '80s were classics in every sense of the word. In fact, you can still see them regularly on the Classic Sports.

Both games were played in Chapel Hill. In 1980-81, we came from down 16 to tie the game on a three-point play (the hard way) by one of the ACC's great clutch players, Jeff Lamp. We then went on to win in overtime to preserve our unbeaten record (19-0) and number-one ranking. Then, two years later, we led by 16, and North Carolina stormed back to close the gap to one. A steal and a dunk at the other end by none other than Michael Jordan—the world's best clutch player—gave Carolina the one-point victory.

While those games were classics, the contest that had the greatest impact on the game of basketball was the infamous 1982 ACC championship game. After losing in Chapel Hill by five in January, we won the February rematch at home by 16. The rubber match in the ACC championship game lived up to its billing for the first 30-plus minutes, even though we were playing without our all-ACC point guard, Othell Wilson, who had been injured in the first-round game with Wake Forest.

The lead changed hands often and furiously until the 7:30 mark. That's when Carolina, holding a one-point lead, went to its Four Corners offense. Our strategy against the Four Corners was to play solid defense and let the clock put the pressure back on Carolina. We had employed this strategy effectively on several occasions, but this time North Carolina had a weapon that we had not seen since the days of Phil Ford.

We played great defense, but even though we made him take tough shots, the Michael Jordan legend began that day. Carolina would hold the ball and finally Jordan would go one-on-one against Jeff Jones (or whomever) and make the shot to give them a three-point lead. We would come back to cut it to one each time, but could never get the lead back. After winning the ACC title, North Carolina went on to win Dean's first NCAA championship, with Jordan adding to his legend by making the winning shot. The final score of 47-45 between two of the most powerful programs in the land convinced everyone in basketball that a shot clock and a three-point shot were necessary for the college game.

The next year, the ACC agreed to play all its conference games with an experimental 30-second shot clock and three-point line. Ironically, neither North Carolina nor Virginia would reap the benefits of this experiment. In a controversial move, the ACC decided to play the ACC Tournament using the shot clock and three-point line, over the objections of those of us who wanted to use the ACC Tournament to prepare for the NCAA tournament. N.C. State parlayed the three-point shot into an improbable ACC championship that not only got them into the NCAA tournament, but propelled them to an even more improbable dream that ended with them as NCAA champions.

As a basketball strategist, Dean was outstanding. His standard multiple defenses always made North Carolina extremely difficult to prepare for. His offensive system paid huge dividends in consistency. There were many who felt that his inflexible offensive approach tended to hurt North Carolina in postseason play. However, I can honestly say that Dean often changed to take advantage of situations, either with personnel or strategy that differed from Carolina's basic game plan. He would invite other coaches to scout his team and make suggestions. He took their advice to heart with great success on several occasions that I am familiar with, and I am sure on numerous others that I know nothing about. He was always the teacher, but smart enough to always remain a student of the game as well.

North Carolina basketball under Dean Smith not only set a high standard for the game nationally, but also raised the bar in the ACC so high that the rest of us became much better than anyone would have thought possible. This was true of individual players and coaches as well as other ACC programs. We all owe Dean a debt of gratitude for these high standards that forced us all to do our best to make ACC basketball what it is today. The 16 years I spent coaching in the ACC were something special. The same thing can be said for all who competed with North Carolina during the Dean Smith era.

AL McGUIRE

McGuire compiled a 295-80 record at Marquette from 1964-65 to 1976-77, defeating Dean Smith and North Carolina in the 1977 NCAA final, 67-59.

The first time I met him, Frank McGuire invited me to come down as an assistant to take Buck Freeman's place. Buck was into the sauce a little bit. Frank had taken Buck down from St. John's with him. I said: "No, Frank, you just won a national championship. If you go someplace else, I'll go with you, leave Belmont-Abbey College" (where McGuire was head coach). They had no place to go but down. I took a pass. I probably saved myself a lot of headaches. It was not my world.

Bob Spear was the head man at Air Force. Dean was his assistant there. I didn't know Dean. But after Frank hired him, he came to my home. He came in the back door. I lived in Chapel Hill, North Carolina. The first thing I noticed about Dean was that his nose was so big, and his crewcut made his nose look bigger.

We had hot dogs and beans. There was something very special about him. You could tell that there were thoroughbred bloodlines in Dean from way, way back. You could just feel it. He was very quiet. Of course, he was caught between two Irish guys, myself and Frank, two New Yorkers. I didn't know exactly what it was about him. I knew there was that intensity, that work ethic, that moral type of excellence.

Dean constantly did me favors. I remember him allowing my team to go down and play the freshman team at Chapel Hill. That was huge for Belmont-Abbey College. It didn't mean much to Dean. But he allowed us to take our bus down there and play.

Dean understood that I was at a small school. Anytime I was ever in touch with Dean at NCAA meetings, he always picked up the bill. He used plastic. The only difference between us is that he likes really good meals. I'm a street eater.

Dean was also the only coach ever to visit my home about my son, Allie. He had his alligator shoes on, and there were five inches of snow outside. Allie only visited one school—Carolina. But of course, he came to Marquette. We're going back 25 or 30 years. Allie has a son at Cornell now. Anyway, Dean was very smooth. When I visited a home, I was more of a kitchen operator. He was more of a living-room operator. Growing up, the only time I got into a living room was when someone died.

There was one thing I felt very sad about. He was the one who inducted me into the Hall of Fame. I gave a two-, three-minute talk, and I didn't thank him. He flew up from Chapel Hill with his wife, walked down the aisle with me. This was the end of maybe 50 or 60 things he had done for me in my life. He even helped me with a recruit once at Marquette—Jackie Burke, from New Jersey. I hate to think I'm a complete New Yorker. I wrote him a letter to apologize. I think I did. I hope I did. If not, I did it verbally. I mean, it's not easy traveling to Springfield (Massachusetts). Who the hell wants to go to Springfield? It's like Fort Apache. You can't go out at night.

I never really ran with Dean. I might have been a little too rough— you can take the boy out of the city, but you can't take the knife out of his hands. But he was always completely cordial. He was just someone special. I've been a loner all my life. Dean's been a workaholic. I've never been a workaholic, except years ago when I was collecting toy soldiers.

Al McGuire (Photo courtesy of Marquette University)

It wasn't strange coaching against him in the 1977 championship game. I've never looked at things like that. To me, the half-court line extends out the buidling. I don't have a love affair with other coaches. I don't have a vendetta. If you want to bury someone and you think about how close you are to them, the last nail you put in will be in your own coffin. The idea is to win, and get out of there.

As far as the game, Dean did have a lot of injuries. Ford's hand was bad, and a couple of guys couldn't play at all. And he probably was in the same situation Mike Krzyzewski was in against UConn in '99. Duke was figured to win. And it's very difficult to win when people figure you to win. It's much easier to win when you're the Huskies, with the world picking against you.

We got a big break when they went Four Corners and missed a shot. We were way ahead in the first half. I knew they'd make a run in the second half. They were too good. It just so happened that we won the ballgame. As for the Four Corners, you live by the sword, die by the sword. He had won so many damn ballgames. He was right to go to it. They came all the way back, grabbed the lead. We were tightening. The only thing was, it gave us a little breathing time. I only played five or six men.

What happened was, they came up dry. Someone took the shot, we got the ball, Butch (Lee) went down and scored. That was all she wrote. They had to come out. It's the same with Mike (Krzyzewski) not calling a timeout (in the final seconds against Connecticut in the '99 final). That's his M.O. Certain things are decided before the game. His M.O. not to call time out was decided October 15. The only adjustments coaches make are in the first seven minutes of the first half and the first five minutes of the second half. The rest is on computer. The rest is automatic.

Even after the game, he handled it like a gentleman, sucked it up. I know in Chapel Hill all the stores were sold out of sky blue. They were ready to paint the town. Again, he showed that constant graciousness. There wasn't that graciousness in the ACC—they were too close, looking for chinks in his armor. Dean was too successful. What you got from coaches, athletic directors and media were left-handed compliments. But once you get known by one name, you're successful. Dean stood the test of time.

I don't think he should have retired. You never give up the badge, or the patch, as they call it in New York. Golf is important to him. His family is important to him. But everything becomes less important when it's overdone. How much golf can you play? How many books can you write? How many commentaries can you do? I thought he did a magnificent job at CBS. But I don't think he was comfortable.

He has his own way of doing things. I found working in television that you can get anything you need from him; if you go about it properly, you've got it. You go through the sports information director, you go through

Bill Guthridge, you got it. You just can't go pound your way in and say, "This is CBS," or, "This is the peacock. We're going to do this or that." It has to be done in the proper way.

I still think—I know—that he dies when North Carolina plays. I wish him luck in his life. I hope he makes a few birdies, and maybe an eagle or two.

Bill Foster

Foster compiled a 113-64 record at Duke from 1974-75 to 1979-80, reaching the Final Four in 1978. He is a basketball consultant with the Big 12 and lives in Coppell, Texas.

I made the comment when I got to Duke that I thought the game was invented by Naismith, but then I found out that it was invented by Dean Smith—one word, Deansmith. I said it in jest, but it seemed like everything someone had come up with, he had done before. We shot free throws before. I didn't know they were invented at Chapel Hill.

Seriously, I always had tremendous respect for him. I always felt that I got along with him. I know he didn't get along with some other coaches. That's to be expected with the rivalries, the intense rivalries. Basketball is so big down there, it's a religion. Tobacco Road is a different breed of cat. People asked me: "Did you go to Chapel Hill often?" I said: "Once a year, only under duress."

One of the biggest things during the football season at Duke was when the ACC basketball handbook would come out. They would announce it, and it seemed like everyone was coming up the steps to buy the pre-season book. I liked to say that if I went to buy a quart of milk, the news would be in the morning paper, and there would be a picture in the evening paper. Hopefully, it was milk. Later on, I think it would have needed to be stronger.

Being at Duke, it got highly competitive. But I had respect for the person, and respect for the coach. I thought he was an outstanding coach. He did a lot of innovative things—the Four Corners, back screens for lob passes at the end of breaks, changing defenses. With some of these things, he was not the innovator. But he used them, and through national exposure with very good teams, a lot of people jumped on the bandwagon. He also built a system, which is copied today, not just by his former assistant coaches, but by everyone.

His players always acknowledged a good pass. I'd like to see that duplicated in more places. His teams—and Michael Jordan was a great example—were the epitome of team, as opposed to individual. You look at his players who have gone on to the pros. Most of them score more than they did at Carolina. They were really taught, encouraged, and promoted to be team players first, and scorers second.

The other thing I had respect for was the type of person he had in his program. I felt he ran a class program. And I never really detected that he was taking advantage of the state of North Carolina with what he did, his camps, whatever. Sometimes you find there is a feeling in the state that the coach at the state level might be exploiting the people. He very easily could have. But I don't think he did. Not to say that he didn't make money—and I certainly don't begrudge him that—but I don't think he overdid it. That's about as high a compliment as I could pay an individual.

I look back when we played them—my gosh, sometimes we played them four times a year, the Big Four tournament, two games in the league, then the ACC tournament. I used to say that with the Big Four to open up the season, you could go from first in the country to dropping out of the top fifty if you went 0-2. We did that a couple of times at Duke. We also won two games, and became the number-one team in the country.

Coming from the University of Utah, I didn't know what I was getting into, not as much as I should have. Duke had always been a favorite of mine. After high school (Glen-Nor in Glenolden, Pennsylvania) I went to a one-year business school as a prep school and played basketball there. I had a clipping that I kept in my wallet that said I had an offer from Duke. I don't know if the coach then had been drug-tested or not. I went to Elizabethtown (Pennsylvania) College. I doubt I could have played for Duke, if Duke wanted to be good.

I was always fascinated by Duke, fascinated that they called wanting me to be their coach, fascinated by the league. After I got there, I wasn't so fascinated by the league, nor anything else. We had talent, but not enough. I was Duke's third coach in three years. I felt sorry for the players, I really did. I wish I hadn't. I wish I had been more demanding.

My first year, we were going over to Chapel Hill, and the business manager thought he'd save money, so he got us a Holiday Inn bus, a big, old green bus. I was so embarrassed. We got over to Chapel Hill. It was a nice day. It seemed like it was 75 degrees. The students were sitting out in the sun. I told the players, "I don't want them to know we're Duke. Put your jackets over your heads, and we'll run in."

We had a long way to go. They had won ten games the year before I got there. I look back, it's scary. After my third year, I thought I must not be the guy for this job. But my fourth year, we were second in the nation. We went from the basement almost to the penthouse. And we only missed out on the penthouse after getting beat by a real good Kentucky team in a high-scoring game.

Duke had had a tradition, but had lost it. The toughest thing was, our only two NBA players were Jack Marin and Jeff Mullins—terrific guys, but they were near the end of their careers. Every team, it seemed to me, had one or two North Carolina guys. They were all over the place. There were a ton of guys who had played for North Carolina.

Getting Gene Banks was very important for us—he was one of the top two players in the country that year, and Albert King was the other. We already had Jim Spanarkel. He wasn't real highly recruited. We were very fortunate with him. And we also had Mike Gminski. For Gene, all the typical schools were in there—North Carolina, Notre Dame, UCLA, Duke, and sort of at the end, Penn. They'd keep calling Gene, and he'd keep adding schools to the list.

He was very pivotal. Those guys at North Carolina, they always came back and played in the summer. Chapel Hill was just the place to be. But when we got Banks, Gminski, Spanarkel, their guys started to come over and play at Duke. To me, that was one of the signs that we were going to be good. I thought: "God, this is great." We weren't allowed to go watch. I always stayed away. But people were saying the games were great. That was a sign we were starting to make a move.

The 7-0 game (in 1979), I should have made copies of the tape for all the players, showing what a great defensive team we were, holding the best team in the country to no points for a half. You think about what an accomplishment that was. They were holding the ball, but no points? Are you kidding me? How many times has that been done? It didn't speak so well for your offense, scoring only seven points. But a coach always has to look at it from the positive side. And we won, 47-40.

One time, Dean and I were over in Switzerland for a coaching clinic, being conducted in four different languages. We were coming down to the village for breakfast one morning from our hotel. The sun was shining down. It was really a beautiful picture. It was almost like an isolated shot of the sun coming down on this quaint little village, this terrific-looking Swiss town. He said: "That reminds me of Chapel Hill." Well, they ran out of water one time in Chapel Hill. I dropped him a note, and said it was really ironic they had to get their water from Durham. I never heard back from him for a long time. His village had everything except water.

At the same clinic, there was a big, tall Russian coach—she must have been 6-foot-9. Dean took over his son, Scott. I took my wife. Dean is so proper, so courteous. We went to hear this band. I got up to dance and left Dean with the Russian coach. I guess he asked her to dance. And I danced with my wife for like two hours. I had never danced two hours with my wife in my whole life. But that night, I did. Dean is so polite, he kept dancing with her. It was the funniest scene.

I can remember another time, being down at the ACC meetings in Myrtle Beach, South Carolina. They were priceless, the league meetings when all the coaches got together. Carl Tacy, God bless him, wouldn't say anything. Lefty (Driesell) would always say: "I ain't going to be coaching that much longer. This is all for you young guys like Terry (Holland)."

One night, I don't know what the heck I was doing, I'm coming back at 11:30 or 12. I'm with Norm Sloan and Lefty. Damn if they didn't have some firecrackers. Lefty has these firecrackers. He's setting them off—bang, bang, bang—and yelling real loud: "Norm, don't shoot Dean! Don't shoot Dean!" Then another one went off—bang, bang, bang. I got the hell out of there. I figured the police would come. That's all we needed, for them to get a hold of me, Lefty and Norm.

Another time—and this tells you about the North Carolina mystique—I'm coming back from the league meetings with Lou Holtz, of all people. He was the football coach at North Carolina State then. And he drives as fast as he talks. We're in the car, and he's driving like hell. I'm sitting in the front seat listening to him. I couldn't get a word in. We're driving back roads. He's got a clinic in Hawaii he has to leave for the next morning. I'm just trying to get home. I can't remember why I didn't bring my car.

It's probably one in the morning, and a cop stops us. I have my shoes off, sitting in the front. The first thing I do is put my shoes on. The cop thinks I've got something stashed underneath. He's going to write Lou a speeding ticket. Lou says: "I'm Lou Holtz, the coach of North Carolina State." And he says, "This is Bill Foster, the basketball coach at Duke." All of a sudden, it hits Lou—this guy is probably a UNC fan. And we're State and Duke.

The guy says: "I could have put down 75 mph, but I'm going to put down 65." Lou says: "What kind of guy are you, giving us a break? You're probably a North Carolina fan. Why not put down 75?" So, the guy puts down 75. It was all because of the North Carolina-North Carolina State-Duke rivalry. The intensity of Tobacco Road.

LES ROBINSON

Robinson played at North Carolina State in 1962-63 and 1963-64, and coached at The Citadel and East Tennessee State before compiling a 78-98 record as the head coach at North Carolina State from 1990-91 to 1995-96. He became athletic director at North Carolina State in 1996.

We go back to when he was an assistant coach at Carolina and I was a freshman at N.C. State. He became a head coach my second year. Then,

Les Robinson (Photo courtesy of North Carolina State)

before I left, I was the freshman coach while he was coaching. I actually was on our staff and scouted him virtually every game when we weren't playing during the '64-'65 and '65-'66 seasons. That was one of my jobs. It was like a dream to me. I had two tickets to every Duke and Carolina game. Back then, the scouts sat right in the stands, good seats. The schools traded off tickets.

I started observing his teams at a very early stage of my career. I would return home and stop at Coach (Press) Maravich's on the highway between Chapel Hill or Durham and here. He'd ask me questions. This is how I learned to scout. He'd tell me what to look for. If I didn't see it, he'd say: "Watch that the next time."

I go back that far. Then I left in '66 and became a high-school coach (at Cedar Key H.S. in Florida). But our relationship continued through the years. I went to the National High School Coaches Association meeting in '67. He was one of the main speakers. It was at the Fountainbleau Hotel in Miami Beach. These were coaches from all over. But because of our previous relationship, he and I spent a couple of hours down by the pool talking one of those days. I remember it vividly. He was en route to Puerto Rico. There are two things I remember that were significant.

He told me that summer that he was going to coach three or four more years at best. He had lined up a job—you know how organized he is. It was through a friend of his, a headmaster of a prep school in New England. He could have the athletic director's job. And he was going to go up there. The other thing, he was en route to hiring an assistant coach. The coach was Bill Guthridge. Bill was coaching in a summer league in Puerto Rico. Dean went down, interviewed him and gave him the job. And you know the rest of the story.

Thirty-five years later, when Bill replaced him, it was so big around here, the media was calling us—(current North Carolina State coach) Herb (Sendek) and me—wanting to do interviews, live. Our SID finally said that we'd have a press conference. That evening, Bobby Cremins called. He asked: "Has the media been hounding you?" I said: "Bobby, this is so big, we had a press conference this afternoon. We had a press conference for him retiring and Bill Guthridge becoming a head coach." That's how big it was. I doubt it's ever happened in the ACC or anywhere else. The only thing that might equate to it is John Wooden retiring and Southern Cal having a press conference. But they don't care enough about basketball out there to do that.

I coached against him both at Citadel and East Tennessee State. At The Citadel, we played in the North-South doubleheader against him. Each year, you'd flip-flop. Citadel and Furman would be at home, believe it or not, against North Carolina and North Carolina State. That was just the way it was set up. It was their doubleheader. But I begged to get in. It was a great recruiting coup. And financially, it was very good for us.

We'd compete against him there. We'd been in it a year, I think. We were at the ABC (American Basketball Coaches) meeting in Chicago. This is like in April. I said to Dean during a break: "We all set for the North-South?" I just wanted to make sure. He said: "Yes, everything's set." The year before, and we had held the ball. He said: "By the way, we're experimenting this year in the ACC with a clock. It's your choice." In the ACC, they were going to have it in all games, but in these games we had a choice.

I said: "You're asking me if we want to use the clock or not? I can make the decision?" He said: "Yes." I said: "Well, we don't want to use a clock, you know that." He sort of laughed. I said: "But I don't want to get knocked out of the North-South. If using a clock will keep us there, use the clock." He said: "No. I'll be happy. I want you to hold the ball. You play however you want to." I said: "I can tell you now—we'll be holding the ball." This was always the first weekend in February. He said: "A month later, we'll be playing a bottom seed—a team like you—and they'll be holding the ball. You can't practice this in a real setting." He wanted it to be held. He was happy to play us.

Then I went to East Tennessee, and we scheduled 'em (in 1986). Buzz (Peterson) was with us (as an assistant). We scheduled 'em at the Dean Dome. We had probably the worst team East Tennessee has ever had. We were on NCAA probation, had our scholarships cut back. We weren't very good. At halftime, we were getting killed. If we had known we were going to be that bad, we wouldn't have scheduled the game. It was embarrassing.

Coming out at halftime, I was just sort of standing there. He walked up behind me. We knew each other well enough that he could be candid. He said: "You're hurting. You've got to get some players." He said: "Is there anything I can do tonight?" I said: "One thing you could do is take off the press. I wouldn't mind seeing the point zone." I'm not too proud. I didn't want the scoring record broken. I wanted to get something out of this game, at least get our kids thinking I know something about the game.

I went in the huddle and said: "All right, men, a lot of times in this situation they're in a point zone. Let's attack the point zone. Here's the way it works." We had been practicing against it all week. Sure enough, they came out in a point zone. Our kids were like: "Hey, Coach knew what he was talking about." We were able to survive. I can laugh now. It wasn't funny that night. (East Tennessee State lost, 118-65.)

Then I come here, and our first meeting was at Reynolds. Other than that we won (97-91), there's only one thing I remember as a sidelight. I had brought back the floor that had been put away for seventeen years, back in the early '70s. We went to tartan. I was going to get a wooden floor. Our SID, Frank Weedon, said: "Les, the one you played on is still down there." I said: "What?" No one knew it was still down in the basement—for 17 years.

The next day, we had it on the floor. It looked awful, but we got it refinished. The lines were off because the game had changed. But they fixed it up in time, and it looked great. And now we're playing North Carolina for the first time. I shake hands with Dean before the game. We're talking, exchanging pleasantries, as they say. He says: "Les, is this the same floor when you were here as a player?" I said: "Yeah. That's it." He got this little frown on his face. He said: "Does it still have all those same dead spots?" He was sort of negative about it. I said: "Yeah, Coach, it does. But think about it. You and I are the only ones in the league who know where they are." He said: "You've got a good point there, Les." That made him happy. It really was trivial. But in his mind, it gave him an edge.

We always had a good relationship. Strangely enough, during our worst times here, we always had good success against him. He was very gracious in defeat. I know a lot of things were said about him, by good friends of mine. But I always evaluate people based on my dealings with them. We were three-and-one against them at one time. Then they beat the heck out of us. We went on probation. We lost scholarships. We sunk.

One night, they beat us like a drum over here. He told the media that Les didn't have ACC-caliber players. Not many coaches would say that. One, you're devaluing your victory. Plus, you've got to play that team again. But he was being honest. He said that we had some young guys who would develop into ACC players, but they were not there yet. I always appreciated that. He told it like it was. I was surprised he said it. But I was right there when he did.

His memory is unbelievable. But I got him one time. We were at Oak Hill, recruiting (Jerry) Stackhouse. Probably because Dean Smith was there, they called it an evaluation. Not that anyone needed to evaluate Jerry Stackhouse. It was a cold, ugly October night, almost November. It was nasty out. Limbs were falling off trees. There were storms. We were sitting up there, talking about old times. You don't get him very often on trivia, especially about his team. There was this kid out there who was left-handed. We were talking about left-handers being different.

I said, "I remember something from scouting that I had never seen before, and have never seen since. You started three left-handers." He said: "No, I never started three left-handers." I said: "Dean, I wrote it down. I know you did." We had a little debate. I was trying to narrow down which team it was. I didn't remember who they were, but there were three of 'em. He said: "You know, you're right. I did start them for a while." I said: "I didn't say you started 'em all year. But the night I was there, you started three left-handers at Carmichael Gym." That was one of the things Coach Maravich had told me—watch for left-handers.

That's the only one I've ever gotten him on. I asked him to help get a friend of mine's daughter into Carolina in the '70s. We were on an NCAA committee together. We had a break. We were getting some lunch. Dean said: "I'm working on Penny Thomas." I said: "Holy mackerel." I had talked to him about it a couple of months before. I had to think for a minute about what he was talking about. But his memory . . .

Once when I was at Citadel, we had an upset. We played Stetson on a Tuesday night and won at the buzzer. It was a huge win for Citadel. We came back that day. We were playing Clemson that weekend. My assistant and I drove to Clemson to scout Clemson against North Carolina.

We walked in, and he was out there having a smoke. It was like two or three minutes before tipoff. His back was to me. As I passed him, I said: "Good luck, Coach." He looked at me and said immediately: "Great win last night over Stetson." And he was a couple minutes away from playing. My assistant didn't even know that he knew me. I said thanks, and walked on. His recall was amazing.

CLIFF ELLIS

Ellis compiled a 177-128 record at Clemson from 1984-85 to 1993-94. He left Clemson for Auburn in 1994.

I always respected Dean. The people at Clemson really struggled with it. Anybody who wins and wins and wins, in our society when you're whipping somebody all the time, people get tired of it. I think people thought that Dean got away with everything, got every call. But out of respect, I never challenged Dean. It was just not my way. Dean didn't shoot the shots or make the shots. And the officials in the ACC were very professional.

My first game against Dean was a win. My last game against him was a win. He won more than I did. But the officials weren't responsible for that. The bottom line was, North Carolina always had better talent. The fact that they won, they became the enemy, so to speak. I didn't go on the attack. A lot of people were offended by the fact that I wouldn't do it. They wanted somebody to attack him. When Rick Barnes did it, he immediately gained popularity with the fans. But through the years, I don't know if it's the right approach. One of the things I was encouraged to do was get a technical foul, get the crowd going. But it wasn't a wrestling match. I wasn't in it for a circus or wrestling match.

The first time I really got to know Dean was at my first ACC spring meeting in Myrtle Beach. The thing that was most impressive is that he was the first person to come and extend a welcome, a handshake. Of course, it may have been a setup for the kill. But I was new to the ACC. I had been at the University of South Alabama, had success with that program. This was in

1984. Dean had just won a national championship for North Carolina—what, two years earlier?

At that time Clemson was really struggling. It was really known as a football school. I was coming in to try to change that. I think we did. Here was a guy that really didn't need me. But he opened his hand up. And he knew a lot about the teams that I had had. His recall was amazing.

We had played in the NCAA a couple of times, played Louisville, Alcorn State. Alcorn State was not a name that you would recognize. But at that point in time, they had a kid named Larry Smith, who had gone on to the NBA. Dean remembered. He's got a memory like an encyclopedia. He can file it. He recalls events, situations that go way back. It was so impressive to me that he could recall the game, tell me about the games we had played. I said, "Geez, here's a guy you're not going to come in with any surprises on."

During the spring meetings, something would come up and he'd remember the situation. In those years, Lefty Driesell was in the meetings, Jim Valvano, Terry Holland, Bobby Cremins. Something would come up, we'd start talking about an issue and Dean would say: "Terry, that's like the situation in 1977 when we played such and such." The recall . . . he knew it like it was yesterday. He has a file in his brain that's next to none.

You were not going to outplan him. He would film you to death. We'd go into the spring meeting, and he was always analyzing game situations, every year. I could remember him taking stacks of films to (ACC director of basketball officials) Fred Barakat. "I want you to look at this film, I want you to look at that film." The situation that would occur, he saw as a mistake. He did it a) to correct the situation and b) to let everyone know he was on top of all this. You weren't going to put anything past him.

The one game that I could remember, well, Clemson has never beaten North Carolina at North Carolina. It's something like a ghost. One year, we were making one heckuva run, all because of Chris Whitney. He hit several three-point shots in a row. We were making a charge. And Dean very simply went to a box-and-one. You don't see him do that often. He doesn't have to. But he went to the box-and-one on Chris, and once he took that away, the game was never in doubt. That game would have been huge, a huge win for Clemson. But the move never allowed it to happen.

RICK BARNES

Barnes compiled a 74-48 record at Clemson from 1994-95 to 1997-98 before leaving to become head coach at Texas. He also has coached at George Mason and Providence.

I don't think I'm any different than most kids who grew up in North Carolina in the '50s and '60s. When you were old enough to get into athletics and follow sports, everyone followed the University of North Carolina. The teams you always saw were North Carolina and somebody. Some things don't change. It's still kind of like that. Like any kid, you had to have great respect for what he did.

I really got into following college basketball about 1965 or '66—around the time he was starting to do the things that he did. I knew at that point that I wanted to coach. I did try to learn and study everything about him. No question, it was a dream of mine to someday coach in that league, just be in coaching. Dean probably inspired a lot of people—not just the players who played for him, but people on the outside looking in.

The thing that I respected most, after being in the business and understanding it, was that every game the University of North Carolina plays, somebody wants to take 'em down. To handle that situation year after year—he did it with not just one or two recruiting classes, but for 30-plus years—that's the one thing I admired most about him after being in the league.

I thought all of the games were important, I really did. I never tried to put more emphasis on one game. But you could tell that when Duke or North Carolina came calling—or when you went calling on them—there was something special about those places. Truth be told, the hardest thing was convincing kids who dreamed of playing at Duke or North Carolina to go out and beat them.

When you took your team in there, when you walked into North Carolina, it was amazing how many of the kids started looking up into the rafters. There was a mystique about it. As an opposing coach, you want to say: "It's not that important." But the truth of the matter is, the kids know what's going on. They look up and see Jordan's number hanging from the rafters. It's there. And it's a real testament to what Dean has built. It's remarkable the way they've sustained it. It's just amazing to me.

The fans get all juiced up every time they'd come in. A team would go on a big run at the start, and maybe Carolina would be down 18-4. They never flinched. They just kept coming. After the first seven or eight minutes, when teams had taken their best shot, they'd say: "OK. Let's play." A lot of it came from the fact that Dean had 'em prepared. I think their players knew that over the years, whenever you wore the North Carolina uniform, teams would play their best. But after four or five minutes, all the emotion would wear off, and they'd get back to playing their game.

He helped other teams in the league get better. He went after it. Other teams started going after it. Duke always had a great reputation. Wake Forest has a great tradition. Then there's North Carolina State. And Gary Williams has done an unbelievable job at Maryland, and Lefty Driesell before him. At Clemson, I said: "We need to get into that game." That was my big thing. North Carolina and Duke set the standard. And in this league, whether you liked it or not, you had to play 'em twice a year.

The situation at the ACC tournament got blown out of proportion. I respected him. It was a situation that happened. He said something to one of my players whom he felt was being too rough. He was basically taking up for his players. I was doing the same thing for my players. It was the heat of competition. Again, it's something you respect—him standing up for his team. And I stood up for mine.

He never made me feel like he thought he was better than me. I've been around a while. I was in awe at my first Big East coaches' meeting—John Thompson was there, Jim Boeheim, Rollie Massimino, Lou Carnesecca, P.J. Carlesimo. Then, as time went on, I felt like I was prepared for a lot of different things. I never felt pressure to beat North Carolina. I obviously wanted to. But I never felt that Clemson fans wanted me to go after him. I would hate it if people thought that was something I planned.

I got sick and tired of talking about it. We kept competing. We were almost like two little kids. We kept going at it. I obviously would never expect him to back down. He knew I would compete and not back down. And Dean was good. He didn't change. He didn't treat me like I was some guy who tried to come in and one-up him. He always had kind things to say after games. It got to be old. People tried to make something out of it that wasn't there.

I finally started joking about it. I was tired of dealing with it. I never lost respect for what he had accomplished, what he had done, what he had meant to basketball. I could sit here and talk the same way about Mike Krzyzewski and Gary Williams. But Dean, growing up in the state of North Carolina, I just know what he has meant to the league.

His greatest legacy is that the program will sustain itself long after his time is up. He's still part of it now. He always will be. He's done a great job with every facet of it. He's taken care of every part of that program. That's the true legacy of what he's done. As time goes by, they'll continue to be great.

JEFF JONES

Jones played at Virginia from 1978-79 to 1981-82 and compiled a 146-104 record as the school's head coach from 1990-91 to 1997-98.

The first time I ever met him was as a high-school senior (in Owensboro, Kentucky) Bill Guthridge had come down, and I think Eddie Fogler. Then Coach Smith came after them and we had a home visit. He actually came by the school as well to meet people there and watch pickup games that day. This was in the spring of '78.

The whole school was buzzing—Dean Smith was coming. Normally, the pickup games might have 14 or 15 guys. That day, we probably had 25 people who wanted to play. Some of them were former and current college players. That day, the teachers, the principal, all kinds of people came down, supposedly to watch the pickup games. Naturally, what they were there for was to get a chance to meet Dean Smith.

He was coming to watch me play in the pickup games. Some of the guys were trying to show their stuff. I remember one guy in particular. He already had gone to college, played and graduated. Now he was back in Owensboro. Finally, someone pulled him aside and said: "Let Jeff get the ball now."

He came to my home with one of the assistants, had dinner with my family. We sat down in the living room and talked about North Carolina, the program, the school. The one thing that surprised me—it wasn't a bad thing, but it stuck with me—was that he smoked. And he smoked a lot. It was just different than anybody else who had been in the home. But he was able even then to talk about all the players who had gone on from North Carolina to the NBA, his graduation rates, those kinds of things.

A really good friend of my brother's who was two years younger had been born in North Carolina. He was a huge Carolina fan, a huge Dean Smith fan. His name was Rodney Agner. And he came by the house to have a chance to meet Coach Smith. The reason that sticks out is that a number of years later—I was already at Virginia for some time—Rodney had gone to a North Carolina game and met Dean Smith again. Rodney said: "I actually met you at Jeff Jones' house when you were there," gave a brief description of the meeting. And Dean remembered him. It wasn't something like: "Oh, I remember you." He said: "I remember you. You did this and that." That kind of told me that all the stories about him remembering people and places weren't fabrications. This was years after.

My best visit by far was to North Carolina. I had a great time. I enjoyed the coaches, players, everything about it. But for some reason, I felt more comfortable at Virginia. A big part of it was that I kind of had a shared background with some of the players —Jeff Lamp, Lee Raker, Terry Gates. I didn't know them, but I knew of them being in Kentucky. It came down to that more than anything else.

I remember the first time we beat 'em at Virginia. It was in Charlottesville. My second year. A huge snowstorm. It was just a great game, going back and forth. I had a good game. I remember walking out of University Hall and bumping into him, him being very gracious with me. He had continued to correspond with my parents, not anything big, just a letter at

Christmas or something of that nature. He had sent me a Christmas card one time. It was nice. It wasn't like: "You went to Virginia, the hell with you."

I remember a lot of great matchups, in particular my senior year in the ACC tournament, the slowdown game (a 47-45 Carolina victory). I was mad. I was mad at them for holding the ball, mad at us for not trying to get them out of it. Afterward, the Virginia players and some of the Carolina players I talked to were disappointed. It was a great opportunity—at that point, we were the two best teams in the country. It was on national TV, for the ACC championship. To be decided like that, it was frustrating. They had Jordan, Perkins and Worthy. They went on to win the national championship. It was a classic game (Carolina led 34-31 at halftime). Both teams were shooting well over 60 percent, going up and down. It had all of the ingredients for being a potentially historic kind of game. It ended up being historic for other reasons.

Coaching against them, it was always tough. They always had very good teams, very good players, great preparation. Going down to Chapel Hill, playing in the Dean Dome, pretty much every year I'd walk away angry, because it always seemed to happen the same way. It was lots of different things.

One thing—real or imagined, it could very well be imagined—is that teams could go down, play them really, really close, then all of a sudden in the last few minutes they'd grind you down. I hope this doesn't come off as sour grapes—they had great teams, great players. But with the officiating, things would always seem to go in their favor, all the key calls. It was always the other team that got in foul trouble. Maybe that was by design. But it had the same ring to it.

It was always amusing and frustrating at times to hear Dean talk about how physical Virginia was. The truth is, for the last ten years or so, even before that, there has been no other team any more physical than North Carolina. They did it in different ways. They were more physical offensively, how their big men would post up, how they set illegal back screens. Yet, they constantly harped on how physical Virginia was. We had some guys giving up two or three inches and 40 pounds across the front line. Yet, we were more physical than them? I never could understand that. They were extremely physical. Clemson was extremely physical, Virginia, Wake Forest. No one was any more physical than North Carolina.

It seemed during the latter years that he mellowed out a little bit. I remember stuff I heard about him, being paranoid. But in the last three or four years when we had the ACC coaches' meetings, dinners where all of us got together, he seemed to be much looser, more relaxed, more comfortable. Talking to some of the guys who had been around longer, they saw it.

Maybe it was that Norm Sloan wasn't there anymore. Terry Holland wasn't there. Lefty Driesell wasn't there. All these people wanted to beat Dean

Smith more than anything else. Maybe with these guys being gone, the new breed coming in, he didn't have to worry that every time he turned around, somebody would be looking to take him out. I remember hearing a story from when he left the room at an ACC meeting. Lefty Driesell said something to the effect of: "We've got to get that sucker." So much attention was directed at him and the North Carolina program.

The aura was always about the program. Even now, Dean won't talk about himself. He'll talk about the program. If you think of other Hall of Fame-type coaches—say, Bobby Knight—I don't know that the Indiana University basketball program has the aura as much as Bobby Knight. I don't mean this as a criticism, but you always hear that Bobby Knight is bigger than the program. At North Carolina, I don't think that necessarily was true. That didn't happen by chance. It was something he wanted.

PAT KENNEDY

Kennedy compiled a 222-131 record at Florida State from 1986-87 to 1996-97 before leaving to become head coach at DePaul. He was an assistant coach at Iona from 1977-80 and the head coach there from 1980-81 to 1985-86.

I remember recruiting Jimmy Black out of New York City. I pretty much had Jimmy wrapped up—he was coming to Iona. I was Jim Valvano's assistant. Jimmy almost announced he was coming to Iona, but you couldn't sign anything back then.

If I remember correctly, Carolina had lost Jerry Eaves to Louisville. All of a sudden, kind of out of nowhere, Dean calls Howard Garfinkel to see if there were any guards available. I had seen Jimmy Black play 28 out of his 28 high-school games. I did not miss one. I traveled with the team to Pennsylvania, did the whole thing. I thought Jimmy was a great point guard. But he played forward for his high school team.

Out of nowhere one day, Dean shows up at his high school. Jimmy goes for about 36. And he played point guard that day— their starting point guard was injured. Jimmy visited Carolina the next week. And we lost him. That certainly showed me the competitiveness and power of Dean Smith.

I'll never forget one time seeing him in LaGuardia Airport. At the time, Jim Valvano was talking to N.C. State about their head-coaching job. He came right up to me. I was amazed he knew my name, absolutely amazed. Here I was, just an assistant at little Iona. But he knew my name. And he knew Jim was involved with N.C. State, which no one knew. Jim's wife didn't know. Jim and I were the only two people who knew. But Dean knew.

I'll also never forget one of the games in Tallahassee. He came over to say hello before the game. He was always so gracious. But he had forgotten my wife's name. If you know Dean, you know that he's got incredible recall. He has an incredible gift for it. It bothered him so much, he made sure that the next time he saw me he apologized for not knowing it. He said: "Please give your wife Jeannie my very best." I've always been a little bit blown away by his recall.

In playing against him, I thought Dean was one of the great recruiters, as all legendary coaches have been. I also thought he was one of the great offensive geniuses. People always talk about their defense, the way they always play hard. But I really felt Dean was an of-

Pat Kennedy (Photo courtesy of DePaul University)

fensive genius. He always made such little subtle adjustments that ended up becoming major positives. Maybe it was the way they would set a screen. Maybe it was the way they would design certain cuts. Maybe it was the way they reversed the ball. You had to study it closely to pick it up. I would spend a lot of time trying to dissect the stuff he did. To me, his program was the IBM of college basketball.

Dean resented a little bit people talking about his system. But I deeply admired his system, his ability to rotate players and keep the same level of play. As much as Dean was in control, his teams played at a frantic pace. It was a little different with the Phil Ford teams that went to Four Corners and held the ball. But there were different rules back then. The one thing Jim Valvano always told me was: "If you play Dean Smith, you'll always be in the game. They never stop playing."

It was an honor coaching against him. I always said he's one of the few coaches in the world that, when you walked into his building, he had his name on it, and he was also sitting on the bench. That's usually saved for guys who are long passed.

BOBBY CREMINS

Cremins played at South Carolina from 1967-68 to 1969-70. He coached at Appalachian State from 1975-76 and 1980-81 before taking over at Georgia Tech, where he was 341-220 through 1998-99.

My college coach, Frank McGuire, and Dean were very close. Dean was great to Frank McGuire during the latter part of his life. He really did a lot of nice things for him. He used to stay in touch with him, call him. He was one of the pallbearers at his funeral. We shared a good friend in Frank McGuire.

I can remember as a player, playing against Dean's teams. We had a great player named John Roche. Coach McGuire loved to beat North Carolina, his old school. We had some vicious games against them. It was really intense. Anybody who played against us, we hated. But I knew as a player that Dean was a great coach.

He wrote me a letter after my senior year. He does that with several players in the ACC. It was a beautiful letter, congratulating me on my career at South Carolina. My greatest game was against Dean Smith—23 points and 15 assists. Dean always fouled at the end of games. He fouled me. I made all the free throws (16 of 17). I was a hero. I was a kid from New York with pimples all over my face. But he made me a hero for one night.

Once I started coaching, if you beat North Carolina, you had done something. I never thought anyone could catch up to him. But I think Mike (Krzyzewski) did at Duke. I can't speak for Mike, but Dean was every coach's measuring stick. They were on top. Our program arrived when we started to beat North Carolina for the ACC championship in 1985 (57-54). Everybody said we couldn't beat North Carolina three times in one year. They led most of the game, but we caught them at the end for our first ACC championship. That was special.

He seemed to be more organized. I called him a system coach. I thought he had a great system. The last few years, in particular when he had (Antawn) Jamison and (Vince) Carter, but even before that, he started to make some changes. He started letting players play more. He opened up a bit. But he had a great system, offensively and defensively. And he was great at special situations, particularly at the ends of games. That was like his masterpiece, at the ends of games. You knew if you had a lead against North Carolina at the end of a game that Dean was going to make it a nightmare for you before you won the game. You might win the game, but he'd make it a nightmare—timeouts, fouls, everything.

Going against him was challenging, not frustrating. I'd gone against him as a player. I was not scared of him. I loved it. I looked forward to playing North Carolina. The first time I ever went against him was at Chapel Hill.

They beat us by about 60. One of my players scored for North Carolina—Lee Goza. I said: "Lee, don't we have enough problems without you scoring for North Carolina?" He said: "Don't worry about it, coach, my mother will be very happy. She always wanted me to go to North Carolina."

The other story I like to tell is from my first ACC coaches' meeting. Dean got up and left the room. Everyone was saying: "We've got to get Dean." I spoke up and said: "Why the hell do we have to get Dean?" Lefty (Driesell) looked at me and said: "Just shut up. Wait until you've been in the league a few years." I would try to figure out why people wanted to "get" him. I guess it was because Dean was a very private person. And he won all the time.

I expected confrontations, crazy confrontations. I had heard so much about all the hatred (directed at Smith). It seemed like when I came into the league there was still some of it, but not a lot of it. I'll tell you one of the nicest things he did. At Bill Guthridge's first meeting, he read a letter from Dean to all of us. It was a really classy letter. He mentioned every coach, just wished us good luck, told us how much he missed us. It was really nice.

We had some tough games against each other, very tough. I remember one game that they were beating us. Everyone thought that North Carolina got all the breaks. I yelled at the officials: "We're playing this game, too." There was a special magic about Dean and North Carolina. They did get a lot of breaks, probably because of their great tradition. Dean was very smart with the officials. All the officials knew that he knew all the rules.

We all looked up to him, but we had to beat him. I personally was very glad to see him break the record. I thought he retired at the perfect time.

GARY WILLIAMS

Williams played at Maryland from 1964-65 to 1966-67, and coached at American, Boston College and Ohio State before returning to Maryland as head coach in 1989-90. His record at Maryland through 1998-99 was 192-117.

My sophomore year was my first year of varsity play—back then, freshmen couldn't play varsity. They had Billy Cunningham and Bobby Lewis. Both he and Cunningham were in the top ten in the country in scoring that year. That was 1964-65. It might have been one of Dean's worst records at North Carolina (15-9, 10-4 ACC). We beat them twice. That's how bad they were.

The next year is when he really made the change into the type of coach he was—multiple substitutions, pressing, all the things he was famous for. There was a big transition in the way he coached. He didn't like the way they played (in 1964-65). Two guys scored most of the points. They didn't play great defense. They let you score easily. But the next year, it was hard to score, and they had five guys in double figures. Not knowing I was going to be a coach, it still impressed me as a player, having played against one style one year, and a different style the next.

The whole thing for him was how the game was played. Even though he didn't lose much, he could accept a loss if his team did what it was supposed to do. He wasn't a guy who would go off on his team after every loss. Sometimes you get beat, that's all. I think that's how he lasted so long.

Coaching against him was hard for a couple of reasons. Number one, you'd walk in and know you were coaching against a legend. You'd worry about that, how that translated to the officials. After games, if you were lucky enough to win, you almost felt bad. He was a guy I learned a lot of things from.

I was 26 or 27 years old when I met him at the old Five-Star camp. I was an assistant coach at Lafayette then.

Gary Williams

I was introduced to him by some head coach he knew. I was in awe. He remembered a couple of games I had played against him at Maryland. He tried to make you feel comfortable. I got up the guts to ask him: "What's important if you want to be a head coach?" He said: "Never take a job if it's a job where you don't have a chance to win the league championship." I always kept that in mind. That stuck with me.

Everyone talked about Dean trying to get an edge with referees, how he'd turn up the heat at Carmichael. So what? This isn't Little League. Everyone doesn't have to play an inning. I kind of liked it that he went after it that hard. By the time I got here it was the latter part of his career. But he was still the way he was when I was playing. He'd do everything he could to win within the rules. If he could go right up to the line, he'd do that. It's basketball, not golf. That's the way the game is played. The great thing about basketball is that you learn to compete. That's underrated. Dean talks about his players, how close they are. But if you look at the players and how successful they are, it's because they learned how to compete.

The coaches before, like Norm Sloan and Lefty (Driesell), they were basically his same age. There were some jealous feelings there. But (Rick) Barnes, myself, the new guys in the league, we didn't have that long a time where we dealt with Dean in the league, how much he controlled the league. I had been in other places, coaching against (Bobby) Knight, John Thompson, (Rollie) Massimino. I wasn't going to be intimidated. At the same time, that doesn't mean you didn't respect what he did. Everyone does some good things as a coach. You can learn things from guys in your league. You might hate someone during a game, but once the game's over, that's not there. It never has been for me.

When you shook hands, he might be ticked off, but he'd always say something positive—if you had lost, he might say: "I liked the way your team ran its offense." I don't think anyone saw that. I doubt people thought he would be that considerate. Dean had this image as being very aloof. But Dean couldn't go anywhere in Carolina. He was like Michael Jordan.

A few years ago, Dave Gavitt was invited to the thing Carolina does every summer, where they all get together to play golf and invite one or two outsiders. Dave said he was standing in the hotel lobby, and Dean was the guy, even with Michael Jordan there. For people in that state, he's the guy. People don't understand where they hold Dean Smith in that state. They feel he's responsible for a lot of good things about the university, let alone the basketball team.

I played golf with him a few summers ago. He ticked me off, too. He brought this caddy with him. He was reading every putt for Dean. Finally, I said: "Dean, who is this guy?" And he said: "Oh, he's the head pro of the club." I could see afterward how hard it was for him to walk into the locker room, the grill room. He didn't stay to have a drink. He felt he couldn't do that. I felt bad about that. I guess home is the only place he could go where he could be isolated with his family.

DAVE ODOM

Odom was an assistant coach at Wake Forest, head coach at East Carolina and assistant coach at Virginia before returning to Wake Forest as head coach in 1989-90. His record at Wake Forest was 199-107 through 1998-99.

The first thing I think about when I think about Dean Smith—apart from his outstanding coaching record, what he's meant to the game—is his remarkable memory, his ability for almost perfect recall.

I've often tried to figure out how he did it. I watched him as he interacted with people at social gatherings like conference tournaments. I

Dave Odom

really believe that he remembers people's names by something specific that they do, some habit that they have, something that stands out, makes them different than any person he knows.

For instance, every time he sees my wife, he always says to her: "Hi, Lynn. How are you doing? Still running?" She's one of the few coaches' wives in our league that runs. That's his way of saying: "I really do know you," which is kind of neat. With Terry Holland's wife, Ann, he'd always say: "Ann Holland was the one to get the wives together in a social fashion." The first recollection he has of a person, he'll always bring that up at the beginning of a conversation to let them know that he really does know who these people really are. The guy has an impeccable memory, almost perfect recall.

He's a master of the bittersweet—he'll give you a compliment, then just before you're able to really taste it, he'd jerk it back. He'd say something like: "Boy, your team really played well against us last night. Of course, Michael (Jordan) was hurt." He didn't actually say that, but that's how it would be. He really throws compliments around pretty good. Just about the time someone starts to puff their chest out, he kind of puts 'em back in their place. It's neat to see how he does that. He does it really well.

I remember the first year we were in the finals of the ACC tournament (1995). He and I have been the only two coaches in the league who go out with their teams for warm-ups. As is our habit, we were out there early. I always enjoyed going down and fraternizing with him and the North Carolina staff. The more you were around him, the more you relaxed.

On that particular day, I said: "Coach, how many Sunday afternoons have you done exactly what we're getting ready to do right now, play in the ACC final?" He said: "Oh, I don't know. I'd have to go back and check." Bill Guthridge was standing right next to him. I said: "I bet you Bill knows how many." He said: "No, he missed the first one." He didn't want to tell me he had been there 25 times, or whatever it was. But as soon as I let him know I was going to try to find another way, he knew exactly how many!

He was, and still is, the most prepared coach—and his teams were the most prepared teams—I ever coached against. I know that helped me as a coach get prepared. You knew he was the one person you could never out-prepare. And to go against him helped you get as ready as you possibly could for every eventuality. You think about Dean Smith teams, you think about the most prepared teams in college basketball. It was almost impossible to come up with something that they didn't look like they were prepared to execute in.

We're all creatures of habit, he more than anybody. You knew exactly what to expect in terms of style. Ernie Nestor, a longtime friend and colleague of mine, we were sitting on the bench watching Eric Montross in his senior year, early in the season. I always got a kick out of watching Dean early, seeing what they were doing, the subtle changes the average fans and media would never notice. As coaches, you'd know if they put in a little change to offset the scouting report of the other team.

They used to run this stack set. They reversed it in that particular game. Almost on cue, Ernie looked at me, and I looked at him—"There he goes again." We ended up winning the game. But he always had 'em prepared. You never felt safe in games against his teams. You never could have a lead big enough. He could work the clock better, work the time and situation better. When they needed to stretch the game, they knew how to soak every second out of every minute. When they were in a hurry, they knew how to do that, burn the clock.

I've lived here pretty much all my life. He's been around pretty much all my life. When you first get into it, you can't help but be somewhat awestruck. But the longer you compete against him, you lose some of that, and the challenge becomes greater. What you realize quickly is that you've got to get better, go to him. He's not going to get worse, go to you. Reality begins to set in. You go to work, recruit. Your team gets better. You need not worry about him being on the other bench. If you're concerned about him being on the other bench, you're almost beaten before tipoff.

Anytime you beat him, there was a sense of accomplishment. What you really wanted was for him to recognize you as a worthy opponent. I don't know if he did. I'm not saying that he did. But competing against me and Wake Forest, if it ever crossed his mind that I was a worthy opponent, that would give me a tremendous sense of pride.

Chapter Seven

OPPOSING PLAYERS

TOM BURLESON

Burleson was the center at North Carolina State from 1971-72 to 1973-74. The Wolfpack went 73-11 during his three years on the varsity and won the NCAA title in 1974.

He is the director of the Avery (North Carolina) County Inspections Department.

Coach Smith was extremely professional in recruiting me. He felt he had a really good shot at me because Tom McMillen wanted to come to Carolina. Tom wanted me to be there. He felt I was a true center at 7-foot-4—7-foot-2 then. That way, he would never have to be considered a center. We talked on the phone a few times, played in the Dapper Dan, things like that. We were both highly recruited. If I had gone to Carolina, then he would have gone to Carolina. That's what he told me.

I know that Lefty Driesell made him sort of a last-minute offer, and then he sort of changed his mind. Part of his decision—not all of it—was that I didn't sign with Carolina. My family had a history at North Carolina State. I grew up on a farm, in an agricultural, rural setting. I had an inborn love for the school. I was very honored to be recruited by Coach Smith and the Carolina program. I just felt that N.C. State had more to offer me because of my background in agriculture, 4H, all that kind of stuff.

My mind was made up probably my junior year. But at that time, I didn't really come out with anything. I could have changed my mind. We would have had a great team with Coach Smith. He already had told me that

Bobby Jones had given him a verbal commitment. Bobby was a tremendous forward. They also were recruiting David Thompson. I knew that David was a great player. But for me, it was just never really in the cards. I was a farm boy wanting to go to N.C. State. It was a dream of mine since I was in elementary school. If I had an opportunity to play ball, great. But that's where I wanted to go. My uncle was in school there at the time. You're very impressionable at that age. My uncle was a role model to me.

Coach Smith was great, but I just wasn't open-minded about going there. I knew he realized that. I was the first number-one player in the state to stay in the state and not go to Carolina. I'm sure he didn't want to see that type of trend happening. It was just a very unusual situation. It wasn't that he didn't have a great program to offer—he did. Today, with their tradition and everything, he would have even more to offer. And it would have been even harder to turn down.

I know I'm one of the thorns in his side. If I had gone to Carolina, his chances of getting McMillen would have been a lot better, and his chances of getting David Thompson would have been better. It was never anything personal against Mr. Smith. We had that love-hate relationship with North Carolina, but there's not a program in the country that I respected any more. I gained a really neat view of it. We played each other. I guess I dealt Mr. Smith some of his longest losing streaks against N.C. State. But I always respected him. I don't have any dislike for the program.

He had a great team of his own while I was at N.C. State. He was very calm and collected. Mitch Kupchak and I were later roommates at the World University Games. Mitch told me that they turned the heat up in practice to like 90 inside the gym before our game at Carmichael in 1973. Then they did the same thing in the game, trying to fatigue us. I remember the fans were dying, we were dying. We were still able to pull it out (82-78). But he was always on top of his game.

The one thing that sort of stands out with me was in my sophomore year. We were beating Carolina by one. I fouled out of the game. Paul Coder came in. He was fresh. Bob McAdoo and I had pretty much exhausted each other. Coder came in, scored seven points in like a minute-and-a-half and gave us the victory at Raleigh.

I remember George Karl on the foul line. I saw a person or two waving. I stood up on the bench and got the whole crowd to stand up behind the goal and wave their arms, try to distract George. It probably was not a nice thing to do. Before then, fans did not try to wave their arms and distract the foul shooter.

Coach Smith made a comment on his show afterward: "I know Tom and his family. I know he didn't mean to do it. That was not a very sportsmanlike thing to do." Every time I see fans stand up today, I realize what I created. I know it was pretty poor sportsmanship. I was a sophomore, nineteen years old. Someone would have done it, sooner or later. But I respected him for saying that. He was always very professional.

When we beat them, he praised me quite a bit. In my senior year, they had us down by quite a bit at Raleigh. I scored about eight points and Mark Moeller scored about eight points within the last five minutes, bringing us back from a six-point deficit to win. People said: "How do you stop Burleson?" He made the comment: "He's 7-feet-4, and he's shooting 15- to 20-foot jump shots. You tell me how to stop him." He was always nice that way.

I look at what happened to UCLA after John Wooden left, and I look at North Carolina. UCLA, that was just an era. The Carolina tradition lives on today. I don't foresee them taking even a semi-nosedive, like the UCLA program did. You almost think it would be a suicide mission to take that job. But it wasn't. He didn't totally walk away all at once. He left his assistants. I'm sure they've gotten his support. He's still there for them. He's sort of weaning them. But he'll always be a part of it.

He was a tremendous coach. He really followed his players once he recruited them, followed them all the way through. Coach Smith has always shown class in everything he has done. Stepping down the way he did showed a lot of class. His loyalty to Coach Guthridge, that's what his whole system is about—loyalty to his players, loyalty to the Tar Heel family. I admire what Coach Smith has done with the Carolina program, how he has affected lives in a positive nature.

He comes up for the ACC sports writers' golf tournament in May. We've sat around and sort of chewed old times. He and I are very friendly. I really enjoy talking to him. He comes up, we joke around. I've got a picture of us holding our drivers up, the big drivers, the Big Berthas. I'm holding my driver up, and of course it's just a little higher than his. But as they took the picture, you could see him holding his driver up to be higher than mine, then me lifting mine up to be higher than his. Just a little competitive fun between us.

DAVID THOMPSON

Thompson led North Carolina State to the 1974 NCAA championship, was a three-time ACC Player of the Year and the 1975 National Player of the Year.

Like most kids in North Carolina, I grew up an ACC fan, a Carolina fan. When I was growing up, they had Charlie Scott and some other guys there. So quite naturally, I was a Carolina fan. Dean Smith actively recruited me. As a matter of fact, he spoke at my high school sports banquet my senior year.

The first time he really noticed me was when I went to the North Carolina basketball camp at the end of my junior and senior years. I played really well. He used to come down to Shelby. It was a small town back then, a lot smaller than it is now. There was only one good restaurant in town. It was the restaurant at the Holiday Inn, out on Highway 74. We went and had dinner there. I heard recently that he still had the receipt.

Coach Smith was just a nice person. I always respected him. It's really a testament to him that all the players who leave always come back and want to be part of that program. A lot of their guys are in the coaching fraternity now. They all go to him. He's like a father figure. They always check with him before they do anything.

One of the reasons I went to North Carolina State was because they had Tom Burleson there. Charlie Scott and some of the other guys had left Carolina. And I liked the guys at State, (assistant coach) Eddie Biedenbach. I just thought my chances would be a little better there. I liked the campus and everything.

Coach Smith took it real well. Even though I didn't go to Carolina, he was always real cordial with me and my parents. He always sent them Christmas cards. It made a big impression on them. And it made a big impression on me as well. At the end of our careers, he sent letters to Monte Towe and me, congratulating us for having great careers. He also mentioned that we always had nice things to say about North Carolina, and he respected us for that. And he also said that he was glad that we were leaving.

All of the games we played against them were very close. We just always found ways to win. Those first few years, we didn't lose too many games to anyone. But they were always well-coached. Any time we played them, we knew we'd be in for a tough night. They played great defense. They used a lot of different guys against me. It was very hard for one guy to dominate. Luckily, we had three or four guys who could take over when we needed them to.

I don't know if things would have been different if I went to Carolina. I couldn't have asked for a better career in college than I had at N.C. State. We lost seven games in three years. It would have been hard to beat that record anywhere, especially in the ACC, with the conference being so tough. Looking back on it, I played on three teams ranked in the top five. We were twice able to go through the conference—regular-season and tournament—without a loss. That's incredible. You've got to be a very talented team, plus have a little luck on your side.

MONTE TOWE

*Towe, the point guard at North Carolina State from 1972-73 to 1974-
75, has spent the past 20 years in coaching. He became an assistant to former
North Carolina State assistant Eddie Biedenbach at the University of North Carolina at Asheville in 1996.*

He always gave me a lot of credit for being the reason that we were
so successful against Carolina during the time that I played there. But I don't
think that was the reason he said that. The real reason was that he didn't want
to give David (Thompson) and Tom (Burleson) credit. State had beaten them
in the recruiting wars for those two. He could give me credit. Maybe he
meant it, but c'mon, without Tom and David, I could have had four other
guys, and we wouldn't have had a chance.

I wasn't recruited by Carolina. I was just hoping to be recruited by
Purdue. I grew up in the Midwest, in Indiana. I was brought up on Big Ten
basketball, not ACC. At the time, North Carolina was a power, but I can
remember a *Sports Illustrated* cover with South Carolina—John Roche, Frank
McGuire. North Carolina State came about because of Norm Sloan's relationship with Dick Dickey, an All-American at North Carolina State who
happened to see me play. When North Carolina State offered me a scholarship, my choices were limited. I wasn't highly recruited. Butler, Bradley, that's
about it.

The games were tremendously heated. The recruitment of Burleson
and Thompson—particularly Thompson—carried over to the games. It
brought an atmosphere to the game that went beyond the game itself. It was
a tremendous time in my life. It was very exciting basketball. Not only did we
have regular-season competition and ACC tournament competition, but we
also had the Big Four tournament. We all played each other in Greensboro in
December.

They were awfully good, awfully big. George Karl was my first
matchup—he was a senior when I was a sophomore. Before that, freshmen
weren't eligible. It was the last year they were not able to play. Our first freshman game against Carolina, we were undefeated, and I think maybe they had
one loss. They beat us. I remember David saying after the game: "I will never
lose to Carolina again." And it about came true. The next game was at
Reynolds, in front of twelve thousand people. David had maybe the best
game he ever had. Then we went on to beat them eight straight (as varsity
players) before losing in the ACC tournament final my senior year.

Basketball-wise, I always thought Dean was very innovative, particularly offensively, which is not usually what you hear. I always remember
Norm and other people copying the things that he did. Obviously, when

you're in their league, and they're so successful, you're going to copy them to some degree. That's kind of what happened. The out-of-bounds play underneath. The back screens for McAdoo, Worthy, the people who could get up around the rim. As much as he appears to maybe be conservative, he was very progressive and innovative with his basketball.

I remember a couple of other things. My sophomore year when we were in the ACC tournament, my father and family were in town. The final was coming up, and Carolina had been eliminated. My father ran into him, probably at a hotel. Knowing my father, he probably went right up to Dean and told him he was my father. And he probably asked him if he had tickets left over. Dean was nice enough to give him what he asked for—four tickets, six tickets, I can't remember. That touched a spot in my heart. It was very nice of him.

I went to Raleigh in 1991 and was trying to start a new

Monte Towe

league called the Global Basketball Association. I needed players. This was September, the league was starting up in October. I called Dean and asked if he had any players available. He mentioned Ranzino Smith and a couple of other guys. I said: "Where are they?" He said: "In Chapel Hill." I asked him if I could come watch them play. And he said: "Can't you play anymore? Come on over and work them out." (Tom) Gugliotta and Chris Corchiani went over with me. He was nice enough to try and help me with what I was trying to get done. He was also trying to help his ex-players get jobs. I know people I've been around from Carolina, their admiration, respect and love for him goes beyond being a person. He's almost like a deity. That has to say something for who he is.

In the field of competition, Dean was no better than anybody else, and no worse than anybody else. He is very competitive. However that comes across to people, so be it. That's the way he is. Don't ever think he's not a competitive person.

Norm had so many run-ins with him in the recruiting wars. He was the head coach at North Carolina State. At that time, Carolina was the strongest program in the league. Norm chose to fight it and fight it and fight it, in recruiting, in games. Because of that, I don't think they are friends. I do think they respect each other and probably care about each other. They shared so many great memories in battle. I can't help but think that both of them, deep down, have a lot of respect for each other.

LEN ELMORE

Elmore, the all-time leading rebounder at Maryland, spent ten seasons in the ABA and NBA after graduating in 1974. He is an attorney and college basketball analyst for ESPN.

I remember getting a call at home, talking to Charlie Scott on the phone. At the time, I just thought North Carolina was too far south for me to go in 1970, considering all that went on. Charlie obviously sung the praises. But he was already accustomed to being there, having been to Laurinburg Prep.

Me, I was a New York City guy. I was politically active in high school. I had preconceived notions about the south. I was a little bit apprehensive about Maryland. But it was so close to D.C., and so many New Yorkers went to school there. I felt a little more comfortable. Coach Smith was an impressive guy. It just never went beyond that telephone call.

I remember the first time we played there my sophomore year. (Tom) McMillen had initiated a controversy. He was all but signed, sealed and delivered to Carolina, and he changed his mind. We met with probably more than the usual difficult crowd. We were playing the number two team in the country—Bob McAdoo, Bill Chamberlain, George Karl, Steve Previs, Dennis Wuycik. We came in there and wound up getting smacked by twenty (92-72).

One thing you had to remember playing Dean Smith teams—you not only had to be on top of your game physically, but also mentally. They were so practiced in the fundamentals, when to go back door, change directions, things like that. You had to be able to analyze it. You had to have outstanding peripheral vision.

My job was to anchor the defense. I had to see who was coming, make sure I didn't get out of position, make sure my man didn't leave me. My junior and senior years, I played Bobby Jones. He was adept at moving without the ball. It made it difficult. But we held our own.

Coach would say some things to you on the court, always with a smile on his face. "Watch your hands. Don't play dirty." Things of that nature. He'd give you a little bit of a nudge here and there, probably with the intention of having you lose focus. I never had any kind of confrontation with him that I would consider out of the ordinary. Worse things could happen. (Clemson's) Tates Locke would send a guy in there to physically take you out of a game. That would bother you. But the mental games, I actually appreciated them. To me, it was kind of incentive.

With Coach Driesell, I can't get into his own mind, but I don't think he had a personal obsession with Coach Smith. I do think he used Carolina as a measuring stick, to measure his growth as a coach, and our growth as a team. Obviously, during that era, they were the team to beat, the team you pointed to—except for N.C. State for a year or so. There was always that apparent animosity that was held in check.

But I remember my sophomore year, the assistants got after it pretty good—George Raveling and Bill Guthridge. They almost came to blows in

the tunnel. George was 6-foot-5, but Guthridge got right up in his chest. I can't remember exactly what had happened. Lefty had a way of inciting the crowd, anyway. The combination of all those things got under the Carolina coaches' skin.

Mike O'Koren was my roommate when we played together with the Nets. I was very impressed by the fact that he spoke to Coach Smith almost on a weekly basis. There were times I would answer the phone when he called back. We would exchange pleasantries. Our exchanges were characterized by a great deal of class on his part. He still had the partisan, Carolina rah-rah stuff. He would make somewhat anti-Maryland comments. It was all

Len Elmore

in jest. I was very impressed by the fact that he stayed in touch with these guys.

As an agent, quite honestly, I never went after Carolina guys. I thought it was sort of a closed-shop situation. It may have been my faulty perception that because of who I was, having gone to Maryland, I would never get a fair shot. In business, it was always viewed as what impact would it have on the Carolina program and the Carolina constituency. Obviously, if one of their guys signed with someone from Maryland, it didn't really reflect well. I just didn't think it was necessary to waste my resources or energy going after Carolina guys.

As I got older, I started to appreciate a lot of the things that he did. During the time I played against him, we were archrivals, and to some extent, archenemies. It was purely an emotional evaluation. As you go on, you're impressed with not only the relationships he had with his former players, but you get to learn a bit more about him, what he was like in the '60s. He may have been ahead of his time, particularly from a race-relations standpoint.

As a television analyst, I always enjoyed the interaction. But when I was working for Jefferson-Pilot, if I said the sky was blue, he'd say it was gray. There were times in a postgame interview where I would comment on his offense, and he'd say, "The defense did the job." Or, I would say something about his defense, and he'd say, "It was our offense tonight." It was as if I could never be right. I couldn't analyze and evaluate a Tar Heel team. It was all part of the PR game some coaches like to play. As time went on, I think he came to respect my analysis. We'd have some detailed conversations.

TOM MCMILLEN

McMillen, a 6-foot-11 forward, was the subject of a heated and well-publicized recruiting battle between Maryland, North Carolina and Virginia. He chose Maryland and became the first of two players in school history (the other is Joe Smith) to finish with a career scoring average of more than 20 points per game. He studied a year at Oxford under a Rhodes Scholarship, spent 11 seasons in the NBA and later became a U.S. Congressman from Maryland.

The following passage combines his memories of Dean Smith from an interview, as well as selections from his autobiography, Out of Bounds, *used by permission.*

It's not so much that my parents disliked Dean. They just liked others better. It was sort of a reverse psychology at work. My dad wanted me to be near our home in Mansfield, Pennsylvania, so he could watch me play. He was more into Lefty's style than Dean's style. And he thought it would be

Tom McMillen

good for me to be close to my brother, Jay, who had played at Maryland and was then in dental school there. My mother was very close to Bill Gibson, the coach at the University of Virginia. He had been in my hometown for years, as the coach of Mansfield State College from 1956 to '62.

My recruiting story is one of tremendous entanglements. I started going to Dean's camps when I was in eighth or ninth grade —my brother Jay was even a counselor there, after he left Maryland. My brother Paul was a banker in Chapel Hill. I had a sister, Sheila, at the University of Pennsylvania. And the coach at Virginia was from my hometown. It was a very difficult situation.

I liked Dean. I liked Bill Guthridge. I liked the tradition. At the end of my recruiting, it wasn't that I was against Maryland, but I was tilting toward Carolina. Dean went out of his way in terms of recruiting me. He was at my house countless times. And Mansfield is not an easy place to get to. I just thought Carolina made a lot of sense to me.

At one point, I called Tom Burleson, thinking it would be fun if we both went to North Carolina. Tom, Bobby Jones, me—what a team. It would have been a big team, anyway. My parents were upset that I made the call. They thought Dean was pulling the strings a little bit. They didn't want me to take that step. They thought it was too much.

On April 14, 1970, I made the decision to attend the University of North Carolina. I was ready to sign a letter of intent. We were going to have the signing ceremony at a restaurant in Elmira, New York, about 20 miles from Mansfield. But my parents said they wouldn't go to the ceremony. And without the signature of at least one parent, even if I signed a letter of intent, it would not be legally binding. So my high school coach, Rich Miller, called Dean at my request to cancel the press conference.

On June 23, I called Dean with the news that I was ready to sign the letter of intent despite my parents' veto; and the next day we went through the signing ceremony, although both of us realized that a letter would be invalid without a parent's signature. Our thinking was that a signing ceremony might diminish the zeal of recruiters from other schools and the hostility of my family. On June 23, 1970, the cameras captured me in the act of signing my name in Dean's presence. The cameras failed to reveal that I was signing not a letter of intent but a napkin.

The next day my parents blasted Coach Smith in an AP story that was carried in newspapers across the country, and suddenly the rift between me and my parents was public. My parents accused Dean of trying to undermine their parental authority and alluded to "valid reasons" for not wanting me to attend North Carolina. Dad described recruiting as a "nasty, dirty business." The same stories carried Mom's vow that I would never attend North Carolina with my parents' blessing. "I do not blame my son," she told the reporters, "he's been brainwashed. I do blame the coach."

Dean was alarmed that the phrase "valid reasons" implied that he had committed recruiting violations, and I was concerned that the situation between Dean and my parents was deteriorating further. Rumors mushroomed that I had visited North Carolina eight times and that a credit card had been furnished to me on those visits. Of course, none of these rumors was true.

Coaches began to snipe at Dean, most behind his back but a few on the record. For example, Jack Kraft, the Villanova coach, leveled the following charge at the press: "I'm disgusted to be associated with a group—I'm talking about college basketball coaches —who are splitting up families. I'm 100 percent in agreement that something has to be done in a strict and serious way. This is the worst case of all, when you are splitting people up."

In mid-August I took a trip to Europe and the Soviet Union with the Olympic development team. Dennis Wuycik was on my team. I spent a lot of time with him. I became even more solid for Carolina. But when I came back from that trip, my father was very, very ill. We didn't know if he was going to live. I felt like I had put a lot of pressure on my family with all this. So, I opened the process back up. I said I'd talk to Maryland. I started shifting to Maryland.

On September 9, I packed for school without knowing where I was going. Dean was in Europe calling every hour. Bill Gibson was in my house playing cards with my mother and father. It's like I was in prison. There was a plane down the road that was going to take me to Virginia. I called my brother, Jay, at Maryland and said, "Get up here." He drove up that night. Bill knew something was up. And I sent a telegram to Dean that said: "Very very sorry. Hope you understand. Going to Maryland for reasons you know."

About a week later, Dean sent me a touching letter that I have kept to this day in which he said that ". . . not being your coach in college after having counted on it has been the greatest disappointment of my career." He also said, "Tom, I have never been through anything like these past five months. I know you have not, either. All of this in college athletics is not worth it. I am talking about the hate letters, phony letters, lies, insinuations, threats of investigation, etc. In fact, Tom, I would get out of coaching, but it is too great a challenge right now, and I never want to be accused of quitting."

Dean was always very professional. He handled everything with such aplomb. I still admire him for the persistence that he showed in recruiting me. It just wasn't in the stars. In retrospect, I'm obviously happy that I went to Maryland. My life could have taken a different turn if I had gone to Carolina. Who knows? I couldn't go wrong at either place.

At the end, what was really good about Maryland is that we got to build a program. They didn't have a program; we built one. We'll always be remembered not for perpetuating a tradition, but beginning one. That was the coup de grace that made the difference both in my decision to go there and in the way it all worked out.

My father, even when he was sick, never missed one of my games at College Park. He'd drive down and drive back with his friends, five hours each way. And he was not a young man. It would have killed him not to be able to do that at Carolina. It would have been very hard.

I still have the highest admiration and respect for Dean. What happened in my recruiting was just an example of the craziness of the process. It's obviously pretty ridiculous when schools spent more time recruiting me than they do the presidents of their own universities.

DAN BONNER

Bonner, a forward at Virginia from 1972-73 to 1974-75, is a college basketball analyst for Jefferson-Pilot, ESPN and CBS.

One of the things that always impressed me about Dean Smith was that he was able to evaluate talent to the point that he never recruited me. There were very few schools in the country when I was a high-school student that did not recruit me. But North Carolina was one that did not. I did not hold that against him. As I realized what my talent level was compared to who I was playing against, I always thought: "Well, if nothing else, that guy's a pretty good judge of talent."

I was very pleased to be able to play at that level. I'm very proud of the fact that I was able to accomplish that. I was not an outstanding player. I only really played my senior season. There was no question that the players they had at North Carolina were better than I. I wasn't excited about going to North Carolina. I grew up in Pennsylvania. I would have been upset had the University of Pittsburgh or Penn State not recruited me. But they did, and they did very hard. I could not have named all the teams in the Atlantic Coast Conference before I came down here. I never had any dealings with Dean as a high-school student. I never really had any dealings with Dean as a player, either.

But it's pretty funny. When they had that controversy with Clemson, Rick Barnes accused Dean of yelling at (Iger) Iturbe. Dean said that he didn't yell, he didn't talk to any of the players. I was amused by that. When I was a senior at Virginia, we were playing down at Chapel Hill. It was a really intense game. They actually beat us pretty good. I held Kupchak, I think, to 40 that night.

Their front line was Kupchak, LaGarde and Walter Davis. Our front line was Marc Iavaroni, myself and Wally Walker. We were very concerned that Kupchak would overpower me in situations where we didn't want to give up an easy two. I guarded Kupchak, but on the free-throw line, we decided when they were shooting a free throw, we would want Kupchak next to Iavaroni, and LaGarde next to me. We were afraid Kupchak would go over me and they would score easily.

It was fairly humorous. It was in the second half. We were down in front of the North Carolina bench. They were shooting a free throw. We line up, and they line up. Kupchak is next to me, and LaGarde is on the other side, next to Iavaroni. I motion to Iavaroni, and we switch. Kupchak and LaGarde switch. And now, I hear Dean yelling at the official. The referee comes up to me. He says: "Look, you guys have to be underneath the basket first. You guys get in your position, and stay there."

I thought: "What the hell is this? What difference did it make?" But obviously, it did make a difference. In our preparation, we thought it made a difference. Obviously, they did, too. But I was not happy about this. We got in our places. Kupchak gets next to me. I hear Dean behind me. Dean says to me: "What's the matter, Bonner? You afraid? You can't take Kupchak?" I thought to myself: "This is one of the best coaches in the world. Why is he bothering me?" I was nobody.

They made both of the free throws. On the second free throw, I hit Kupchak as hard as I could hit him. I had decided, the building could fall down, but there was no way he was getting the rebound. As I turned, I told Dean what I thought. I was a smart-ass, twenty-one-year-old. I said some things and ran up the court. That was the only dealing I had with him. It was sort of in the heat of battle. I never thought much about it. That story, I remembered it, when they all had that controversy with Clemson.

I covered the game where Clemson and North Carolina played at Clemson the first time Rick Barnes was the coach, and Barnes got thrown out of the game. Rick and I had a little controversy about that. I said on the air, I thought that was very poor sportsmanship. Rick got mad. He didn't stay mad. He just told me, he thought I was wrong, I could always talk to him about it. I think North Carolina shot 56 free throws in that game. They could have shot 156, as much as Clemson fouled.

As a broadcaster, I was always a little bit intimidated by Dean, by his presence. I've dealt with an awful lot of people who played for him and worked with him. I was always impressed by the fact that he generated this tremendous loyalty. There is nobody who I have ever spoken to who has ever played for Dean who will tell any stories about him that are in the least bit negative, who would criticize him at all. They are very protective of him. Somebody who engenders that kind of loyalty must really work hard for the people he deals with.

As a broadcaster, I probably worked in the league ten years before he addressed me as anything but Mr. Bonner. I felt like it was really a big thing when he started calling me Dan. It would be so insignificant for Dean that he wouldn't recall it. It tells you how much I respect him, or how much I'm intimidated by him. I'm not sure what the proper term is.

You have to understand, I didn't really have that many dealings with him, North Carolina was always up there, I've never been the top-gun broadcaster. For many years, I would go the entire season and not do a North Carolina game. It's only been within the last five or six years, with all the games on television, where I would do a couple of North Carolina games before the tournament.

Dean watches a lot of tape. He's very well prepared. He's always impressed me as one of those coaches who would tell you that it didn't make any difference what you said, but he paid very close attention to it. On the Raycom/Jefferson Pilot games, we used to have the Holly Farms player of the game. Nowadays, we have two players of the game, one for each team. In those days, we just had one. I was working with Marty Brennaman on a Saturday game at North Carolina. I was doing one game a week then on Saturday. It wasn't like now, when I'm doing two or three games a week.

Marty had done a Thursday night game at North Carolina. He was staying over to do the Saturday game at North Carolina. He went to practice. Now Marty is a graduate of North Carolina. He's very excited about this. He goes to practice. And after practice, a North Carolina manager comes up to him and says: "Coach Smith would like to see you in his office."

For Marty, this is like a nun called into the presence of the Pope. He's really thrilled by this. He goes into Dean's office. It's in the Dean Dome. According to Marty's version of the story, Dean doesn't say hello, goodbye or go to hell. Dean starts in with him: Why did Marty make J.R. Reid the Holly Farms Player of the Game? Dean could have told him to kiss his ring, and Marty would have done it. But now Marty is dumbfounded. And Marty, if you know him at all, is not the kind of person to stay dumbfounded very long.

Now Marty gets mad. Marty says to him: "What are you talking about?" Dean says: "Well, I don't really care who you make the Player of the Game. But it's important to the players, yadda, yadda, yadda." Well, J.R. Reid is a freshman. One of Dean's big things was, he didn't want to push his freshmen. He and Marty get into this discussion. Marty explains he didn't determine the Holly Farms Player of the Game—Billy Packer did.

But Marty is so mad. He tells this story to me, and I think it's pretty funny. And Marty tells this story to Billy Cunningham, who was doing games at the time. Cunningham and I, we decide that every game, we should make J.R. Reid the player of the game. Brennaman and Mike Patrick were the play-by-play guys. Packer was doing color. Cunningham was doing color. I did a few games here and there. It was the funniest thing. Of course, J.R. had a pretty good year. But we went out of our way to try to make J.R. Reid the

Player of the Game. I don't know that it was anything but juvenile. But it was Cunningham's idea. It wasn't mine.

My direct dealings with Dean were very limited. I've never been to a North Carolina practice other than at an NCAA tournament game. A couple of years, Dean was angry. It was after the ACC tournament. They had won the ACC tournament, beaten Virginia in the title game. It was Junior Burrough, that crew, at Virginia. It was a very physical, very competitive game. I'm doing the game for the ACC network. I jump over the table, and I'm supposed to interview the head coach.

The coaches always get a little bit frustrated. They drag them over right after the game. They want to be with their players. I understand all that. We're in a commercial. I'm standing there with Dean. I say to him: "That's a great win, coach." He was very angry. He says to me: "I liked the result. I didn't like the way the game was played. But you liked that. You liked that."

He has always felt for a long time that the game has become too physical, that there's too much pushing and shoving. I never minded that type of basketball. That was the only kind I could play. The difference was, I was 6-feet-6 and 195 pounds. There was little pushing and shoving that people in my era really accomplished. Nowadays, these guys are so big and so strong, and they all teach this physical play. Dean always felt it was a little overboard. He was very angry, I think, because he thought that it got out of hand.

Now I don't know what to do. Here I have this man who obviously is upset, and I've got to interview him. I'm thinking: "Oh no." They say, "OK, ten seconds." I don't know what to ask. I thought: "Well, I'm going to do it. It's going to be safe. I'm just going to say the same thing I just said to him. I don't want to make him mad. He's obviously upset. I don't want to look bad on TV. I sure don't want him to look bad on TV." I said the same thing. He reacted in pretty much the same way, turned around and walked off.

I'm thinking: "How am I going to get out of this without looking ridiculous?" I turn around, look at the camera and say: "Back to you, Bob!" There's just this dead silence in the (production) truck. Finally, the guy who is producing the game gets on and says: "What the hell was that all about?" I said: "I do not know." But I surmised it. Dean and I never talked about it. But he was just upset with the way things went.

I think Dean always associated me with not only Virginia, but Terry Holland and Virginia. Dean never said that to me. I think that Dean always regarded me as a Virginia guy. He has such intense loyalty to his North Carolina people, and his players and coaches have such intense loyalty to him. I think it's beyond Dean's capacity—this is not really a criticism—but it's beyond his world view to believe that someone could actually work games that involved their alma mater and have any sense of objectivity at all.

We did have a little bit of controversy about some of the things I said on the air. It entirely was about what he felt was criticism of his players' behavior. And it was. I would agree. I try very hard as an announcer to see the players as college kids. I know that they're big, physical specimens, they run up and down, this is a multimillion-dollar business. But I've always tried to keep in mind that they're kids. I've tried very hard not to say: "That was a stupid pass. That was a stupid shot." Decision-making is sometimes a hit-and-miss proposition.

But the one thing I do criticize players for is if they hurt the team because they are not able to control their emotions, or they don't hustle, something like that. I said a couple of times, when Rasheed Wallace was at North Carolina, that he, in my opinion, hurt the team by his reactions. I said it not because I had anything against Rasheed Wallace. But when I was a player, all I did was jabber at the referees. That made the referees angry.

I didn't really pay attention, but a little light came on when I was a senior. Since we had nobody else, I was the starter. In our first five games— my last season, the last time I knew I'd be playing basketball—I fouled out of three games, and I was in deep trouble the other two. I spent long periods of time in all five of those games where I didn't play. I started thinking about it. We watched films. The thing I was getting called for didn't seem to be any more serious than things other people were getting away with. I tried to analyze, why was this happening? I decided, because I was jabbering at the referees. I said to myself: "That's it." I kept my mouth shut. I never got more than three fouls the rest of the year.

That taught me, you just don't talk to the referees. You don't show the referees up. You just go and play. Things happen on every play. If the referees want to, they'll blow the whistle. I would say on the air: "Look, you just can't talk to the referee." I made that comment a couple of times about Rasheed. I made that comment a couple of times about Jeff McInnis. Dean and I did have a discussion about that. In fact, he sent me a videotape, clips in which he thought I was overly critical. I explained what I felt. We never really had any problem about it. But it gets back to one of his main tenets —he was going to protect his players. While maybe he could criticize, he didn't want outside people criticizing without some response on his part. I guess that's one reason he generates such loyalty.

I've always been impressed by the way that he did things. Unlike Terry Holland, I don't know what his private persona is vs. his public one, because the only one I've ever seen is his public one. But you look at the success they had, and the way they had it. They had kids who played hard. For the most part, they graduated. You look at their media guide, and they're doctors and lawyers and leaders of their communities, right down the line. To sustain that kind of success in such different eras—the '60s, the '70s, the '80s, the '90s, how much the game changed, how much kids changed—you just have to be very impressed. And I was always very impressed. I always felt a little intimidated in his presence.

MARC IAVARONI

Iavaroni, a forward at Virginia from 1974-75 to 1977-78, spent seven seasons in the NBA and played for the Philadelphia 76ers' 1983 championship team.

He became an assistant coach with the Cleveland Cavaliers in 1997.

My first year, he gave an honest assessment of how he thought we were going to do at Operation Basketball. We had just lost an ABA player, Gus Gerard. He didn't see us winning any games in the ACC.

I don't think he meant any malice. But it ends up on our bulletin board. I would have loved to have gone to Carolina. I got recruited by Duke, and by Maryland late. I really found the perfect place in Virginia. You always had a desire to beat the best. This added to it.

The first time we played them, they schooled us pretty good. They had pro players. Phil Ford, the ACC Rookie of the Year. Mike O'Koren. Tommy LaGarde. Ed Stahl. Walter Davis. On and on. They got to Charlottesville, and we somehow beat them. We used that (quote) to our advantage.

My recollections beyond that go in little snapshots. In four years, we never beat them at Carmichael. The closest we came was my sophomore year. We really had 'em. Then one of our subs gave up a rebound, and they hit a shot at the buzzer to beat us by two (73-71). We took that, rode that into the ACC tournament, and beat 'em (67-62).

I don't remember anything negative about Coach Smith until my junior year. I used him as a motivational tool. I certainly didn't have anything against him. But I used the things that he said. And if he didn't say them, maybe I made them up. I was a young kid. I couldn't control it. At times, I could go overboard. I was always trying to prove myself. One time, I had a picture of Dean Smith in my locker. It kept me motivated. Coach (Terry) Holland asked me to please take it down. I understood why.

I remember my junior year, feeling very brash, very confident that we could beat them at Carolina. I was playing pretty well. We got involved in a jump-ball situation. The way it was with the old jump balls, if you couldn't get position on someone, you'd either put your foot in front or behind him. Bruce Buckley had position on me. I kind of flopped. Everyone was heckling, booing me. Dean's pointing at me. I winked at Dean. I was going to have fun with it. I wasn't going to let him psych me out. When I winked at Dean, I'll

Marc Iavaroni

never forget the looks on their bench. They couldn't believe it. It was like I had winked at God, like I was trying to pull a fast one.

I'll preface everything by saying that I always thought he was a great coach, one of the best of all time. I also think he's a human being. He has done a great job with his program, keeping contact with his players, which I know is important to them. But I do know that like anyone, he has fallacies. He probably has gone overboard with that in a negative way on occasion.

One of those occurred in 1977, the year after we won the ACC tournament. We were in the finals with them again. At halftime, I was at the end of the court, near the corral in the Greensboro Coliseum. Our bench was at the far end. Their bench was at the near end. We came off, and all of a sudden we were being funneled into maybe a five-foot-wide corral toward the outdated, undersized locker rooms.

As we went, the crowd was right in our face. He was yelling at me, jabbing me with his finger in my ribs. He was heated. His assistants were heated. It was very emotional. What prompted it was that it was pretty close at halftime. I don't think they liked the idea of losing two years in a row to Virginia. This was his opportunity to gain a psychological edge. He continued to say stuff to me. I was at least cognizant enough of the events to know this was a dangerous situation. I put my hands up in the air. I wanted to make sure that if anything happened, everyone was going to know where my hands were.

Anyway, we got to a certain point, and I was on the wrong side to get to my locker room. I had to cross his path. I didn't speed up. I didn't slow down. I stopped. He stopped. I don't remember what he said, if he said anything. But he finished it off with a rabbit thing in my gut. Not hard. Not to hurt. But his emotions had run the gamut. Call it whatever you want, but he struck me. It shocked me. Maybe it helped them on the backdoor out of the Four Corners. I was determined to stop Mike O'Koren. They went backdoor on me twice. But that was one disappointment I had with Coach Smith. I'm sure he would say he regretted that. He did send me a letter at the end of my career wishing me the best, saying that he thought I'd make a fine player in the pros. It was totally unsolicited. I never asked for an apology.

I have a lot of respect for everyone that has been through the Carolina program. Brad Daugherty. George Karl. Larry Brown. Doug Moe. Michael Jordan. They were all team players. Phil Ford. I can't name 'em all. They were all really good guys. I think that spoke highly of Coach Smith. I just think it's important that I always tell the truth. I tell my children, there are a lot of good stories about people I want them to emulate. I always preface it and finish the stories by saying that these are not perfect people, that they all have faults, too. You emulate the things they do well, the habits they develop. I'm not a perfect person, either.

RICK ROBEY

Robey, a forward at Kentucky from 1974-75 to 1977-78, told reporters after the 1977 East Regional final that Smith called him "a sonuvabitch" late in North Carolina's 79-72 victory. Smith later said: "Maybe someone in the stands called Robey a name and he thought it was me."

Anytime Kentucky and North Carolina met, it was a huge game, due to the traditions of both schools. The game I remember most is when we got beat by them in that East Regional Final. They got an early lead—14 or 15 points. Back then, there wasn't a shot clock. His big strategy was the Four Corners.

In that game, we finally got back to within four or five points, but we just weren't able to win. They made something like 35 of 36 free throws. That's when Dean and I had that little altercation. I fouled John Kuester with 15 or 16 seconds to go. He thought it was a flagrant foul, and came down and had a few choice words for me.

After the game, I asked Coach (Joe) Hall: "Should I tell them (reporters) what he said to me?" He said: "Go ahead if you want to." After getting beat, you're not a happy camper, anyway. He came all the way from his bench to the end of the floor. Looking at the film, I just kind of pushed him off and went to the bench. In those kinds of situations, everyone does things that they regret later. But a lot of people have talked about that for many years.

I played in the World University Games after that season. We played a game in Chapel Hill. He came up to me and said: "Well, Rick, I don't think I said what you said I said, but what I said, I'm sorry." That was the end of it. Dean Smith was one of the all-time great coaches. That was just the heat of battle.

I always enjoyed playing North Carolina because of the two traditions. I can remember my freshman year playing them at Freedom Hall in Louisville. We beat them (90-78). That was a big win. After my college career, I became good friends with Mike O'Koren, and played with Tommy LaGarde in the Pan American Games.

It was always a lot of fun. We would tease each other. I knew Phil Ford pretty well. I always told him: "Oh, you had to go Four Corners. You couldn't play us like a bunch of men." But heck, it was a good strategy back then, kind of like the three-pointer is today. If you didn't use it, shame on you.

JIM SPANARKEL

Spanarkel was the point guard at Duke from 1975-76 to 1978-79 and the captain his junior and senior years. The Blue Devils went 27-7 in his junior season and lost to Kentucky in the NCAA Final, 94-88.

My freshman year, we were one game under .500 (13-14). My sophomore year was about the same (14-13). We hadn't turned it around as of yet. My junior year, we had (Gene) Banks, (Kenny) Dennard, (Bob) Bender, (Mike) Gminski. That's when it really got started.

I knew coming in that it was a top-notch rivalry. People really got wound up for Carolina, even those first couple of years when we weren't that competitive. You could tell there was a little extra sting in the losses, a little extra excitement in the wins. Right from the beginning, you could tell it was different from Duke-Wake Forest or Duke-Maryland. Everyone stepped into it knowing that they were the big kids on the block.

Mike O'Koren and I were both from New Jersey. I remember the first game that he came to play over at Duke. I went to talk to him, gave him a hug. And I had people ask me: "Why are you talking to him?" I said: "It's only the fact that I've known him since the sixth grade." But bringing our program up to their level meant a lot. The people at Duke wanted to be competitive. It's a very competitive school. Regardless of what they're doing, they want to be successful at as high a level as possible. And now Carolina tries to compete with them. If you look at it, how many guys are better than Mike Krzyzewski in the United States?

The game they held the ball was my last game as a senior at Cameron. I think both of us were ranked in the top five. We were a little stunned by the fact that they sat on the basketball. That was one of the places the "air ball" chant began. They threw up three or four shots in the first half and didn't hit iron on any of them. We were up, 7-0. Ironically, that was the difference in the final score (Duke won, 47-40).

We were a little shocked. The fans were shocked, also. You figured they were ranked about the same, they would try to beat our butts on our home floor. We were more puzzled than anything. The Cameron Crazies were still wound up. They probably got wound up even more so because of that.

I wasn't fond of the Four Corners. It was all within the rules. But I think it was tweaking the game a little bit. Obviously, it worked. They had Phil Ford, and nobody could guard him. I don't know if it was straight-up basketball, but Dean was always in command. They

Jim Spanarkel

always ran a lot of guys in off their bench. He was in command at all times.

The one thing that stood out was that he always carried himself as a classy individual, whether he was losing or winning. He never lost his pride, never let his guard down. He always carried himself as a gentleman. He was clearly a great coach. He was clearly a great success. But he always conducted himself like a gentleman.

They always went ten deep with All-Americans. I always found it interesting how he kept all ten happy. Maybe that's one of the secrets of his success. He had All-Americans sitting on the bench for two and a half years, yet they were happy. I always found it interesting that he could get guys to do that. Most guys want to play. They don't want to stand up and be cheerleaders on the bench. If you're a first-year or second-year coach, I don't think that would fly. But when you're an institution like Dean Smith, you could do it.

MIKE GMINSKI

Gminski, the Duke center from 1976-77 to 1979-80, spent 15 years in the NBA with New Jersey, Philadelphia, Charlotte and Milwaukee.

I went to Carolina on an unofficial visit between my sophomore and junior years in high school. I was going to graduate early. The tallest center I played against was 6-3. I thought I'd benefit more from my freshman year in college than I would from my senior year in high school. I was in an accelerated academic program. I only told a certain number of schools, to take a little bit of control of the recruiting process.

Eddie Fogler had seen me play, come up to visit. We were getting pretty far down the road. During my weekend, I had a meeting with Coach Smith. He asked me what my expectations would be. I said one of the things I was looking forward to was playing a lot as a freshman. Well, all the bells and whistles started firing off somewhere. We ended the meeting cordially. But a week or so later, I received a letter from Coach Guthridge informing me that they were no longer recruiting me.

It was a little abrupt, but there were still other schools in the picture. Being 16 years old, you kind of shake those things off pretty easily. Duke was not among the original schools I contacted. But they were the first school where I had an official visit, and it was love at first sight. I knew that's where I was going to go. A week or so after I made my decision, I received a letter from Coach Smith congratulating me, saying he was looking forward to playing against me for four years.

I didn't understand what the rivalry meant until I went through the first couple of games. I had a completely different mind set. I grew up in Connecticut. The Big East did not exist then. The focus was completely on professional sports. College sports in the Northeast was kind of an afterthought. If you wanted to play big-time basketball, you went elsewhere. I was not prepared for the intensity of the rivalry. It certainly took some getting used to.

I remember walking into the Greensboro Coliseum for the first time for the Big Four tournament, when they still had that. I asked someone off-handedly if the place was sold out. That got a chuckle out of some of the Duke people and media. My hometown, Monroe, Connecticut, had seven thousand people in it. You could have fit my town in there two-and-a-half times. It was pretty hard for me to fathom.

Minus the shot clock, the Four Corners was a big part of what they did. They'd wear you down, get a lead, give the ball to Phil Ford and off they went. It was very tough to play against. Obviously, during those years, point guard was a critical position for Coach Smith. The key was to break out on top, try to take control of the game that way, at least keep them on the attack. It was frustrating to play against the talent more than it was frustrating to play against the system. But when you have a weapon like the Four Corners, and great players executing it, it obviously makes things difficult.

After recruiting, the other time our paths crossed in college was in the weirdest night and game I've ever been involved with— the 7-0 game. It was Jim Spanarkel's senior year, his last home game. Obviously, it was a very emotional time for all of us, especially for him. If memory serves, we got the tip and came down and scored. Then they sat on the ball for six or seven minutes. Carolina took only two shots in the first half. Both were by Rich Yonakor. Both of them were air balls. I'm almost positive that's when the "Air ball" chant started.

Mike Gminski

It was 7-0 at half, a very surreal kind of halftime. Then they came out in the second half and played. The final was 47-40, so it was 40-40 in the second half. Toward the end of the game, they were in a score and timeout mode, or if they missed, foul quickly. They missed, I got a rebound. There were probably about 15 seconds to go. I was getting hammered. The referees weren't blowing the whistle. I started clearing out some space for myself. I had my arms out. I was spinning around.

As I was trying to clear space, I hit Al Wood right in the nose. It was a pretty good shot. He went down like a sack of potatoes. They finally blew the whistle—on me. And Dean Smith came charging off the sidelines, got right in my face: "How can you do that to one of my players? You know what we're trying to do. We're trying to stop the clock." I said: "Coach, I know what you're trying to do, but the refs aren't blowing the whistle, and I've got to protect myself."

We were in front of our bench. He had come running all the way down to our end of the floor. But he didn't get a technical. I got thrown out of the game, on my homecourt, but he didn't get a technical. I'm convinced to this day that the refs were intimidated. It's the only game I've ever been thrown out of, on any level.

The thing that can be honestly said about both sides is that there probably was not much love lost, but there definitely was a healthy respect. I certainly respected him. Looking back, I even respected him for getting out of the recruiting process when he did. He might have continued to recruit me to muddle the picture, keep me from going to Duke. I don't know if it was a perceived attitude problem on my part. But he made the decision that I wasn't a guy who could play there. He got out, and that was fine.

I look at those Carolina teams and think: "With me on those teams, they would have been pretty good." They were pretty good without me. But they would have been that much stronger. It's kind of ironic. Mike O'Koren was in my group on my official visit to Duke. I got to meet him. Duke thought that they had a pretty good "in" with him, because Spanarkel had played with him in high school. But Mike went to North Carolina. We wound up beating each other's brains out for four years—and then we both got drafted by the Nets. We roomed together as rookies and every year at training camp. He wound up being my best friend from my playing days in the NBA.

We look back on it. The Duke students were really pretty brutal toward Michael. They really got after him. After we got drafted, he had to convince his mom that I was OK. She had heard all the things that were said. It took a while before she warmed up to me. It took a long time before she warmed up to my wife. My wife had been a student at Duke. Mike's mom thought she was sitting up in the stands, saying all those things about her son. But after a while, we all became really good friends.

KENNY DENNARD

Dennard, a forward at Duke from 1977-78 to 1980-81, spent three seasons in the NBA with Kansas City and Denver. He became the managing partner at Easterly Investor Relations in Houston in 1997.

I was recruited by Carolina and chose to go to Duke because I felt I could play earlier, have a chance to play as a freshman. At Carolina, you had to be a Phil Ford or Mike O'Koren, a world-class type player. I wasn't coming out of oblivion, but I wasn't on anyone's top 50 list. They didn't have those rankings in 1977 like they do now. But I was a fairly well-known player. I had about 150 offers.

I chose Duke, and it turned out to be a great move for me. During my four years at Duke, Coach Smith was always very complimentary of me in the press. He was what you would call a class guy. I had learned that not every coach was like that.

I grew up in Winston-Salem, then moved just outside of Winston-Salem for high school, out on a farm in King, North Carolina. I went to a rural county school, and was recruited heavily by Wake Forest. They thought I was in the bag. Being so close, I played down there all the time. I knew all their players. They thought for sure I would come to Wake. They didn't recruit me very hard.

Carl Tacy was the head coach at the time. I went out during recruiting, visited a lot of schools, had a lot of fun, saw a lot of places. Duke was the one that hit me. I made a pre-season commitment to Duke in November 1976, before my senior season. I got a Christmas card from the Wake Forest staff. It said: "Hope you're having as much fun next Christmas as you are this Christmas."

Well, my freshman year, our first game against Wake was at the Big Four tournament. I went 5-for-5 from the field and 5-for-5 from the line, and I think I had 10 rebounds. My revenge was that I didn't miss a shot. And I wasn't brought to Duke to be a scorer. I was there to be a role player.

The difference with Coach Smith was that he was always flattering to the other teams. He would never do anything to motivate the other team like I was motivated to whup up on Wake Forest. That shows the contrast between Coach Smith and a staff that doesn't have any legacy.

It wasn't until later that I realized what a good guy he was as far as caring for his players—and not just his players. I was going into my second year with Kansas City when I learned that I had testicular cancer. I had a three-year contract. It became a legal problem. I had to sue them. They put me on the suspended list without pay because I basically went out and saved my own life through early detection, then surgery in September 1982 and four weeks of radiation treatment.

The summer after the season ended, I was playing at Carolina. Coach Smith always watched the pickup games. It was an interesting time. Michael Jordan was still around as a college player. Mike O'Koren, Tommy LaGarde, Walter Davis and Phil Ford— those guys came back and played. They were great games. And that's when Coach Smith recommended to Doug Moe that he give me a chance to play in Denver. Doug mentioned it to me later.

Those kinds of recommendations are pretty powerful. Doug took a shot and traded for me, and I made the team. I got the third year out of my contract in Denver. I won the lawsuit after my Denver career was over—it took a couple of years to get through all that litigation. The point was, there was no way I could go back to Kansas City and play. I was suing them. I never would have played. But Coach Smith helped me get the chance with Denver.

He's always been like that. He was competitive. During games, he'd yell at you if you touched one of his players. But he was always professional. Carolina guys and Duke guys are pretty much friends after their college careers are over. You have almost a war-time camaraderie. I played with Phil Ford in Kansas City. You have something in common. It's not like what the fans have.

When I was finished playing basketball, I had to put my résumé together. I thought enough to call Coach Smith and see if he would be a reference for me. He was so kind to be a reference for me when I was a player. I thought it would be cool if Coach Smith, my biggest competitor in that world, would be my reference. This was in 1988. I called him up and asked him if he would do it. He said yes. People asked: "Why didn't you use Coach K as a reference?" I had played for him his first year. But there was more value to Coach Smith at the time.

In 1993, I was working for a New York investor-relations firm and staying out in San Francisco when I got recruited by a company back in Durham. One of the stipulations of me coming to work there was that they would pay for my executive MBA. The guy who was the CEO was a Duke guy. Some of the guys in the management team were Carolina guys. We always had fun around the Duke-Carolina game.

I needed to submit applications for the MBA programs at Duke and Carolina. Both were in the top ten. Duke cost twice as much as Carolina, but the company was willing to pay for either one. I used Coach K as one of my three references on the Duke application. And I had Lee Shaffer and Coach Smith as two of my three references for the Carolina application. I thought I had three good references for both applications.

I get a call from Duke saying: "You need to get another reference." I said: "I submitted three with my application." She said: "What does Coach K know of your career?" I said: "Excuse me?" And she said—this is a quote— "Coach K's reference won't work here. You need to get another one." I eventually got rejected for the Duke executive MBA program. The next week, I did the interview at Carolina and got accepted to the Kenan-Flagler executive MBA program the next day. They didn't call back and say: "Coach Smith's recommendation is no good."

I didn't graduate from the program—it was for two years, and I left after one when I got recruited by another company in Houston. But Coach Smith's recommendation helped me get into Carolina. This isn't to bash Duke. It just shows you about Coach Smith, his ability to be heard.

Here's a guy who helps his players in life, yet also helps players from other teams. I'm an example of that. And I doubt I'm the only example. It goes beyond what people would typically think a coach does. He's more of a guy who builds relationships. You can't use the word "legend" enough.

SIDNEY LOWE

Lowe helped lead North Carolina State to the 1983 NCAA title. He was head coach of the NBA's Minnesota Timberwolves in 1993 and '94 and became an assistant coach with the Cleveland Cavaliers in 1994-95.

Certainly one memory that I have is testament to what kind of person he is. Put aside the coaching aspect. We all know he's a great coach. I played on the World University Games team in 1981, after my sophomore year. And the way I got nominated was Dean Smith.

Dean Smith talked to Dr. Tom Davis, the coach of that team. They talked about players around the country. Dean Smith told him there was a very good point guard at North Carolina State. That ended up being one of the great experiences of my life, being able to represent the United States in the World University Games.

I got an opportunity to go to Yugoslavia and on to Romania, where the games were held. I ended up winning a gold medal at the games. I had some very memorable moments there with friends, players, coaches. I had highlights—a length-of-the-court shot, a big three-point play in the championship game over the big Russian. I never would have had that opportunity if it weren't for Dean Smith.

It was amazing to me that a coach from another university would call on my behalf. I had gotten wind of it before I went. After I got there, it was confirmed that Dean made the phone call. I wonder if Dean even remembers that. He wanted to do something for a kid. For him, it's just natural. Dean always stands in the background. But I called him and thanked him for doing that.

He could have been all over the TV screen. But he was always saying: "Take my player. Take this player. Work with this guy." That's something special. There are a lot of coaches that wouldn't do that. I think the way players come back to see him, keep in touch with him, the way they give him credit for their careers, being the individuals that they are, that's the true testimony. That's what makes him feel good. The fact that his players come back and keep in touch, that's important. That's why they have such a tradition. And it's not just his players that feel that way. I respect him unbelievably.

I actually never took a visit there. I had predetermined pretty much where I was going to go. The only two schools I visited were Penn State and North Carolina State—Penn State because one of my assistants from DeMatha

Sidney Lowe

(H.S.) was going there as an assistant. I had known about Dean obviously from (DeMatha coach) Morgan Wooten's relationship with him. But I had never really met Dean until I went to North Carolina State.

As a freshman, it was obvious there was a big rivalry between North Carolina State and Carolina. But the thing for me was Dean Smith. He was such a legend. At that time, even though there was a great rivalry as far as the players were concerned, it was much more the coaches, Dean Smith and Norm Sloan. I was more in awe of Dean Smith than I was of playing against Carolina.

Dean was Dean. Dean was a legend. Dean was the man. I'm sure that in Norm's heart, yes, he wanted to beat Dean. But I couldn't sense any animosity. With Coach Valvano, there wasn't as much of a rivalry with the coaches. It was more Carolina-N.C. State. I'm sure maybe in Coach Valvano's mind, he wanted to beat Dean as well. When you're on top, everyone wants to beat you.

After a game, he'd shake hands with the coaches, and if we crossed paths, he would say: "Good game." We never really talked much, other than the time I called him after the World University Games.

JAY BILAS

Bilas, a forward and center at Duke from 1983 to '86, is an attorney and college basketball analyst at ESPN.

I didn't realize the power the University of North Carolina wielded around the state until we went out barnstorming after my senior year. I had no clue. I just thought it was a bigger school. They had fans. We had fans. But that's not the way it is. It's like nine-to-one. The people in Durham like Duke. But you step out of Durham, you had better watch your ass.

We would drive to these small towns in North Carolina on the barnstorming tour, sometimes go to South Carolina and Virginia. They would pay us to play in these ACC All-Star Games. It's mostly for people who wouldn't get a chance to see ACC games otherwise. You'd be in high-school gyms. You'd play, sign autographs and go on home.

We played in the national championship game in 1986 on a Monday night, and on Tuesday we were in New Bern, North Carolina. Talk about bizarre. But anyway, we played one night in Lenoir at Lenoir-Rhyne College. It was a huge barn of a gym. It reminded you of the gym where they played the final game in *Hoosiers*. At halftime, there was a dunking contest. There was a huge trophy no one cared about. What everyone cared about was the money.

I was geeked up just to watch. Johnny Dawkins was in it. Speedy Jones from Maryland. And Len Bias—what he could do was outrageous. Then there was Warren Martin, a 7-footer from North Carolina. He was a really good player, just huge. It took you five minutes to get around him. But he couldn't jump over a pair of shoes. He could dunk, but nothing that elicited more than a yawn.

They decided in advance that they would decide the winner on crowd applause. Dawkins was great. Speedy Jones was even better. And Len Bias, they should have just stopped the contest right there. Then Warren Martin squeaked one in. Everyone on the bench kind of giggled. We thought: "What's he doing? Seven-footers don't win dunking contests. They're won by 6-foot-2 guys doing 360s."

After each guy dunked two or three times, there was no question it came down to Dawkins or Len Bias. Speedy Jones got a nice ovation, Johnny Dawkins a little more, Len Bias a little more than that. But for Warren Martin, the roof flew off the joint. The guy walked away with the money and that huge trophy. And I walked out of there thinking: "Someone cheated. That's cheating. That's un-American." But then I got it. I understood. North Carolina in this state is all things to all people. It's the mecca, the Wailing Wall, all in one. It was an eye-opening experience. I'll never forget that as long as I live.

The first thing I remember about Coach Smith was the first time I played at Carmichael. It was one of those dream sequences. I knew we were going over there. I knew we were going to play North Carolina, all it entailed. But I didn't fathom being that close to Coach Smith.

I had a chance to steal a look over there at what he was doing while we were warming up. On the free-throw line, I'd look behind me to our bench, then look behind me to their bench and think: "That's Dean Smith!" It was really weird.

Being from Los Angeles, I got a job with ABC during the Olympics in 1984. I had just finished my sophomore year. The job was great. I got to work at the scorer's table at the basketball venue with a headset on. I had to work just about every game. That got to be a pain. But the plus side was that I got to work every U.S. game.

It was at the Forum in Inglewood, where the Lakers played, 15 minutes from my parents' house. A half hour before a game started, we were just kind of shooting warm-ups. I looked up and he was sitting seven or eight rows up in the stands from our broadcast position. I thought I needed to go up and say hello, pay my respects.

I went up and said: "I'm Jay Bilas. I play at Duke." He said: "Jay, how are you doing? I forgot this was your hometown." I would have been impressed if he recognized me. But the fact that he remembered I was from

California, and put that in the context of why I was there, I walked away thinking, "How nice was that?"

I was 19 or 20 years old. We played against them every year two or three times. To this day, it's the most intense basketball I've ever played. Playing against North Carolina was more intense than playing in the Final Four. It was a different kind of intensity. But the way he remembered me was the one thing that stuck out in my mind.

You know how coaches work officials? He would always work them pretty hard. But he did it in a way that was nonconfrontational. He was able to get his point across without really being seen. At the time, Coach K was not able to do that. It was early on in Coach K's career. Coach Smith would get demonstrative sometimes, pull on his arm. He seemed to do that with me a lot. It always seemed that after I did something good, he was making that motion.

I didn't understand the dynamic when I got there. But North Carolina had dominated that league for so long since Coach Smith had been there, it got under your skin. Beating them, that was the benchmark. If you beat North Carolina in the ACC, you were the best. It was unspoken, but that's the way we looked at it. For me, as a former player in the league, it feels different without him being here. You can't tell me it doesn't feel different for the coaches, too. It's odd for me as a former player to see my ex-coach as kind of the elder statesman of the league.

I was in school in 1984, when Coach K said there was a double standard with North Carolina. They beat us at our place by five. Something had happened in the game, I don't remember what. I think he hit the scorer's table, and the old scoreboard at Cameron went nuts for a second. I don't remember exactly what it was.

After the game, Coach K said something to the effect that: "We all know there's a double standard in this league, and it's got to stop." Right now, I will bet you any amount that people are saying that about Duke. But I remember walking out of there thinking: "My God, you say something like that, it'll start a firestorm. Half the world will say you're a whiner. The other half will say it's about time someone said something."

We finally beat them my sophomore year in the ACC tournament. They beat us by five at our place. In Jordan's last game at Carmichael, they beat us in double overtime. And in the ACC tournament, we beat them again. They had Jordan, Perkins, Kenny Smith. You say those names, you go: "How the heck did we beat those guys?"

We lost to Maryland in the final for two reasons. Len Bias was one. And we ran out of gas. But we got back to town, and everyone's bumper in the city of Durham had a bumper sticker that had the score. Someone had printed up bumper stickers right away. It's the only way I remember the score. The bumper sticker said, "Duke blue 77, Carolina blue 75." I remember being so mad when I saw that. I remember thinking: "They don't print up bumper stickers when they beat us. They expect to beat us. We need to get to the point where we expect to beat them." I was really fuming over that.

In the early '90s, Carolina beat Duke at the Smith Center, and they stormed the court. When was the last time you saw that? That was the time I thought it became a little more even. But I'm not sure there's a program in the ACC that doesn't have a horrific record against them. They've dominated the league.

As a broadcaster, I would sort of shake hands with Coach Smith and his staff before a game. He was always very complimentary. But I never went to him to get information. I knew he wasn't going to tell me anything. They are tight-lipped there. That's just the way they do it. I respect that.

I've heard all the stories about other guys getting phone calls about things they said, maybe a letter. That never happened with me. If it did, my response would be: "If you're not going to let me into practice to watch, how can you be upset if I said something wrong?" They would let you watch practice, but their policy was, you couldn't watch the day of a game or the day before a game. Well, you're not going to go in there three days early. No one has the time for that.

At the same time, I've seen them play so many times, I know what they do. None of their coaches is a toastmaster. That's OK. I never had a problem with that. When I listen to guys complain about no access, I could care less. They just do it the way they do it. But if you watch them play, watch the way they run their system, and walk away from that complaining, you need to find another business. They don't do the work for you like some places, telling you all these stories. But if you like basketball, you'll like watching them play anytime.

When I was in school, I spent some time with the Carolina players. We were so close together, we would play pickup games. I played on a U.S. National Team with Joe Wolf and John Brownlee, who later transferred. We were together two or three weeks. With all of the guys I've run into from North Carolina, all of them had nothing but positive things to say about Coach Smith publicly. But to me, the measure of any person is what people say about you privately.

To this day, I've never heard one North Carolina player say anything negative about him privately. That's not true of other coaches. You'll be together with players, everyone gets talking. It's a forum for guys to complain about why their careers weren't better. You'd talk about coaches' idiosyncracies. But not once did I hear anything negative about Coach Smith. That's the God's honest truth. And that, to me, speaks volumes about the guy.

DANNY FERRY

Ferry, a member of the Cleveland Cavaliers, was the National Player of the Year at Duke in 1988-89. He was the subject of a well-publicized recruiting battle between North Carolina and Duke, and later found himself in the middle of a controversy with Dean Smith.

On January 18, 1989, Smith noticed a sign in the Duke student section that said, "J.R. CAN'T REID." Prior to the team's rematch in Chapel Hill, he said that the combined SAT scores of Reid and his African American teammate, Scott Williams, were higher than those of Duke's white stars, Ferry and Christian Laettner.

I was really surprised, and kind of disappointed. It put me in an unfair position. One, they had my SAT scores because they recruited me. Two, when you put the two scores together, you didn't really know how I did.

I did all right on my SATs. If you want to compare me to J.R. Reid, fine—I think I win that comparison. If you want to compare me to Scott Williams, fine. But I didn't agree with him doing that. It didn't fit with my perception of Coach Smith.

I forgot about it pretty quickly. The day after it happened, I didn't worry about it. It was the only experience I had that was a negative with Carolina. Other than that, it was a good, hard-fought rivalry. With the two schools being so close together, you couldn't breathe without feeling the other one's breath.

I have good memories of Coach Smith, going back to when he recruited my brother, Bob Jr. When they signed Michael Jordan, they said it was probably best if my brother didn't come. They dealt with him in a very honest and respectful manner. Within my family, that was very much appreciated, the way he handled the whole situation.

Growing up, I always wanted to play at Carolina for Coach Smith. When they recruited me, it was a big thrill. They came on a home visit, and I also went on a school visit. My final two choices were Duke and Carolina. Had I signed early, my guess is that I might have signed at Carolina. But I was uncertain, so I waited.

I got to know Coach K. To see the program he had built, what he was about, the relationship we built, I just knew Duke was the place for me. It was the right place at the right time. Carolina was a great place. But it probably wasn't right for me. And it wasn't the right time for me, either, with the players that they had at the time. Playing time definitely was part of the equation.

If you had asked me to pick between Duke and Carolina the year before, I would have picked Carolina, just because of the respect I had for Coach Smith, the program he had built, my natural urges. I cheered for Caro-

Danny Ferry

lina. But definitely, the opportunity to develop at Duke, with playing time, was on my mind. Duke was getting ready to lose many of their players after my freshman year. I saw myself being someone who could really help Duke sustain and build on what had been started.

More than anything else, I just felt really comfortable at Duke— more comfortable with the players overall, more comfortable with the school overall, based on my visit and my experience. It ended up being everything I expected and more. I really enjoyed my four years. I never regretted going to Duke.

When I told Coach Smith of my decision, he was great. He thanked me for letting him know, and thanked me for showing sincere interest in the school. As everyone would expect, he handled it with class. I very much respect him and the program that he built. My high-school coach at DeMatha, Morgan Wootten, publicly but quietly always held Coach Smith in very, very high esteem. It was almost like DeMatha tried to be a little bit like Carolina. That was a great compliment. That was always an undertone of the DeMatha program.

My freshman year, they had a great team, and so did we. It was a great year in the ACC, with Georgia Tech being so good, and Maryland having (Len) Bias. To start off your college career with that intensity, my taste for the rivalry and competition with Carolina only grew. I think it was brought out more than any other year I could have been at Duke.

It was very competitive between Coach Smith and Coach K. It was hard for Coach K at first. He was never looked at as a peer or on a level close to comparable—at first. I don't think that really stands any longer. Coach always respected Carolina and Coach Smith. But he very much wanted to beat their butts, too.

Three games stand out, the first one being the one we lost when the Smith Center opened (95-92). It was my first experience playing against Carolina, playing at Carolina. The arena had just opened. Duke and Carolina were unbeaten, ranked one, two. That really stands out.

My junior year when we beat them in the ACC tournament (65-61), that was a great win for us. For Billy King, Kevin Strickland, Quin Snyder, Robert Brickey and me—the guys who came to Duke after the (Johnny) Dawkins class—it was a signal. It legitimized what we were doing. We were able to sustain what the guys in front of us had done. We were a good team. And that's when we really started to believe it.

Lastly, I remember the loss in the ACC tournament my senior year (77-74). That was really hard. It was just a battle, as physical a college game as I had played in. It was heartbreaking for me. I really wanted to win. It was a good, hard-fought game. But it was a big letdown when we lost.

Coach Smith always said hello to me. It was always cordial. Nothing more than that, though. I'm one of those people who kind of keeps to myself in that situation. I'd go say hello and shake his hand. But that was it.

Grant Hill

GRANT HILL

Hill, a star at Duke from 1990-91 to 1993-94, was the third overall pick by the Detroit Pistons in the 1994 NBA draft.

I was always a big Carolina fan, a big Dean Smith fan. Growing up, I always wanted to go there. The first game I ever saw was Georgetown-Carolina in the '82 Finals. I taped it. I still have it on tape—on Betamax. Georgetown and Carolina became the two teams that I watched. I followed Patrick Ewing's career. We had Georgetown season tickets from '83 to '90. I loved Georgetown. I loved Carolina. But I knew I couldn't go to Georgetown—it was too close to home. I still loved John Thompson, but I wanted to get away from D.C.

It came down to Duke and Carolina. I put Duke on the list almost as a courtesy. I wanted to go to Carolina. But my first visit was to Duke. After the visit, I wanted to go there. My mom and dad seemed to think that if I had visited Eastern Michigan first, I probably would have ended up going there. Duke was not the team I had always loved. But it was just a perfect fit. It made sense for me to go there. And I'm glad I made that decision.

At the time, I think my dad (former NFL running back Calvin Hill) was upset—not that I chose Duke, but that the recruiting process was over. He wanted me to go where I wanted to go. But he wanted me to drag it out a bit longer. He was a big Dean Smith fan. He enjoyed Dean calling him, talking to him. It was good for his ego.

I had a little bit of contact with Dean. I had made an unofficial visit my junior year. But I really had more contact with him when I went to Duke and played against him. There was a respect there. I had so much respect for him, and it seemed like he had respect for me. We would talk before games. A couple of times, I went over there to shake his hand, and he'd say: "I've got a uniform in the locker room waiting for you."

He still spoke with my parents, sent them letters. And when I graduated from Duke, he sent me a letter, saying that it was fun competing against me, that I was a class person, that he thought I'd have a great career in the NBA. It was kind of unheard of. Carolina people don't do that with Duke people, and vice versa. It said a lot as to what he was all about. I thought it was pretty classy.

There were a lot of similarities between the programs, and a lot of differences. I'm not saying one was better than the other. It just goes to show you that you can be successful doing it two different ways. Both were adamant about people being student-athletes. It wasn't so much a basketball experience. It was about a Carolina experience, a Duke experience. That every student-athlete had a social life along with basketball. It was part of the growth that took place at both universities.

As far as playing, there were different philosophies. The most telling thing was how they ran their offensive sets. Dean Smith had a very structured offense, which Billy Cunningham ran, which Michael Jordan ran, which Kenny Smith ran, which Jerry Stackhouse ran, then Vince Carter and Antawn Jamison. It has remained pretty consistent. Coach K was a little different. I wouldn't say one's predictable and one's unpredictable. Both were very successful.

The game I remember most is the first Duke-Carolina game my freshman year. All the upperclassmen kept saying: "Wait until we play Carolina. The intensity will go up another level." I couldn't believe that Cameron could go up another level. I didn't play particularly well. I had a facemask on because I broke my nose. But we won (74-60). I don't think I've been in a game as intense since.

Chapter Eight

REFEREES

DICK PAPARO

Paparo was an ACC official from 1982 to 1998.

He always acted like a gentlemen. In 17 years in that league, I never heard him curse. He was from the old school. His biggest asset was that when he was working an official, it never looked like he was screaming and yelling. But he was really working you over.

I was in the league 17 years. He had only four technicals in 17 years. I called every one of them. He would clap his hands in your face after a call. That used to drive me crazy. I used to always have to warn him. But of all the people I've ever worked for, I probably had more respect for him than any-one.

Usually when he had something to say, you'd let him go. He knew the rules. He knew what was going on. I think deep down inside, Dean feared strength. If you knew he was Dean Smith, respected him, but weren't afraid of him, he respected you. If he figured that you might do something to him, he wouldn't bother you. But if he thought you were going to do nothing, he'd crucify you, like all coaches.

That's the relationship I had with him. I respected him. I liked him. I really, really enjoyed refereeing his games. He was a special person. But like every icon, he wanted people to fear him. He knew how far he could go with certain guys.

A lot of officials used to get caught up in the North Carolina tradi-tion. They'd say: "I worked the Dean Dome. I worked Duke-Carolina. I worked Duke-Maryland." It sort of works against the officials, and helps the team. But why did the coaches complain? They complained because Dean won almost a thousand games. If you sat around talking to Dean, he'd tell you Duke got all the calls the last few years, because they won national championships.

The greatest story I remember was a game Carolina had against Notre Dame at Madison Square Garden. They were much superior to Notre Dame. I think it was (John) McLeod's first year. The following Wednesday, I got Dean in a game at Chapel Hill. Always before a game, you go up and shake hands with the coaches. I go up, and Dean said: "I just want to apologize for how badly our team played against Notre Dame in New York. Our team didn't play very well. Also, I want to tell you that that wasn't one of your better performances, either." I just turned around and walked away.

Another classic story is from about five years ago. They were playing Virginia. They were down six or seven points with seven minutes to go. Their captain comes up to me and says: "Coach Smith would like to see you." I said: "What?" He said: "Coach Smith would like to see you." That was the rule—the captain would come over and ask you to talk to the coach.

I walked across the floor to talk to Dean. He stood up from the huddle and said: "Dick, I want to ask you something: Who's going to win the national championship?" I said: "What are you talking about?" He said: "Who's going to win the national championship? I know—Virginia, if you keep letting them hold like they've been holding us!"

That's just the way it was. I walked away.

HANK NICHOLS

Nichols, the national coordinator for NCAA men's basketball officiating, was an ACC official from 1971 to '86.

He was a helluva competitor. It was always obvious that he was really competing every night. You could just tell by the way he operated on the sidelines. Just from his attitude, you could tell that winning was important. In more recent years, after watching him, listening to him talk, playing well was important, too.

One thing I always thought was that he took losses better than most coaches. He got beat, he gave credit to the other clubs, the referees were OK, that's the way it goes. I suppose in retrospect, when you only lost once every six months, it was easier to take. But he was really good about losing.

Early in his career, he had a habit of slapping his hands together, clapping right by your ear when you ran by. He didn't do that later. Sometimes when he got frustrated or angry, he did point his finger across the court.

But when you compare that to some of the stuff that other coaches did, it's all relative.

He wasn't actually very bad on the sidelines. He got his Ts. I probably called as many on him as anyone, especially at Duke and N.C. State during the Sloan years. Those games, he really wanted to win. For whatever reason, he was more intense in those games, in my opinion—especially at Duke in his later years. His behavior would not be as normal at Duke. When he came into the Duke gym, he was wired.

He would get his Ts for just aggravating you after you asked him to quit. He never would swear at you. Sometimes he would be so competitive, get into the game so much, he would say stuff to you that would really just get you. It wasn't so much what he said. It was just that he would get going, and wouldn't stop. He didn't do that often. Don't get me wrong. He got his share of Ts, and he took 'em. Just like he took his losses well, he took his Ts well, too. I don't think he got many in comparison. He wasn't a guy who led the league in Ts, or anything like that.

The thing about refereeing North Carolina with most of his teams is that they didn't grab and hold very much. They played defense with their feet more than most teams. Their fouls usually came from trying to block shots, taking charges, occasionally reaching for steals, being aggressive. They didn't come out with their hands all over you. As referees, you weren't always making decisions on hand-checking. Other referees always commented on that. Their style changed with their players. When they had (Tommy) LaGarde and (Mitch) Kupchak, they were a little tougher than when they had Walter Davis and more finesse players. From a referee's standpoint, you took what you had.

When he was young, he'd come over before the game and tell you what happened in the game before. He'd say, "Player X grabbed Kupchak." We'd have to get the other coach. That was the procedure. He would have to say that in front of the other coach. That was hard. But he was a film nut. He prepared for everything. It was part of his preparation, to make sure the referee understood what concerned him about the opponent. To me, that was always part of the way he got ready.

He's not the only guy who did that. And later on, he didn't do much of it. He decided that the referees weren't going to decide the games. He decided if his team played well, it would win. If his team didn't play well, it would lose. He was different the last half of my officiating career. I just assumed as everyone matures and grows, they put emphasis on different things.

LENNY WIRTZ

Wirtz was an ACC official from 1959 to '95.

I never knew, until about the time I retired, that he was a math major. Maybe that's why we were so polarized. I happened to be a math major. We repelled each other once in a while.

When I started in the league, he was still an assistant to Frank McGuire. That's when we got to know one another. After another year or two, McGuire left and went to South Carolina. Dean got the head coaching job. And, of course, assistants always treat you different than the head coach.

Like most coaches, he was very competitive. They're always looking for an edge if they think they can get one with the officials. And he was always a stickler for the rules. He wanted the rule book to be called almost literally. I always refereed realistically. If you enforced every rule, you wouldn't have any players left.

He was always very analytical. He analyzed everyone, and every situation. Someone told me that Dean used to have his assistants watch all the TV games and have them grade the officials, so he knew how to coach his team when it had those officials. He was a great psychologist. He was always trying to play head games. You'd come on the floor, and if you had worked a game for him two or three weeks earlier, he would mention a call that went against him. He would ask you if you were sure you were right. He would be trying to get inside your head, wanting me to give him something. He always wanted to know why you did something.

I can remember an instance with John Kuester way back when. I was working a game at North Carolina State. John Kuester was the Carolina captain. He comes up and says: "Mr. Wirtz, Mr. Smith said that Dr. Steitz—the late Ed Steitz, the national rules interpreter—said this is the way the rule should be." Well, it wasn't the way we were told. I said to Captain Kuester: "Go back and tell Mr. Smith that I'm sorry, but Mr. Wirtz said this is the way it's going to be called." I looked over, and he made a face. But for the most part, he was very unemotional.

I was fairly quick with Ts. But I don't think I called a technical foul on him as long as I refereed. He was very concerned about his public image, how he looked to the fans, how he looked on television. For me, he was never overly friendly. He was cordial. But he didn't go out of his way to crack a joke. He was always business. I always got the feeling that he thought of us as a necessary evil that he had to put up with.

I had a ritual that I went through, always trying to protect our crew. It was something I learned a long time ago at the old St. John Arena at Ohio State. They had six or eight game clocks, all over the place. I always liked to have one face as the officials' face. Every time you walked in there, you would ask: "Is there a master face?" They would say: "You don't have to worry. We've never had a problem." But one night, Ohio State was playing Purdue, and all of a sudden, we had a situation where there were different times on every face. I said it was never going to happen to me again.

Every time I'd come in, I'd say: "Coach Smith, if anything goes wrong, and we can't get it straightened out from the play-by-play—the time is recorded every time the whistle is blown—we'll use this clock as the officials' face." He'd say: "Lenny, you're the only one that does that. I don't know why." I said: "Coach, to cover my tail from people like you." He'd say: "Sure, you're giving the other guy a break, looking at the other face."

But I always liked to referee North Carolina games. They were one of the best-coached teams in the league. You'd go out, referee the game, call the rules, and you shouldn't have any problem. And if the league office didn't tell me I had a problem, I didn't go asking to find something out. I don't know if he accepted me as an official or hated my guts as soon as I walked on the floor.

One night—and I had a lot fun with this over the last five or six years I worked in the league—he didn't particularly like the way I officiated. A reporter came to me and said: "I'd like to tell you about a quote from Dean, and see if you have any comment." Now, we're not allowed to comment on anything but rules interpretations. We're not allowed to comment on behavior, or anything like that.

Coach Smith said something like: "Lenny and I have been together 25 years, and maybe now is the time for a divorce." I said: "My goodness, I feel like I'm married to all of our coaches. But if he insists on a divorce, I get the house." And the Dean Dome had been built then. This guy printed that, and I never had so much reaction from people and coaches. People would ask: "Did you get the house yet?" Even *Sports Illustrated* called. I told them I hadn't been served with papers yet.

I remember the very first game that Florida State played in the ACC—it was at North Carolina, at the Dean Dome. Pat Kennedy had a really good basketball team when he came into the league. They won that first game, and they must have thought it was pretty easy. I was working a game two or three years later when their team was all seniors. They were really good. They got Coach Smith down by at least 20, the last ten or eleven minutes of the second half.

Instead of milking that, they kept playing and running with them for some reason. All of a sudden, things turned around. Carolina mounts a charge, and now Kennedy can't stop it. He loses the game. Midway through all that, I had to hit him with a technical foul. He thought we were favoring Dean with the calls.

Way back when, I worked a game when Valvano had the same problem. He was kicking the hell out of Dean one night at Carmichael, beating him by at least 20 points. Valvano said afterward that he was shell-shocked. He never thought he could lose that game. But he did. Smith was so competitive. He never gave up. He always tried to analyze what was going on, find a way to beat his opponent.

The game needs more Dean Smiths, coaches of that stature. Everett Case and Frank McGuire really put the ACC on its pedestal. Those two guys were great coaches. And then Dean. Our league has had such a good reputation with the NCAA on suspensions and expulsions and all that. I always thought it was a real privilege to work in the league. I tried to keep my reputation as clean as I could.

When I retired, every coach wrote me a letter but Dean Smith. I don't know if that's his nature or not. Over the years, coaches accept you or reject you. If they reject you, you hear from them just about every game. They get on you more on the road than they do at home. Dean Smith, if he worked me, I sure as heck didn't know about it. He was a model of deportment most of the time. He would say: "Lenny, you missed a call." They would all give you that. And you did miss them, too.

Chapter Nine

THE MEDIA

BILLY PACKER

Packer, the college basketball analyst for CBS, played at Wake Forest from 1960 to '62 and was an assistant at Wake under Jack McCloskey from 1966 to '70.

Surprising as this might be, when I came to Wake Forest as a freshman, I was not knowledgeable about the history of the ACC. I wasn't even that much aware of what North Carolina had accomplished in '57. It's a lot different today. The national championship game was not even televised then.

In my freshman year, when I wasn't eligible, I obviously got to know who Frank McGuire and Everett Case were. They were two giants of the business. I joined a team that was in a losing situation. When we became sophomores, we became a very good team. Dean was assistant to Frank McGuire my freshman, sophomore and junior years. McGuire was such a dominant figure, I couldn't have even told you Dean Smith was his assistant coach. It wasn't like: "Wow, they've got an assistant coach there who is going to be a giant."

We had great competitions between the two teams, some tremendous fights, things like that, my freshman year particularly. McGuire obviously was a big focal point of the scandal of '61. He left to coach the Sixers. Carolina basketball was left in the real doldrums. Not only did they not have powerful players—York Larese and Doug Moe were gone—they were going to be left with a relatively weak team for them, a weaker schedule, weaker recruiting. It was quite a black mark on their tradition. To us, it was almost like they might have named Dean on an interim basis. Why was this guy hired? It wasn't like: "Wow, they really got someone special to take over their program." And you look at his record the first couple of years, it was anything but sensational.

When we played against them my senior year, they weren't a real good team. They played nice basketball, but they weren't that good. They weren't competing for the ACC championship. Then I got out of school, and

I was a blatant Wake Forest fan. I remember hearing about their first big recruit, Billy Cunningham. When Wake Forest beat that team in Winston-Salem, I was at that game as a fan. That was the night they hung Dean in effigy. At that point, I figured: "This guy is not going to make it." I wasn't covering games then. I was looking at it as guy who used to play in the league. They weren't getting it done. You've got to remember how dynamic Frank McGuire was. And the alumni were not happy.

I became an assistant coach at Wake almost at the time he turned it around, when he got Larry Miller and Bobby Lewis. Duke was the most powerful program in the ACC then. They got Miller away from Duke. To get someone away from Vic Bubas, that impressed the hell out of me. Then, with (Rusty) Clark, (Dick) Grubar and (Bill) Bunting, all of a sudden, they started getting some really good players. We wondered what he was going to do with them. It was obvious that he could get players. But there was a lot of skepticism about whether he could coach at all.

It became obvious quickly that not only was he getting players, but he was also doing innovative things, and was tough to beat. It was the first time it dawned on me that this guy is here to stay. McGuire was one of those guys, you were either his enemy or his friend. There was no in-between. My first impression of Dean Smith was that he followed the same concept. He was always at arm's length. Now I have a different relationship with him. For the longest time, way after when I was an assistant, he was at arm's length.

I'll never forget a game in Raleigh when I started announcing. This was in the early '70s, when both Carolina and State were really good. In those days, the announcers used to introduce the starting lineups at center court before the game started. I'm standing on the floor at Reynolds Coliseum, and Dean walked by me and said: "I don't appreciate the red tie." I hadn't even thought about it. But I looked down, and I was wearing a red tie. I thought, that guy has a screw loose if he's worried about what kind of tie I was wearing.

But he was like Coach Wooden. Looking back, you realized that the things they did went deeper, and the average guy didn't even know what was going on. He was very smart. He was saying: "Be aware of what the hell you're doing." And as time wore on, I gained tremendous respect for him. I didn't gain as much respect for the record as I did for his ability to develop a family. Players, managers, coaches, alumni—it was incredible, not only his loyalty to that family, but the incredible memory.

I remember a player I recruited at Wake Forest—Dickie Walker. He was playing ball in Sweden. He came home and said that he got an amazing call when he was over there. Dean Smith was on the line, Dean Smith from the United States. He thought: "The only Dean Smith I would know is from North Carolina." This was in the early '70s. Dean called him to ask about the league. Dean had a player, Donald Washington, who was going to leave school early. He was an outstanding player who never had a great career. Dean was always good about placing players, even when they had a problem. He wanted to make sure the players were being treated right in that league. And he knew to round up Dickie Walker from Wake Forest.

Once I became known as an announcer, we got along really well. I don't have personal relationships with coaches, and he didn't want one. Sometimes guys try to get to you. But I always felt it was not in my best interests. Dean would have no reason to want to get to me. He was always professional. When I had to ask a question, I could. But Dean Smith is not a good interview. He's always somewhat guarded. And he always has a notion where he's coming from.

I used to say to people: "Why do you interview him? I can tell you where he's coming from. I can tell you in the postgame interview what his second sentence is going to be. It's going to be about a guy who's not doing well, but really made a great contribution." Say it was Tommy LaGarde. His stat line could be oh-for-one, four rebounds, three fouls. And Dean's second sentence would be: "We got the kind of play from Tommy LaGarde that is going to help us win a national championship. He blocked out, played well in the trapping defense." He was a master of all that stuff. It used to frustrate the other coaches. Let's face it, the press in North Carolina are mostly North Carolina graduates. It used to frost a lot of coaches in the league. I got a kick out of it.

I always admired the fact—and this is probably why he doesn't have more national championships—that he never sacrificed a game, or a point in the game, for the program. And I don't think any of the games jump out at me more than the '84 regional final against Indiana in Atlanta. They had Jordan, Perkins, Kenny Smith. That, to me, was the most pure talent he ever had. And he didn't get to a regional final.

In that game, it would have been very easy to say: "They can't stop Michael. Tell (Dan) Dakich to hitch up the damn wagon, we're clearing out." But he never sacrificed one moment to win if it went against his system. He never put the focus on one individual. And he never changed. You've got to admire the guy for that. And I think all the players respected that.

I remember the Marquette game in 1977. It was an incredible accomplishment for North Carolina to get to the Final Four. Al McGuire is a good friend of mine. But Al's team actually had a mediocre two-thirds of the season. They were going nowhere. Al had announced he was going to retire. Looking at it, you said: "This guy is not getting much out of that team." Not to take anything away from Marquette, but you've got to remember all the injuries that Carolina had (Phil Ford and Walter Davis played hurt. LaGarde was out after undergoing knee surgery).

In the semifinals, they had beaten, I thought, the best team in the Final Four that year—Las Vegas. I don't think Marquette or UNC-Charlotte could have beaten Vegas. In the final, McGuire knew exactly what Dean was going to do if they ever got the lead. When they went Four Corners, Al said: "There's a lot of time left. I don't mind playing in the 50s." He sat back. It was, who is going to blink first? And it was smart strategy on Al's part.

The famous Jordan shot (in '82), it's funny how things work, how revisionist history sometimes takes over. Dean saying: "I told Michael to bang it in"—I always suspected that was B.S. But the legend kept growing. I finally went to Dean one day, and had the guts to say to him: "Coach, let's review that timeout. You've got James Worthy inside, the number-one low-post player in the country. You've got Sam Perkins, who can step out or play inside, as a second option. No way you could have gone to a timeout and said: 'OK, let's set up Jordan.'"

He went through the whole timeout. Jimmy Black would have the ball. Dean said: "Here's what happens if it goes to Worthy. Here's what happens if it goes to Perkins. Michael probably will be open on the side. Michael, just knock it down if the ball comes your way." It wasn't like: "Now it's time for Michael Jordan to hit the first big shot of his career to win a national championship." But that was the way it went.

Was I surprised he retired? Yes and no. I always think he has a plan. As a matter of fact, I don't think we really know what his thinking was. There's probably more to the story than any of us know. I think he had a lot more to offer the game. It's just conjecture on my part, but if he had retired at another point in time, there may have been some people who said: "We've got to go through a process, open up the position." Then all of a sudden, he would have been put behind the eight ball.

He would have been put on a screening committee, which he never would have wanted. Word would have gotten out—"Dean wants Roy. Dean wants George Karl. Dean wants Larry Brown." All these things he doesn't like to do, he might have been forced to do. But how he retired, it enabled him to orchestrate, out of desperation, exactly what he wanted. He has never given the outward appearance of being power-hungry. But he has great confidence and knowledge in what he wants, as he should.

If he had done it another way, there would have been a bombardment of press. No matter who got hired, they would have said: "Dean favored Larry over George Karl, or Roy over Larry." He never put himself in that situation. He was like Coach Wooden in that respect. If you ask Coach Wooden: "Who was better, Kareem or Walton?" you would never get that answered. It was smart, the way Dean did it. I just hope he did it when he was really tired of basketball. Because I know he really loves the game.

WOODY DURHAM

Durham, a 1963 graduate of North Carolina, has been the play-by-play announcer on the Tar Heels' radio network since 1971.

I was an undergraduate when he became head coach in August of 1961. It was late in the summer when Coach McGuire decided to take the Philadelphia coaching job. We were four years removed from a perfect season, a national championship, the match that sort of lit the fire for what is now ACC basketball. I give Everett Case at N.C. State his due credit. Everett was the guy who brought big-time basketball to the Atlantic Coast Conference. But the entire state got caught up in what Carolina did in 1957. That was kind of the thing that really got it going.

It was not a pretty situation when Coach McGuire left. There were NCAA sanctions being imposed. Then they named this three-year assistant coach. He was in the shadow of Frank McGuire. Very few people knew much about him. So here's the NCAA sanctions, then they name Dean Smith. Everybody said: "What's this? A former assistant at the Air Force Academy coaching North Carolina?"

Everybody was under the impression that we were trying to get out of the big-time. We played only 17 games that first year. He couldn't recruit off-campus. There were just a number of things that you would have thought: "This is not going to last long. He's not going to be able to come out from under this. Then what's Carolina going to do? If they're really going to take this big a dive, what's going to happen to the program?"

When he was an assistant, he was a guy that was easy to like. He was friendly. But it was already very, very evident that he was conscientious. He was very attentive to detail. If you gave him a time and a place to do something, he was there. To this day, Phil Ford jokes that he keeps his watch on Dean Smith time, which is five minutes ahead.

If the bus is leaving to go to the airport, the bus leaves at 6:13. If they say 6:15, that's sort of going to slide right by you. But 6:13, that's going to stay with you. If everybody's there a couple of minutes before or right at 6:13, the bus rolls. If other people who are supposed to be there are not there, that's tough.

Last year, we brought the '67, '68 and '69 teams back for a reunion. My wife and I were invited to dinner at the Carolina Club, which is our alumni center. That night, they passed the microphone around. It got down to one of the managers. I can't remember which one. The manager started telling the story of the night that Dean was hung in effigy, Cunningham getting off the bus and cutting the dummy down. It got real quiet. There were a bunch of round tables. There was no head table. Finally, Dean said: "Well, it helped us beat Duke three days later." Everybody broke up and started laughing. They did beat Duke—three days later in Durham.

Along the way at that particular time he was having some occasional big wins, like Indiana or Kentucky. Coach Rupp signed a ten-year agreement with Coach Smith his first or second year. Carolina won seven of the ten games. Before his first Final Four team in '66-'67, wins like that were happening and proving that he did know what he was doing. It's interesting how much in later life, being together with him, talking with him, we talked about that. We talked about what the transition was like.

As an assistant, Dean was always the heavy. Coach McGuire would go recruiting and leave Dean in charge of practice. Dean would run 'em like the devil. He really made 'em work hard. Practices were very disciplined, right to the minute, just like they were up to the day he retired. They may not have liked him as an assistant. If there was punishment to be dealt out, he was always the guy who did it. When Coach McGuire left, some of the guys talked about not coming back, about transferring. They finally decided: "Let's go back, see how things work out." I think they all got some feeling the first year that he really did know what he was doing. He had virtually no talent on that first team. To win eight games with that group of guys . . .

I specifically remember Carolina coming to play in Greensboro. I was doing some TV games then. The Coliseum asked me: "How about doing the PA for us?" Carolina would come to Greensboro and play a couple of times a year, as would Duke and N.C. State. At that time, the Coliseum seated 9,500 people. It was the biggest arena outside of Charlotte in the state. Anyway, I remember doing the starting lineups: "Now at forward, now at guard." This was in 1964-'65. I said: "And now the head coach of the Tar Heels," and the crowd booed. It was tough. It really was. Not many people talk about it now, but some of those early years were tough.

In 1965, that class of Rusty Clark, Bill Bunting, Joe Brown, Gerald Tuttle and Dick Grubar all came in. Rusty was actually on a Morehead scholarship, a very prestigious scholarship at the University. But he was being very heavily recruited by Davidson with Lefty Driesell. In later years, I heard Dean say: "If I hadn't gotten that big man, I might have lost my job."

For years a lot of people got on him about not going to the Final Four, never winning the national championship. But you had to understand him. He wanted to win. He was disappointed he didn't. But other things that happened in the lives of young men were much more important to him than sacrificing principles, doing other things that might have been needed to win a basketball game. The people who didn't know him missed all of that. They missed really knowing a unique individual. Charlie Scott said: "A guy like this comes along once in a lifetime." Well, that's a former player—he's going to say that. But that's probably pretty close to the truth.

He does have sort of an idiosyncracy about him. He doesn't like public attention. If he's going to a function tonight and the dinner starts at 8:15, he'll get there at about 8:10, 8:15, maybe even 8:20 after people are sitting down. He's uncomfortable with cocktail-party conversation. And the one characteristic that he has, if he's uncomfortable with something, he touches his face. Somehow, some way, he touches his face. I don't think he's even aware of it.

There are countless examples of his memory. Dave Hanners told me a great story. As the years have gone by, one of the things Dean wanted to do was give each player who played for him a videotape of some of the old game films that showed this guy in action, from the stars right on down to the last guy on the bench. That's been an ongoing project for several years. First off, they had to get all the game films transferred to tape for easier editing, things like that.

One summer Dave Hanners was in the tape room watching tape of a game played back in the '60s in Madison Square Garden, I think against Notre Dame. He was looking for specific plays of a certain player to put on a master tape. He said Coach Smith walked through. And he stood there and watched the tape for about a minute. He said, "Hmm. Notre Dame. The Garden." Dave said there were no markings on the court back then to indicate that it was the Garden.

Dave said: "Coach, that is phenomenal that you just walked by and recognized this game." He said: "Dave, watch this, in about a minute now there's going to be a perfectly executed backdoor play, and we're going to score." He told him who was going to throw the pass. Dave said: "Coach, are you sure you haven't watched this tape?" He said Dean stood there, looked at the screen and said: "Well, I know we graded it." Sure they did—but that was 30 years ago!

The fund-raising for the new arena started after the '82 championship. That's what allowed them to raise $5 million more than they needed. The building cost $33.8 million, and it was all private donations. You know what it would cost today. They go to him, and he was very much opposed to the idea of naming it after him. He said: "I want it named after the players." So they finally compromised—the Dean E. Smith Student Activities Center is the proper name of the building.

Now it's been picked up by the media—you hear people call it the Dean Dome. One night he jokingly said to me: "Every time I hear Dean Dome, I think about a guy with a bald head." I've never said Dean Dome in his presence. To this day, you never hear him call the building the Smith Center. He calls it the Student Activities Center.

PETER GAMMONS

Gammons, a baseball analyst for ESPN and the Boston Globe, *began his sportswriting career at the* Daily Tar Heel, *the student newspaper at the University of North Carolina.*

He arrived at Chapel Hill in 1963, took a year and a half to play in rock 'n roll bands and graduated from North Carolina in January 1969.

I covered him. As a young guy, in some ways, he treated me the same way Gene Mauch treated me. Because I was interested, he treated me great. He always seemed to care. One time, Frank Deford was down there, writing for *Sports Illustrated*. He brought me in to introduce me to Frank Deford. I think he was hoping it would rub off on me.

He was really very good at explaining things. I found him a good person to listen to. It was really hard for him when he went down there. Frank McGuire had a lot of stature. It was a real New York team. They were on probation. My freshman year, Bobby Lewis came down from Washington. They still had freshman ball. He averaged like 37 points per game as a 6-foot-2 center. That was some of my favorite basketball of all time.

Dean had tremendous disadvantages. They were on probation. (Billy) Cunningham and (Bill) Galantai and all those New Yorkers were Frank McGuire guys. Dean was a Midwesterner, a complete kind of opposite of what North Carolina had become. But the one thing he had, he was entrusted with power.

The chancellor of the university—J. Carlyle Sitterson, who took over in 1966—was the one who really wanted McGuire out of there (Sitterson was a dean and vice chancellor before becoming chancellor). Basically, it was: "Dean, make this a good program. But make the program right." Sitterson was a basketball fanatic. But he was also a make-it-right fanatic. And he also loved Dean because Dean was so big on the civil-rights movement.

My freshman year, I was involved in the marches in Chapel Hill in January of '64. When I went to Chapel Hill in September of '63, it was segregated. That's where Martin Luther King and so many people came. It was considered the left-wing town of the south. Frankly, it was the only political university down there. Duke was never political. And Dean was in the middle of that. Sitterson loved the fact that Dean was very political.

Probably the thing I like best about him is that he really tried to make his players political, make them care about civil rights. Having Charles Scott as the first big black scholarship athlete south of the Mason-Dixon line, that was very important to him. He thought it was very important for students to be political. And secondly, he signed the antiwar petition at the university.

At a lot of schools, people would have said: "What is the basketball coach doing signing an antiwar petition?" Bill Dooley was coming in as the football coach. He was the exact opposite. All my friends who were football players got run off the team because they wouldn't run into walls. Dean was very much like a professor. He encouraged people to be something other than basketball players. Those two things—the civil-rights movement and the antiwar petition—that's probably why I like him so much, why I respect him. He believed in something deeper than basketball.

Now when he coached, it wasn't quite that way. There was a guy on the team—and he later became a friend of mine—named Bruce Bowers. He was like a backup center. Guys like that, they were McGuire guys. Dean liked that very tight system, that shuffle offense, kind of a Kansas style. They kind of made fun of him. I think it was very frustrating for him at first.

It was always my belief that the guy who really made his transition possible was Billy Cunningham. Cunningham was such a great guy. He loved to win so much. I was actually at a fraternity party at the Deke house the night of the NBA draft when he got taken by Philadelphia. He was so upset. Cunningham's values were: "I want to be a Celtic. That's my idea of the way to play basketball." Because of his love for the game, he really helped bring Dean through it.

Then, when Dean got Larry Miller, that was the first time he got a recruit that somebody else wanted—Miller was Duke's number-one guy, too. That was a turning point. Then he got Dickie Grubar and Rusty Clark and Bill Bunting and all those guys the next year. Larry Brown came in to coach them, which was a very big deal. But he went through a big transition.

I was on the bus the night he was hung in effigy. I had covered the game. We were coming back from Wake Forest. They had really gotten killed. That night is really exaggerated. I think the story is that Cunningham climbed up and tore the thing down. They just stopped the bus, and a couple of guys went out. As I remember, one of the players went out and yelled something, and someone got a rake from the dorm and pulled it down. I don't even remember what dorm it was. It was right near the old gym. It was not that big a deal.

But it also did symbolize something. It really seemed that Dean was in trouble at the time. He was never defensive about it. He was always very optimistic. He was such an ungracious loser, because in his mind, he couldn't lose. It would never dawn on him he could lose. That's one of the things that got him through that period. People were really on his case. The fans were booing him all the time. Duke was a great team then.

It actually helped that the ACC was still white. Duke couldn't go out and win national championships. Duke was a great team, but it was still Jeff Mullins, Hack Tison, Jay Buckley, guys like that. They were good, but they were still all white. UCLA was black. Texas El-Paso was black. That took a little heat off. Duke wasn't winning the national championships they might have.

CURRY KIRKPATRICK

Kirkpatrick, a 1965 graduate of North Carolina, writes for ESPN The Magazine.

I started the same year Dean started as head coach—in 1961. I came to Chapel Hill from upstate New York. The basketball thing really intrigued me. I remember listening to the 1957 national championship game on the radio. I was just intrigued with the whole North Carolina tradition. I wanted to go to the south, get in a warmer area. I visited Duke and North Carolina. I went to Chapel Hill because they had a journalism school. Duke didn't.

I loved college basketball. Frank McGuire was a guy I thought was so cool. But entering my freshman year, McGuire had left. They hired this guy, Dean Smith, who I knew nothing about. He seemed, at the time, so uncool. Here was this dull-looking guy with a big nose from Kansas who I had never heard of. He was going to be the coach at my school. I was very disappointed that the ultra-cool, sophisticated, great-dressing Frank McGuire was gone. Here was this kind of little weird guy who was going to be the head coach. That was my initial impression.

Then I was in college, working for the *Daily Tar Heel*, covering the team. I think Dean would even agree with this—his first big victory was at Kentucky (68-66 on December 17, 1962). I don't know if it was the very first use of the Four Corners, but it was the one that got all the attention. They had Larry Brown at guard, Billy Cunningham inside. I had gotten to go on the trip, which was very unusual for a college kid on a college paper. It was a daily paper, but it wasn't a big deal. They played Indiana on a Saturday afternoon and got killed (90-76) by the Van Arsdale twins. They played at Kentucky on a Monday night, and were big underdogs.

I was on the trip. It really meant a lot for a kid like me to be at Kentucky. I knew we would get absolutely destroyed. But they ended up playing this amazing game, totally slowing it down. They won the game. He beat Adolph Rupp. That was the first noise anyone heard from Dean Smith. He kids me to this day. On the video of the game, I'm sitting at the press table with all these legitimate newspaper guys. And I'm jumping up and cheering when Carolina is making big baskets at the end of the game.

I got out of school, went to *Sports Illustrated*, and they went on to great things. Everyone thought I had some kind of in. I had been that close to the program, that Dean would take me in his confidence. Nothing could have been further from the truth.

He always thought that because I was from North Carolina, I bent over backwards to go the other way at *Sports Illustrated* —I was far too objective for his taste. He thought I was too objective to the point of being against them. He was always suspicious. I think he's intrinsically suspicious of the media, anyway. He was always suspicious of me—he felt I was being ultra-objective to the point of being a contra, basically.

When Michael Jordan was a freshman, we made them number one and put them on the cover in the pre-season basketball issue. They had Worthy, Perkins and Jimmy Black, and Jordan was going to be the freshman starter. The cover was supposed to be the starting five and Dean. But because Jordan was a freshman, he refused to let Jordan appear on the cover. Of course, they went on to the national championship, Jordan hit the winning shot and became the greatest player who ever lived. Dean wouldn't let him be on the cover, which basically would have introduced him.

There's an aside to that story. The college cartoonist at the *Daily Tar Heel* at the time sent me a cartoon after the season that they had done in the newspaper. It was a reproduction of the cover with Dean and the four starters standing there. And this cartoonist drew a little tiny Michael Jordan child peeking in, trying to get in the picture. It was a really clever cartoon. I still have it.

When J.R. Reid was a freshman, he was a huge deal, a huge name. He was like the high school player of the year, and Carolina signed him. He was going to be a great player for the program, and he became such an important part of the team. Late in the season, I went down to do a story on him. We were going to put him on the cover. And Dean, the whole time I was down there, insisted J.R. Reid was not that important to the program, and didn't deserve mention. But we had to do the story.

The cover said: "North Carolina's Main Man: Freshman J.R. Reid." This was late February, right before the tournament. He really was the main man. Nobody doubted that. But Dean used to play down freshmen so much. When the cover came out, he apparently was furious. I don't know if he failed to realize that we were going to put J.R. on the cover. But the next time I saw him was at the first round of the NCAA tournament at the Meadowlands.

He was upset. It wasn't just a minor thing. He was upset to the point that at the press conference, he singled me out. Out of the blue, he started talking about his team, and how J.R. was a freshman, and not that important. Then he said: "Curry Kirkpatrick of *Sports Illustrated*, as a Carolina guy, should know better than to say J.R. Reid is the main man. No freshman at Carolina is ever the main man." I was embarrassed. I thought he was joking, maybe just putting the needle in like he sometimes does. But he wasn't joking. All these press people are in there. Instead of confronting me later privately, he said it there.

Afterward, I went up to him and said: "Dean, what are you upset about? We put the guy on the cover." He wasn't joking. He said: "You know that was not good journalism. He's not the main man. He's not our main player. No freshman is ever our main man." I told him that number one, I'm not responsible for the cover. And number two, I thought he was their main man. We sort of had a little tiff. But at least that showed friends of mine that I didn't have any real in with Dean Smith. He didn't give me much of a wide berth, or any so-called scoops.

I've never felt badly that we were at that arm's length. I would have liked to have had a closer relationship. But that's the way he wanted it. I don't know if there's anybody in the "objective media" that he is really close to. I don't know that there is anybody he has brought into his confidence. Not to say that's good or bad. That's just the way it was. People thought I was one of them. That wasn't happening.

FRANK DEFORD

Deford, senior contributing writer for Sports Illustrated, *profiled Smith after he won his first national championship in 1982. Smith declined to be interviewed for the piece, headlined, "Long Ago, He Won The Big One."*

I had known Dean for a long time. One of the first stories I did was when he turned the corner with Larry Miller and Bobby Lewis. I went all the way back with him. I was very friendly with him. I still am friendly with him. I was going to do this story. I called him up and very politely said: "Dean, I want to do a story on you."

There was sort of a chill on the other end. I don't remember how the exchange went. But he did not like a piece I had done on Bear Bryant. I guess they were circling the wagons in the coaching fraternity about it. The story on Bryant had not been critical. It had just been frank. It just made him human.

At that point, Bear Bryant was held up as a demigod in Alabama. Among other things, I wrote that he had bladder problems, just like a lot of older men do. He joked about it. But in Alabama, he's a god, and I was talking about bodily functions. You'd hardly call it a rip job on Bear Bryant. But Dean felt that it was. He said he would not talk to me.

I called him back and tried to talk him into it. He wouldn't bend. At some point, I got my back up. I said I was going to do the story anyway. He accepted that graciously. There was none of this: "You just try it!" He never, from that point on, told anyone not to talk to me. It was just a matter of principle that he would not talk to me. But he had no compunctions whatsoever about allowing anybody else to talk to me, except for his wife. And that might have been the case under any circumstances.

I talked to Christopher Fordham, the chancellor then and one of his great friends. I can remember sitting in Coach Guthridge's office talking about Dean Smith while Dean Smith was ten feet away. But Dean Smith wouldn't talk to me. He was never ungracious. We had a pleasant phone discussion before I got down there.

It made me work hard as hell. I had to go see everyone, because I had to fill in all the blanks. After the story was written, I don't think I saw him for a couple of years. On subsequent occasions when I saw him, there was no problem. I've never heard anyone say: "Boy, that Dean Smith hates your guts. He said something bad about you." I don't think he ever did.

The only funny thing I heard was from his wife, Linnea, who I've subsequently talked to two or three times on other matters. She's a psychiatrist. And she asked this very good friend of mine: "Did Frank Deford have problems with his father?" You can see where that came from—coaches are father figures. I had written critically of Bear Bryant; ergo, I must have had problems with my father. That just made me laugh. And by the way, I did not have problems with my father.

When you write a story like that it puts pressure on you. If you write critically, if feels like you're doing it to get back at him. It's almost like you have to bend over backwards. It wasn't like I set out to do a rip job. I had great admiration for Smith. The thing I always said—and it would have been the only critical thing in the story— was that everything was so even with Dean Smith. He could never get up for a game. Everything was done the same way. He tried to take all the passion out of things. That was a criticism right to the end of his career.

He would always win 20 games, always finish first or second in the ACC. He'd get to the big game, and it wasn't that he couldn't win. It's just that every game was as big as every other one. Playing Citadel in December was just as big as playing in the Final Four. I always hated the Four Corners. I thought that was representative of his personality, too. And there was the old joke about him being the only coach to hold Jordan under 20 points per game.

But hey, it's pretty hard to argue with success, isn't it? John Wooden won all the championships. But Smith, in many ways, had a superior record. If you really look at it, Wooden would always come out of the West Regional. It was an easier road. With Smith, you could certainly make the argument that he was the greatest coach, playing against the competition he did. And he never had Bill Walton or Lew Alcindor, either. I could have won with those guys.

The story I did, it gave me great insight into him. It was all done in a philosophical and civil way. I appreciated that. I'd much rather have that than a lot of phoniness.

MARK WHICKER

Mark Whicker, a 1973 graduate of North Carolina, was a Morehead Scholar who worked for the Daily Tar Heel *and later the* Chapel Hill News. *He is a columnist with the* Orange County (California) Register.

The thing that always stands out is the extreme loyalty that all of the players have had, and still do toward him, on into life. They knew, beyond anything else, that he was serious when he put them first, above everybody else. If any of them had a problem, it didn't matter who was in his office, they could call and be patched right in. They were a very prideful, close-knit group.

In '71, they had a team picked to be in the second division of the ACC, and they ended up winning the regular season, which was a big surprise. George Karl was a sophomore then. The day of the last game at home, they were supposed to honor the seniors—they were the first with Senior Night. They were also going to honor Don McCauley, an All-American running back, probably the best football player in the ACC in some time.

In the *Daily Tar Heel*, we billed it as "McCauley Night." That was the day before the game. I went down that afternoon and talked to some of the seniors about their remembrances. They were all livid. This was their night. They couldn't believe anyone would take their thunder away. A couple of them wouldn't even talk to me.

They were always using stuff like that. Dean was ahead of his time in terms of motivation, using external forces to motivate. They were probably one of the first basketball programs to say in some form, "We don't get no respect," which is what you hear every day now.

They always had coats and ties on. You knew who they were at all times. There was a distinct identity in their program. They were apart. They didn't stay in regular dorms. They stayed in Granville Towers. They were royalty, and Dean encouraged that. They went to class, did all that stuff, too. But they were a breed apart. They weren't just a basketball team. And I think that was very deliberate on Dean's part.

Back then, the ACC was really tough. To get to the NCAA tournament, you had to win the ACC tournament. They were competing with (North Carolina State's) David Thompson, (Maryland's) John Lucas, (Virginia's) Barry Parkhill, South Carolina teams that were great, outstanding players at Wake Forest. Everybody by then had acknowledged that Dean was the guy. When he came there, nobody knew who he was. Vic Bubas was the Dean Smith of his time.

Dean picked up a lot of things from Vic Bubas in terms of national recruiting, running a program apart from just a basketball team. Then Carolina kind of superseded Duke when they signed Charlie Scott, Larry Miller, those guys. By then, Carolina was the number-one rival of everybody, the team that everybody wanted to beat, even though State and Maryland had great teams, too, probably better teams in the '73-'74 era.

I remember the huge recruiting flap over Tom McMillen. We had guys from our fraternity house go to the Carolina-Maryland football game at Maryland that year. They had this huge sign that said: "Tom, say hi to your mom." His mom was the one who was blamed for this. Anyway, he plays his freshman year with Len Elmore. He's public enemy number one. He's Beelzebub in Chapel Hill, the Antichrist. They finally come to play Carolina on a Saturday afternoon game at Carmichael, which to this day is the loudest arena I've ever been in, and the hottest.

The day before the game, Dean made sure in all the papers, including the *Daily Tar Heel*, to say: "We want our fans to give Tom a big hand. We don't want them to boo or throw things." So, we're all waiting for this outrage to pour forth. But they introduced him, and he got a huge standing ovation. It was a great example of Dean's mind control over the whole community. It screwed McMillen up so much, he ended up scoring about five points the whole game. Billy Chamberlain was guarding him. He was about five inches shorter. And he shut him down. Tom McMillen went to one NCAA tournament, and the only reason they won that was because State was on probation. He never went to the Final Four.

I gave Dean a carton of 200 cigarettes after he won his 200th game (on January 8, 1972), a carton of Kents. He thought that was outstanding. But generally, there was a distance. It was just like any other writer. It was: "We're going to portray the program this way." He was very contentious about anything written that was different from the party line. The kids talked the way he wanted them to talk. They were very seldom spontaneous in the things they said in the media. They all spoke with one voice. Guthridge was very reluctant to talk to us—it was Coach Smith's program. When Roy Williams and Eddie Fogler were there, they were a little bit more outgoing. And Dean changed over the years, too.

The thing about him is, he is so incredibly competitive about everything. I think that's what set him apart. I think that's why his teams played to the buzzer. That's why they were able to wipe out an eight-point deficit in the final seventeen seconds against Duke. That's why they made so many comebacks, and never gave up. He was so incredibly competitive. He would never let anything go.

A primary example of that was in 1982 when they finally won the national championship. You would think that would have been the peak moment of his life. He got in the interview room and said a few complimentary things about Georgetown, which is how he started off every interview. But within about five minutes, he mentioned a story that Frank Barrows had written in the *Charlotte Observer* five years before—Frank Barrows is now managing editor of the *Charlotte Observer*.

He had written a series or big story saying that North Carolina would never win a national championship because Dean's system would not allow them to do it—his system was a good regular-season system, but it would never let them win a tournament. That was based on what happened in the Marquette game, when he went to the Four Corners and shouldn't have, in many people's opinions.

Dean said something to the effect of: "A great writer named Frank Barrows wrote that our system would never allow us to win a national championship. I've always thought that was ridiculous." Then he said something like: "I shouldn't have said that, but I did." That was just the way his mind worked. He would never let anything get by. And it would stay there.

Another example was in 1976. He was coaching the Olympic team. Virginia's Wally Walker didn't make the team, and four Carolina players did—Walter Davis, Phil Ford, Mitch Kupchak and Tommy LaGarde did. Half the team was ACC players, and four were Carolina players. And everybody was raising hell about that.

They win the gold medal. And Bill Millsaps of the *Richmond Times-Dispatch* is there—he's now the executive editor at that paper. He's overcome with patriotism and pride over the fact that we won the gold medal four years after getting screwed. Dean is on top of the world. He brought it back. Dean comes out, and Bill says: "Congratulations. That was great." And Dean says: "Thank you. By the way, do you still think Wally Walker could have made this team?" That's just the way he is.

He was just competitive in every sense of the word, all the good senses of it, all the bad senses of it. His players always played hard. They never took a game off. They were consistent in their effort. They always did the right thing. They always executed the same way. They always had a poker face. Very seldom did they get technicals—if they did, they were punished in some ungodly fashion. They were always the same. You could count on it. They would always win the games they should win, and a few they shouldn't.

Even in interviews, he would take a word out of your question—if he didn't want to answer the question—and make an issue out of that. He was a contentious conversationalist. That's not a criticism. That's just him. He was totally devoted to the program, totally devoted to the image of the program. If writers didn't like him, if other coaches didn't like him, that didn't bother him. And guys hated him. Tates Locke hated him. Norm Sloan just despised him. And I think Terry Holland was quoted as saying he was a hypo-crite, or words to that effect. I'm sure Dean never forgave him for that. A lot of people said: "Here, here."

It was a much more tempestuous time in the ACC. There were fights. South Carolina's John Roche stepped on George Karl's chest during a game. There were more crowd incidents. The Duke students threw stuff all over Frank McGuire one time. Maybe because I was younger, it just seemed that way, but there was a real feeling of menace in some of these arenas. And Carolina brought that out in people.

I remember one game in Clemson when Dean got tossed for some reason. Of course, the students loved that. He had to leave the court, but he was watching the game from the locker-room area, which was in the end zone, and there were bars there. He was watching the game like a prisoner, hands on the bars. George Karl kept going over there trying to get instruc-tions from him, and pass it back to Guthridge. The students would block Karl. He couldn't get to where Dean was. It was like WCW or something. And there was always stuff like that going on.

They had some ups and downs. Duke got good. For a while there, they lost a little bit of their recruiting edge. They signed some guys who weren't really Carolina players, in my opinion. Then they got that straight-ened out. I think George Lynch was very important in that. He was more of a traditional Carolina player, very disciplined, unselfish and hard-working, a little bit more consistent than some of those guys in the J.R. Reid-Scott Wil-liams-Steve Bucknall period. But those teams still went like 28-6 every year.

And look at all the players they've lost early. For him to keep that thing going, with all the lottery picks they've lost early, is really remarkable. The '82 team lost Worthy. The '83 team would have had Jordan, Perkins, Brad Daugherty—and Worthy. I don't think you would have heard of Jim Valvano. I don't think the myth of Jim Valvano would have existed.

After the '84 season, they lost Jordan. He would have been a senior in '85 with Kenny Smith, Daugherty, Steve Hale and some other guys who were pretty good players. I'm not sure you would have heard of Rollie Massimino if that team had been playing in '85. Maybe I'm wrong. Maybe they would have lost to Georgetown in the final. But I think those teams would have been Final Four teams, without any question.

Then Stackhouse and Wallace left after the '95 season, and the '96 team didn't get to the final 16. Then they lost Carter and Jamison after the '97 season. That's not an excuse for them. That's just a fact. Duke has kept all of its players, which I admire. I think that's great. But you have to look at the facts. The fact that they kept those teams together was a real big factor in them repeating. If they had lost Laettner, I don't think they would have won the '92 national championship. But they did, and more power to them.

He's a fascinating guy. He has no groupies. Most of these coaches, they have confidants. He doesn't. He keeps people at their distance. He treats everybody pretty much the same.

DICK WEISS

Weiss is the national college writer for the New York Daily News. *He previously worked for the* Philadelphia Daily News.

I was at the East Regional in 1972—Penn and Villanova were there. I was a young sportswriter. I had just gotten into the business. Carolina beat Penn for the regional championship to go to the Final Four in Los Angeles. I went up, congratulated him and introduced myself to him. The next week, I show up in California. We go to Pepperdine—the old Pepperdine, in the city—for practice. He comes right up to me and says: "How are you doing, Dick?" I was like: "This guy has an encyclopedic memory."

Here I am, I was still in Camden (N.J.) at the time. It wasn't like I had any big name. I was amazed a guy of that stature would remember my name. When you're a young writer, that leaves an enormous impression. It took me a long time to actually call him Dean. I used to call (former Villanova coach) Harry Litwack, "Coach Litwack." I used to call Dean Smith, "Coach Smith."

I still remember being there the night he won the national championship, talking to him out in the corridor in New Orleans before the game. He was cupping a cigarette so nobody could see him. He had gone through that same thing that Jim Calhoun went through where they're close, but they never win the whole thing. I remember being really happy for him. He had been there so many times. It took a great shot by Michael. But it took a predictable shot by Michael. It was like, all of a sudden, he had this huge monkey off his back.

He set the standard for a long time, made people measure up to him. Even when Duke went through a stretch where they dominated play in the ACC, they were always competing against Carolina. It wasn't Carolina competing against Duke. It has since changed. Mike (Krzyzewski) obviously is in total control of Tobacco Road right now. The gap is probably widening.

So many coaches came into Tobacco Road, and no one was able to overcome the whole mystique of Carolina. He became too big and chased a lot of coaches out of the business. Krzyzewski is the one person who stood up to him, and was able to succeed. But even at the end, when you thought Duke was in total control, Carolina came back and won the '93 national championship. You always felt that he was always there.

He was an enormous magnet in recruiting. He made that special trip to Philadelphia the day they were supposed to have the parade after the '93 championship, just to go to Rasheed Wallace's house. The next day, we started hearing that Rasheed was going to North Carolina. It was over. But it wasn't like he had ever recruited that many players from Philadelphia before. He had recruited (Gene) Banks a little bit. But he hadn't really been to our city a lot.

Whenever I walked into his office, I felt like I was walking into this huge boardroom. But he would make himself accessible to you if he knew you. I remember I needed him one day, and they had a game. He said: "Why don't you come up two hours before the game? I'm not doing anything." So I went into his office, and we talked.

But I also remember how private he was. I went to his office to do an interview right after John Feinstein's book on Bob Knight had come out. He said to me, "Geez, can you believe that Bobby opened the door completely for anybody?" There were certain things in his mind that were very private. He liked to be in control of his program, at all times.

I remember the day of his retirement press conference, the massive crowd that made the pilgrimage to Chapel Hill. I was stunned at the amount of media who showed up on short notice, but everyone understood the significance of his leaving at that point in time. It was a huge story. He had just broken Adolph Rupp's record. And all of a sudden, he decided he was going to step down on his terms. What beat him up wasn't the coaching, but all the things he did in the off-season, all the responsibilities he had being Dean Smith.

They held the press conference in the natatorium. Kids were peering in through the windows. I still remember signs outside: "Don't leave, Dean—say it's not true." People writing in chalk on the pavement outside his office, "Don't go." It was unbelievable. There were signs throughout Franklin Street. He obviously had made an enormous impact on the community.

One or two days after he retired, I stayed around and went to lunch with him at the Faculty Club. We talked, and he gave me what turned out to be almost an exclusive interview. He was wonderful. I loved the fact that he has been so involved. I almost feel sad that he's out of it. I don't think we're going to see coaches spend extended periods of time in one job again.

S.L. PRICE

Price, a writer for Sports Illustrated, *worked for the* Daily Tar Heel *and graduated from North Carolina in 1983.*

Understand that I was coming at it then from the standpoint of a student journalist, not breaking stories, just sort of like: "Oh my gosh, I'm covering the Tar Heels. I can't believe I'm doing this." Dean was incredibly professional. He dealt with you exactly like he dealt with everybody else. But on the other hand, he's not a very warm figure. And when you're in college, you sort of have a tendency to gravitate toward the outlaws—or at least anybody who'll talk to you.

At the same time, Jim Valvano was over at State. I went over and did a bunch of stuff on him as well. Valvano, you were like his long-lost son. It was easy to love Valvano as a character. By comparison, Dean came off as sort of this cold schoolmaster. I appreciated what he did as a coach. But I didn't really like him. I didn't feel warmly about him. I thought Valvano was cool.

Dean never said anything of interest whatsoever. After a game, he was like: "We'd like to congratulate Furman for their 97-point loss." He was incredibly gentlemanly and eminently unquotable. I wouldn't say I had a negative view of him. Everyone else was worshiping the heck out of Dean Smith. I thought he was really good at what he did. And I understood that he won a lot of games. But that was it.

Then I wrote this piece about the Dean Dome. It just ripped the Dean Dome. It was a typical college thing. "I'm going to burn the house down. Everyone is going to get ticked off. Look at me." A typical sort of attention-getting thing, although I believed it completely. I still believe it. They were pouring tons of money into the Dean Dome. I said that was a travesty, and not only that, but sports at North Carolina, they think they're doing things the right way, but actually it's overemphasized. There are jock dorms—even though they aren't officially called jock dorms—training tables, so on and so forth.

Everybody went nuts about this story. How could you say this? The chancellor calls me on the carpet. How could you say such a thing about our august institution? Roy Williams rips me—he was an assistant then. And I get a letter from Dean, saying: "Look, I'd really like to talk to you about this at the end of the season." I'm covering the team at the time. A letter from Dean Smith—it was sort of like: "Wow, gods do send letters." And I'm sure that Dean is going to pull the same thing everyone else did. How could you dare to even think of criticizing us?

Understand, I'm a full-of-myself, 20-year-old journalist. But at the same time, I understand that Dean Smith needed me not at all. He doesn't have to take any time with me. The student newspaper. Who cares? I'm full of piss and vinegar, but at the same time, I'm woefully insignificant—and should be.

But he completely blows me away. I expect a tirade. He says: "Tell me what you know. Tell me what you mean by what you wrote. There may be something going on here that I don't know about. Why do you think that we have jock dorms? I don't think we do. You live on campus. Tell me what you know. Tell me what you see. Why do you think this institution is more sports-minded than we think?" He actually wanted to know what I thought. He didn't have to call me in. There was no need for him to butter me up or work me in any shape or form. He's Dean Smith. I'm not.

I walked out of there thinking: "Here's the one guy in the entire state who does not buy into Dean Smith as God." He thought: "I don't know everything. Even this kid might be able to tell me something." I don't know that I did, but his approach was incredibly refreshing and one that completely took me by surprise. Again, he's not a warm figure. But I left there with an enormous amount of respect for him, and have retained it to this day.

It told me why he was such a great coach in many ways. Unlike so many people who achieve a measure of stature, he still felt: "I have things to learn." That went a long way toward explaining why he remained fresh and innovative and able to adapt to changing players through the years.

It's funny. Valvano died, and he was romanticized. But a lot of people forget that he left Iona in disgrace, and State was a mess when he left. In terms of crooked coaches, you could throw Valvano in with them, too. He was a wonderfully lovable guy. But the fact is, I came away respecting Dean as a man. I never warmed up to him. But I realized that the respect was far more important than the general affection you feel for somebody like Valvano. And that's exactly why Smith is who he is.

JOHN FEINSTEIN

Feinstein, a 1977 graduate of Duke, is a best-selling sports author.

I vividly remember the first time I met him. It was my junior year. I was the sports editor of the *Duke Chronicle*, and I wrote a column before Duke went over to play at Carolina, saying that if Bill Foster needed a role model on which to build the Duke program, he should look ten miles down the road to Chapel Hill—it is ten miles, not eight miles, no matter what anyone says.

Duke went over and played there, and Carolina killed them, of course. I was in the locker room, working on a story on Tate Armstrong, who was just having an unbelievable year. I wanted a quote from Dean on Tate, because Tate had 33 against them that day, or something. I walked up and said: "Coach Smith, my name is John Feinstein, and I'm with the *Duke Chronicle*." He said: "Oh yes, I read the column you wrote. I was going to drop you a note to thank you. That was very fair, especially coming from the *Duke Chronicle*." I was like: "Wait a minute. You read something in the *Duke Chronicle*?"

John Feinstein

I later found out that one of their coaches is assigned to clip newspapers, and to put anything relevant to Carolina or Dean in any way on Dean's desk, so that when he would travel, he would read it on airplanes. Obviously, they got all the student newspapers in the league. But I was just floored that he knew who I was. I did several stories down there my junior and senior years stringing for different newspapers. You always wanted a quote from Dean if it was a league issue or something. He would always call me back.

In 1981, I did this big two-part series on him in the *Washington Post*. Of course, it took forever to convince him to let me talk to him. When he finally agreed to do the interview, he said I could interview him in the car driving to Charlotte. They were playing in the North-South double-header. The way it was set up, I was going to drive with him in the car to Charlotte, and I had to cover Maryland-Duke in Durham the next day, so I would drive his car back to Chapel Hill. He gives me his license and registration. I said:

"That's great. If I get stopped by a cop and I hand him the registration that says, 'Dean Smith' on it, what chance have I got?" And he says: "With your luck, it will be a State fan."

We're driving down. He smoked back then. It was the winter time, so the windows were rolled up. We got about an hour out of Chapel Hill, and he said: "Do you want to stop and get a Coke?" I said: "Oh God, yes." We pull into this gas station, and there's this good old boy behind the counter. He looks up, sees Dean and says: "Oh my God, it's Norman Sloan." And Dean says to me, "I told you I was just another guy named Smith."

He wrote me this really nice note after the series came out, said he really didn't want to do it, but he thought I was very fair to him, and that it was a really good job. I wrote him back and said: "I'm glad it worked out. And someday, when you're ready, I want to write your book." He wrote me back and said: "You'd be the first person I consider."

The next year, they won the national championship. I called him and said: "I want to do the book now. I can come down during the summer. We'll do it at your convenience. We can do it on the golf course, if you want." And he said: "Let me think about it. I want to talk to Linnea." A week later, he called me back and said: "I'm just not ready to be as honest as I know you're going to want me to be." I tried to fight him for a minute. I knew it was a lost cause. He said: "I really feel bad about this. Is there something I can do? Can I get you tickets or something?" I said: "It's OK, Dean, I don't need any tickets."

I remember another story, from 1989 or '90. I was talking with Dean at Operation Basketball. We were talking about Lefty Driesell. I said: "Well, I know you've hammered him through the years, but he did put the first loss on you in the Dean Dome." And he goes: "It's funny you should mention that. Dave Gavitt and I were watching tape of that game this summer. Did you know (Len) Bias double-dribbled on that steal from Steve Hale?" First of all, I was wondering why he was looking at tape of that game. And I said: "Dean, Len Bias is dead and buried. Can't you let him rest in peace?" And he said: "Lots of dead men have double-dribbled." It was unbelievable.

We had two major problems. In '91, I wrote a column in *The National* after the ACC tournament final. The headline was: "Dean Smith, a winner and a whiner." It was an accurate headline. It wasn't like one of those headlines where you said: "I didn't write the headline. That's not what the story said." It was what the story said. He was going on nine years having not made the Final Four. That was the year they had the great freshman class with Montross and those guys that eventually won the national championship in '93. But I think as it got to be March, he was beginning to suspect that Duke was better than they were. Duke beat them twice in the regular season, and won the regular-season title.

At the ACC tournament that year, he was just wild, taking his little shots at everybody. He yelled at Dan Bonner about something Dan had said about a Carolina player, told him he said it because he was a dirty player when he was at Virginia. He refused to do any pre-game interviews with Jefferson-Pilot, because Jefferson-Pilot had no one working for them who was a Carolina graduate.

After they killed Duke in the final (96-74), he came in and the first thing he said was: "I just saw Mike (Krzyzewski) in the hallway. I asked him where we were going because I figured he had already talked to (Duke athletic director) Tom (Butters). Which is a direct shot, saying Duke has a guy on the committee, as if Jim Delany hadn't been chairman of the committee. He was obsessed with that '89 thing, natural regions and all that: "I wish we could have played Minnesota." (Duke was assigned to the East Regional and two games at the Greensboro Coliseum that year, while North Carolina was assigned to the Southeast. Duke faced Minnesota in the regional semifinals and advanced to the Final Four. North Carolina played Michigan for the third straight year, and lost.) So I wrote this column saying it was beneath him, as one of the five greatest coaches of all time, to be so snippy. We had a problem there.

It was just one of those things that eventually went away. He was mad for a while. I didn't back down from anything I said. Roy Williams wrote me a long letter that summer about how much he respected both of us, and that he didn't want to see Dean and me fall out. Dean was the best at what he did, and he thought I was the best at what I did, blah, blah, blah. But it never reached the point where Dean and I sat down and thrashed it out. The next year when I saw him, we were cordial. And we just went on from there.

The second problem was over Rasheed Wallace. In '95, I was doing "Under The Boards" for ESPN2. I did an item in which I said that Rasheed was going to turn pro at the end of the year, and that the Carolina coaches were simply worried about keeping him eligible until the end of the season, because they knew he was going.

Apparently, Rasheed's mother went crazy. She thought the leak came from directly inside the Carolina basketball office, which it didn't. It came indirectly. It came from a Carolina person, but not from somebody inside the office. She apparently screamed and yelled at Dean. And Dean later told me that Mitch Kupchak told him that I had said in the same little item that Rasheed had some Derrick Coleman in him. Dean said that really ticked him off. What I did say was that Wallace would probably be the first player chosen in the draft, except there are some scouts on some teams who think he has a little Derrick Coleman in him, and that might drop him to three or four. He eventually was the fourth player chosen.

Jackie Wallace, I guess, started calling newspapers ripping me, including in Philadelphia, Rasheed's hometown. Some reporter in Philadelphia called Bill Guthridge for a comment, because he was in charge of quote-unquote, "academics." Dean returned the call. He said something to the effect of: "John's just saying this because he's a Duke graduate, and he's out to get Carolina."

That infuriated me. What further infuriated me was the press down there, all those Carolina guys. They hadn't reported anything on my initial report, which was fine, no big deal. But they all went with these huge stories, Dean ripping me, Jackie Wallace ripping me. Not one of them ever called me for a comment. Rasheed said it was me trying to get my 15 seconds of fame. I was just getting killed. The guy in Philadelphia was the only one who called me for comment.

Then, Carolina comes up to play at Maryland, and I'm standing in the runway before the game, and there's a tap on my shoulder. I turn around, and it's Dean. He puts out his hand and says: "I owe you an apology." I say: "You're damn right you do." And he said: "I never should have said that the story had anything to do with you going to Duke. I know you better than that." I said: "That's what really upset me. We've known each other for 20 years. When have I ever done anything based on where I went to school? You and I have had our disagreements, but they're only because I'm a reporter, and you're a coach." He said: "You're right. I'm really sorry."

Then he told me about how he got upset because of what Mitch had told him. I told him exactly what I said. And he said: "Oh, that's a lot different, isn't it?" And he asked if there was anything he could do to help. I said: "Yes, if you would make the apology public, that would help." He said he would do it after the game. I said that would be great, very nice.

They lost the game to Maryland. It was a nine o'clock game. He came in. They were rushing to get out of there. He talked about the game. I figured that he forgot the apology. I didn't expect him to do it. I walked out of the interview room, and Jim O'Connell (of the Associated Press) came running after me. He told me that Dean wanted me to get back in there. I went back in there and Dean said: "John, you left before I had a chance to apologize." I said: "I'm sorry, Dean, I thought you forgot."

I can't remember exactly what he said, but basically he said: "I want to apologize to John because I said that he went with the story because he was a Duke graduate. I've known him long enough to know that's not true. We think Rasheed will be back next year" —a non-denial denial—"but I know John didn't say that because he went to Duke." He said: "John, you cheer for all the ACC teams, right?" And I said: "Absolutely, Dean." I thanked him, told him it was very nice to do. None of the papers in North Carolina reported the apology. But that's not Dean's fault. He did the right thing. From that point forward, we were fine.

He was, for him, relatively cooperative when I did "March to Madness." (Smith and North Carolina State's Herb Sendek were the only ACC coaches to deny Feinstein total access.) He gave me a lot of interview time. But the last time I went down to see him after the season was over, it was classic Dean. I called up, made an appointment, came down and went to lunch. As we're driving to lunch, he says to me: "Are you still doing that book?" And I said: "Dean, why do you think I'm here? I mean, I really like you a lot, but I wouldn't come down just to have lunch with you." But he was pretty good about it, and dropped a number of hints during the year about retiring. When he did quit, it wasn't like a shock. I didn't have to rewrite anything. I just had to add on to the epilogue. The hints were there in the book because of stuff he had said.

He always saw me as a Duke person. He couldn't get away from that. He would always say to me: "You've always been fair to us—for someone from Duke." He couldn't help himself. Once, he got really mad at me. There was a game in Durham, and the students were really funny that particular night. They held up signs that said: "Please miss," instead of waving their arms. They gave Dean a dozen roses before the game. Instead of chanting, "Bullshit," they chanted: "We beg to differ." After the game, he looked at me and said: "You think they're funny, don't you?" I said: "I do. They are funny, Dean." And he said: "Aw, that's because you're from Duke." And I said: "Dean, I really think there are people who aren't from Duke who think they're funny, I really believe that."

To me, the first sentence in the history of coaches is John Wooden. I leave Rupp out, because Rupp stood for everything that was wrong about college basketball. But the next sentence, take your pick, it's Dean Smith, it's Bob Knight, it's Mike Krzyzewski. I think those are the three guys. History will ultimately judge the order, but Dean is right there.

Chapter Ten

ON THE
PERIMETER

TOM KONCHALSKI

Konchalski, a recruiting analyst based in New York, is editor of the
HSBI Report.

I met him mainly through Five-Star basketball camps. He'd come occasionally. Part of his allure, part of the Dean Smith mystique, is that he wasn't always there. It's not as if you became good friends with him. Part of his allure in recruiting was that when he showed up at a summer camp, it was almost like Zeus coming down from Mt. Olympus.

Because of the expression, "familiarity breeds contempt," he never made himself that familiar. His assistants would be out there seeing kids during the summer. He would show for one of the Orange-White classics at Five-Star, or show up at Nike camp maybe for one day or so. It was a special occasion when he came. You realized you were in the presence of basketball royalty.

It wasn't always that way. Obviously, when he took over for Frank McGuire, he had some lean years. But for two or three years in the early '80s, every player they brought in on a paid visit, they signed. The standard line was that they used to call recruits collect. It wasn't just true. But it just showed that it was almost an honor to be recruited by North Carolina. Part of it was that they were selective. They wanted a certain type of kid.

Anyone who ever played for Dean Smith speaks of him in tones of reverence. He had a great relationship with his players. No one ever badmouths him. Even some of the kids who transferred—there weren't a whole lot—didn't have bitter things to say about him the way some of (Bobby) Knight's players did about him. He treated players the right way. He really helped them. He was like a one-man placement agency, if you wanted to stay in coaching, play in the pros—and beyond that, if you wanted to find employment outside of basketball.

North Carolina represents the highest standard of excellence in the sport. It's a program that does things the right way. It's not going to cheat. And no matter how big a player is who goes there, he's not going to be bigger than the program, as we witnessed with Michael Jordan. You're going to be part of something bigger than you.

The priorities are set straight. The most important thing is to get an education, get a degree, represent the school well. When they start out with their conditioning program in the fall, they're not talking about winning national championships. They're talking about making a certain time in the mile, or running a sprint in 17 seconds. The emphasis is on winning all these little battles before you can even dream about winning the war. You're putting one foot in front of the other, building in a developmental sense.

That's why they have such success. They don't go in there filling kids' heads with dreams. They go in and demand one hundred percent excellence and effort. And when they get that from good players, success is going to result.

HOWARD GARFINKEL

Garfinkel is the founder of the Five-Star Camp.

My first real recollection would be when he came to the camp to lecture. I'd say it was probably 1969. He came to Camp Rosemont in Honesdale, Pennsylvania. He did a shooting lecture. I have pictures of it still.

What I remember more than the lecture is that he came into the kitchen—he hadn't eaten in a couple of hours. We made him a cheese-and-tomato sandwich. You would have thought he was eating a sirloin steak.

That's him. He was so appreciative. The kitchen wasn't open. I was embarrassed. I felt lousy about it. The guy in the kitchen threw together a little sandwich, and he treated it like a sirloin. He really enjoyed it.

He did two lectures at the camp over the years. Of course, he came to camp sessions to watch the players. I've been very fortunate—more than 50 of our Five-Star kids went to Carolina. He always gave us credit for finding players for him, whether it was true or not.

He'd come every summer. (Eddie) Fogler would come first, or Bill Guthridge. Dean would come in for the All-Star Games. I asked him for tickets one time. I sat two feet from the Carolina bench. He just treated people like they were kings. That was his secret. He knew how to treat people. He was always nice.

One thing the assistants did—which most of the others didn't do—was go to the stations in the morning, the teaching stations. I don't know if it was Dean's orders or not, but Fogler and Bill Guthridge always went to see the drills, how the kids went through the stations. That's how kids practice. You'd watch how they'd practice. Carolina was always there the whole time. Now they all are. Carolina started that trend.

The year Michael Jordan came? Roy Williams was a third-string assistant, like a graduate assistant then. He called me up and said: "We have a player. We want to see how good he is. Would you take him for one of the weeks? We'd like to see him against good players. But don't take him the best week—we're not sure he's that good."

I said I'd love to help, that we'd take him for two weeks, and he could work as a waiter. The first week he tied another player for the outstanding player of the session. He was MVP of the All-Star Game, won like five different things. The second week he would have won 'em, but he got injured.

I read that Dean was irritated with Roy for exposing him. I don't believe that version of it at all. Roy Williams said that he was going to come, anyway. His coach was about to call me, ask me to take him. He was coming anyway; why not have Carolina get the brownie points? He wanted to see him against better players. I remember the conversation like it was yesterday.

We smoked a lot, Dean and I. We always said we were going to quit together. He sent me some Nicorette gum. He was using it, and I should use it. He used it, and quit. I didn't use it, and didn't quit. But he never told me he quit. I was kidding with him, faked being mad at him. I might have quit too if he had told me, and then I would get to live forever, too. The man is definitely going to live forever.

We're not close personal friends. I'm not going to say that. But everything I've had to do with him in the 30 years I've known him has been positive. There's never been a negative moment.

BOB VALVANO

Valvano is the brother of the late Jim Valvano, the coach at North Carolina State from 1980-81 to 1989-90. A former college basketball coach, he is now the color analyst on University of Louisville telecasts, and a host of "Game Night" on ESPN Radio.

I talked with Jim about his relationship with Dean a couple of times. It was always something very positive. He was determined to do that largely because Dean and Norm Sloan kind of had a rough relationship. Jim didn't want anything to do with that.

I remember when Jim was really seriously thinking about taking the UCLA job. One of the guys he talked to about it was Dean Smith. That kind of surprised me. I didn't know coaches in the same league discussed career decisions like that. But he had a lot of respect for Dean, his longevity in the game. They had a long talk about it on a plane. That was kind of neat.

Not that Dean was old, but Jim wasn't a contemporary of his. Jim was a fan of Dean's before he started coaching in the ACC. He looked up to him as an elder statesman. That made a difference in their relationship. Not that Jim didn't work his butt off trying to beat him. But in a situation like that, with the UCLA job, he would listen to Dean. Dean had been at it a lot longer.

I remember the last game at Carmichael. It was against State. When the game ended, Jim ran to the referee, took the basketball away and ran to the other end of the court dribbling. He wanted to be the last one to make a basket at Carmichael. He did it, and then he flipped the ball to a ballboy and ran off. It was on TV. I said: "What the hell is he doing?" He told me, "I wanted to be the answer to a trivia question." That shows some reverence for a guy's program.

Jim Valvano

A lot of people talk about the (public-relations) activities Jim did. One of the reasons was Dean. The guy ran a program as well as you can run it. The thing they did in the summer, bringing everyone back; a guy pointing to a teammate after getting a good pass—those kinds of things, they did so well. Who could do it better? But one of the things Dean didn't like a lot was public speaking. Jim thought that the only way to compete was to get out there, make people at least know him. People thought he was looking for money, doing commercials, those kinds of things. Jim just wanted people to see him, to give him a level to compete with Dean.

I do know this: Most of the writers in Carolina went to Carolina— they've got the bigger journalism school. It would drive all the other coaches crazy. When push comes to shove—I know it might be hard for some coaches to believe this—but writers are human beings. Sometimes rooting interests come into play. The coaches would get together at the ACC meetings and say: "See what this guy wrote? See what that guy wrote?" If Dean exploded a bomb, they'd talk about what a wonderful job he did clearing park land.

PAM VALVANO

Valvano is the widow of Jim Valvano.

The thing I remember most is coming into the league, and the respect Jim had for a man who had accomplished so much. Of course, the rivalry was there between State and Carolina. But the fans, the people who had grown up in the state, felt it a lot more than Jim or I did. We were the new kids on the block.

Jim had so much respect for him. He definitely wanted to beat him, but he wanted to beat everyone. It was different for North Carolina State fans—Carolina was the biggest rival. If you beat them, it could make your season. Jim was very frustrated that so many years went by, and we couldn't get a break, couldn't win a game against them (Valvano lost his first seven games to Carolina, and did not win in Chapel Hill until his tenth and final season at North Carolina State). I remember the first time we beat them. It was a great feeling.

Recruiting was also very tough. Although North Carolina State had won a national championship in 1974, it had been a long time. Kids were dying to go to Carolina. Dean might have all these All-Americans sitting on the bench, but they were there to wear the Carolina blue. They were at the school they wanted. They had the coach they wanted. Dean was Dean. Dean was the man.

It was very important to Jim to have a good relationship with Dean. You're filling somebody else's shoes (Norm Sloan's). But what was then was then. You wanted to establish your own identity. Dean had a lot of respect for Jim. He used to laugh at Jim all the time. He thought he was funny, because Jim was funny. Dean got a kick out of him. They were very, very different people. Dean was an older, established coach who had proven himself. Jim had yet to prove who he was, where he was going. They were on different pages. But the mutual admiration was there.

When Jim got sick, certainly it was not the same between Jim and Dean as it was for Jim and Mike (Krzyzewski). Jim and Mike had a shared background. They played against one another in college, coached against one another at several different schools. Jim happened to be at the hospital where Mike was (Duke). They were the same age. It was a natural fit. We had arrived at the same time. As far as all the other coaches in the ACC, they were all very supportive. They all felt terrible. They all would call and ask how he was doing. Dean, Bobby Cremins, Dave Odom—they all showed concern. Their hearts were all breaking.

Since then, Dean has come to the (Jimmy V Foundation) golf tournament every year, been very supportive. Anything he can do to help the foundation, he's always there. I have total admiration for him. I wouldn't hesitate to call him for anything I wanted. He's the kind of person who would do anything for us and the foundation. Anytime I see him, he's just wonderful. He always wants to know how the girls are. He's sincerely interested in how we're doing.

Chapter Eleven

FROM THE INSIDE

ROBERT SEYMOUR

Seymour was Dean Smith's pastor at the Binkley Baptist Church in Chapel Hill, North Carolina.

Dean Smith came into my life in 1959 or 1960, I'm not sure. I was pastor of a new congregation in Chapel Hill. Dean came here as an assistant coach. He was looking for a church home. He comes from an American Baptist background in Kansas. He felt that our new congregation could emerge into something similar to what he had known previously. He and his family became active members.

In the '60s, the church became very much involved in civil rights. Black students were beginning to come to the University, and we reached out to welcome them. The major concern of the community was having black students on the university campus in a town that was still segregated. We tried to effect a public accommodations ordinance, a municipal ordinance, prior to the federal government's legislation. We almost succeeded in doing that, but in the last analysis failed. There was what you would expect, the usual protests, picketing, marching and so on.

There were still about a dozen restaurants that were holdouts, and did not comply until they were forced to do so by the federal government. It was at that point that the deacons of our church—and Dean was one of them—began to test these restaurants to make sure they were willing to comply with the law. In those days, the basketball team was all white. They had their meals at the Pines restaurant. This was one of those segregated holdouts.

So it was very logical that Dean would go there, and he and I and a black student—I'm embarrassed that I don't remember the black student's name—went there together. After some hesitation, they opened the door and served us. The restaurant was open thereafter.

This was typical of Dean's willingness to be involved in the church, and his willingness to stick his neck out on some controversial issues. But that incident has been magnified out of all proportion to its significance. This was a very quiet thing. There was no fanfare. There were no cameras there. It was part of a much larger effort. There were other teams going out to restaurants all over town at the same time. I've read some press reports that seem to suggest that Dean single-handedly integrated Chapel Hill. That's absurd. But he certainly did lend his influence and his name and his presence to the effort. That carried some weight.

Dean had a little anxiety about recruiting the first black (Charlie Scott). We talked about that. Of course, I encouraged him in doing that. It now seems strange to think that there was ever a time when there were not blacks on the team. My wife and I went to Alaska with the team (in November 1997). When the University of Alaska team came out on the floor, it seemed strange. They were all white. I thought: "Wow! I didn't know there were any of those left."

Later in the '70s he was willing to let his name be used in connection with the movement to abolish nuclear weapons—the nuclear freeze that people were advocating at that time. Another cause to which he is dedicated is the abolition of capital punishment. I work with an organization called People of Faith Against the Death Penalty. We try to get people who have some name recognition to lend their influence and support. Dean was one of the first to step forward and sign on.

(In November 1998) he and I went to see the governor together with a delegation from the North Carolina Council of Churches. We discovered, much to our surprise, that he had been corresponding with a man who was to be executed. We did not know that. That's why we asked him to go with us. We said: "Here's somebody you know. Would you go with us?" He was quite willing to go, though he made it very clear from the outset: "I'm going not because I know this man. I'm going as a matter of principle. I would go to protest any person's execution."

Dean is a very self-effacing person. He doesn't like to be out front. He tries to avoid the limelight, but he can't succeed in doing that. He always gives credit to other people. He can find something good to say about the worst of games. He has a wonderful way of perpetuating personal relationships. He's not interested in the players just while they're here. He follows their careers, counsels with them and is a lifelong friend of these young men who come here to play with him.

Perhaps his greatest achievement has been his insistence that all of these players get a college education. Even those who leave early and go pro are mandated by Dean to put in their contracts that they will come back and finish their educations. It's very impressive to see how these young men still have such high regard for Dean. He is a pivotal influence in their maturing, and their life and career.

There's a very winsome consistency of character. I knew him before the rest of the world did. I think he is essentially the same person today that I knew 40 years ago. He is a very generous man. He gives of his resources to many good causes. He's a strong supporter of the homeless shelter, the YMCA, Childhood Trust, which is an organization that works with sexually abused children. He's a good citizen of this community. Any cause that comes along, you can count on him doing his part.

JOHN LOTZ

Lotz was an assistant coach under Dean Smith from 1966 to '74 and became North Carolina's assistant athletic director for campus and community relations in 1979.

My brother was on the 1957 national championship team at North Carolina. He was captain in 1959, and I'd come through here. I met Dean, and I would visit with him. I was a pretty successful high-school coach (on Long Island), but I would say I basically got the job because he knew my family. He knew that I would be loyal. Loyalty was the key word. Besides everything else, that's what he was looking for. He thought he would get it from me, and he got it.

This was in 1966. He had been hung in effigy the year before. If he were coaching today, I don't know if he would be very much different. He would probably say that we had established a tradition. The things that we did then were things we did over and over and over again every five years. It has become Carolina basketball. If you played or coached here, you under-stood the basic facts—you were going to play unselfishly, and you were going to play hard.

In those days, it was a little bit different. He wasn't the big name that he was ten years later when he had All-Americans, all kinds of prestige. But I just knew he was going to be successful. If you spent any time with him, you knew that he had a great mind, a great basketball mind. And he had a great sense of humility. He wasn't in coaching to become Coach of the Year or get his name in headlines. If you would visit his home, he wouldn't have any trophies, any pictures, anything like that. He just stayed with his principles.

He really tried to put his talent in the types of offenses and defenses that would get the best team results.

I remember scouting Northwestern (in 1966-67). Kentucky beat 'em, 116-114. Dean said: "We'll play Kentucky to a 60-point game." We beat 'em, 64-56. Then we were playing NYU four nights later. He said: "We'll roll it up." And we scored 95. He could go look at film for three hours, and he would only give the players two minutes. He would have enough in his mind to give what he thought they should know. But on the sideline, he was thinking ahead. It was like Tom Landry, thinking ahead to the next play. His first couple of years, I think it would be normal that he'd feel pressure. I would say the last ten years of his coaching career, the pressure was off him. The only pressure was for himself. He wouldn't worry about alumni or what anyone else thought. He enjoyed the competition. He really liked it if it was tied with ten seconds to go. We'd be going nuts, but he would love it.

Nobody would know how many people he has helped. Nobody would know what he's done. No one deals with Dean's personal life but Dean. He doesn't do it for that recognition. He wouldn't want to say: "Well, I gave $10,000 to this organization, $20,000 to that organization." It's something we respect, his privacy in that area.

My father was a Baptist minister in New York. Dean comes from a Kansas background where both his mother and father were Baptists, and his mother was a church organist. They had a strong faith. Dean is not a legalist. He is not rigid. He is very tolerant, open-minded. He is a caring person. He truly believes and lives out his faith in how he deals with people.

He has been a great mentor to a lot of people. It's hard to realize how many phone calls he gets from players and coaches. He's just one of the kindest men I've ever known. He's not in awe of himself. At this time, I think he just doesn't understand why he's still famous. I think he thinks he's going to fade into the wild blue yonder. But he's going to be famous until the day he dies.

BILL GUTHRIDGE

Guthridge, a 1960 graduate of Kansas State, became an assistant coach under Dean Smith prior to the 1967-68 season and replaced him as head coach on October 9, 1997.

He went to the University of Kansas. So did my sister. They knew each other. They dated some—not a whole lot, but some. I met him through her. The first college basketball game I saw, he played in. I think I had maybe met him before that. I talked to him after the game. We followed each other through the years.

Bill Guthridge

We played back here in December of 1959 when I was a senior at Kansas State. We played N.C. State one night, North Carolina the next night. He was an assistant at Carolina. His wife was from Manhattan, Kansas; I became an assistant coach there. He'd come in the summer, and we'd play golf; we stayed in touch. When Larry Brown went to go play in the ABA, that summer I was coaching in Puerto Rico. He located me down there, wanted to know if I'd be interested in being his assistant. I was.

We grew up in the same environment. Both of his parents were teachers. My dad was a teacher, then a superintendent of schools. My mom was a teacher, although she didn't teach after I was born. We both had older sisters named Joann—spelled J-O-A-N. We do have similar backgrounds, but I don't know how much that really meant.

When I came here in '67 from Kansas State, I wanted to be a head coach. I thought it would be good training for me to get another philosophy. I had played for Tex Winter. I was an assistant to Tex Winter. I thought I'd be an assistant to Dean Smith for a few years, then become a head coach. That was my goal. Because of the success of the program, I had opportunities in the '70s, and turned down several jobs.

I did take the Penn State job (in 1978). It was never announced. My assistants were going to be George Karl and Mickey Bell. We had lost at the NCAA tournament in Phoenix, lost to San Francisco (68-64). I was going to tell the team after the game that I was leaving. I told Dean that I didn't want to tell them anything. I made the decision on the way back. I took the red-eye back. I just checked my bags to Chicago. I'd decide on the flight where I was going, Penn State or back here. I decided I was coming back here.

I never interviewed after that. I made a decision that I had the best job. I loved it here at Carolina. It was a great university. Dean Smith was great to work with. We had players who were enjoyable to be around. My family was happy. I thought: "Why leave such a good situation?" Dean has always treated me so great, just like everybody he's ever dealt with. You have loyalty to people like that. I certainly didn't stay around with the idea that I'd eventually be the head coach here. My goal was to retire when Dean did. I really thought Dean would go four or five more years. But that's not the way it turned out.

He told me every year for about the last ten to get ready. He always said that when October 15 came around, if he wasn't ready, wasn't excited about starting the year, he'd know it was time to retire. For about ten years, he would do that after the season was over. Usually as time went by, by the end of August, he had played enough golf, and was starting to draw up plays. The last year, it kept going. He kept saying: "I don't think I could do it." I really thought until the last couple of days that he would reconsider.

We had our annual get-together with coaches—Roy Williams, Eddie Fogler, Buzz Peterson, George Karl. He really enjoys that. I thought that might get the fire burning again. Then he went with the athletic director to see the chancellor. I knew at most two days before that it was going to happen.

I'm my own guy, but certainly there's a lot of him in me, working with him for so many years. He wanted me to think like I was the head coach in game situations, give him suggestions. For many years, I thought as a head coach. I'd give him suggestions. Some he'd accept. Some he'd turn down. That was a real advantage through those years. In the planning of practice, the execution of practice, he was always in charge. But I felt that I had a lot of input. I want to do the same things that he has been doing. I have the same philosophy.

He's been great to me as head coach. He never has said to me: "Why don't you do this?" or: "Why don't you do that?" If I go ask him, he'll give me his opinion. It's kind of different. The roles are reversed. It used to be that he wanted my opinion on things, then he'd make a decision. Now I'm asking his opinion on how to do things, and I make the decision. It was a lot easier making suggestions.

We've worked together for so long. I think it's a real asset. I'm glad to have him around.

PHIL FORD

Ford, the first freshman to start under Dean Smith, was a three-time All-American at North Carolina and the school's all-time leading scorer. He also was a member of Smith's 1976 gold medal-winning U.S. Olympic team and was named 1979 NBA Rookie of the Year.

He joined the North Carolina coaching staff in 1988.

Coach Smith was one of the very few coaches who came to my home and didn't make any promises about playing time. As a matter of fact, the first time we met, the term "basketball" didn't come up until a full hour into our conversation. We talked about being the best citizen you can be. We talked about race relations. We talked about poverty. We talked about so many things about life instead of basketball. That was very impressive to my family and to me.

Other coaches were telling me that the ball was going to be mine for four years. I was going to start my first game. But Coach Smith told me I might have to play junior varsity. At first, that caught me by surprise. My mom and dad sat me down and told me he was being honest with me because he didn't know how I would do at the collegiate level. On the good side of that, if I did choose the University of North Carolina and happened to be playing a lot, he wouldn't be promising my playing time to another high-school player.

As a point guard, you tried to think along the same lines as Coach Smith, as far as making certain calls on the basketball court. The point guard was never in charge here. Coach Smith was always in charge. As a player, I was taught by Coach Smith what calls to make in certain situations. Later in my career, sometimes I'd be making a call, and he'd be making the same call.

Four Corners? That was just an offense to us. I've heard people say, we won a certain game, but we had to play Four Corners. Four Corners was legal. It was part of the game. I don't think people understood that it's not easy to hold the basketball. I got a lot

Phil Ford

of undue credit for that offense. You had to have five very good ball-handlers on the court, five very good free-throw shooters, five very good defenders. It was an offense we practiced, another brainchild of Coach Smith. He was using our team's athletic ability to the best we could to win basketball games. He was using our strength.

It was a way to win. What made the Four Corners work is that it was a snowball effect. We'd tease, as I liked to call it, run some time off the clock and either get fouled or get an easy layup. The other team would come down and take a quick shot. We'd get the rebound, come down and tease again, maybe get another free throw or layup. The other team would come down and take a quick shot. That was the snowball effect. Before you knew it, we had a comfortable lead.

Whether you like North Carolina or not, you have to admit that he's the greatest mind to ever coach basketball. His vision, and his ability to break down other teams, visualize what other teams were trying to do—and the things we had practiced to offset that—was just unbelievable. He was always doing things strategically. The thing that he relayed to us was his calmness. He always says that players won games, and that he lost games. But as players, each of us always knew that if we could execute the things Coach Smith said, we were going to win. We didn't always execute—there were other players out there. But Coach Smith knew exactly what it took to beat anyone.

As an assistant, I remember playing Cincinnati in the regional final the year we won the national title (1992-93). There was like one second left on the clock. Coach Smith drew up a play. The defense came out and was set. The defense called time out. But Coach Smith got an opportunity to see how their defense was set. When our guys were running over to the bench, I kind of heard him say to himself: "We got 'em." He drew up a play. Derrick Phelps was supposed to throw Brian Reese the ball, lob it right in front of the goal. He told Brian: "I promise you, you'll be open. Go up, just tap it in the goal. You don't have time to come down. But I guarantee you, you'll be open." We ran the play. Brian came down with the ball—I guess he was so shocked he was open. Then he went up and missed a dunk. The game went into over-time, and we won (75-73).

It's hilarious to me that people tend to talk about the North Carolina system. I don't think there's a system here at North Carolina. With a system, I tend to think of something that doesn't bend, something that's very rigid. There's definitely a philosophy here of how we like to play basketball, how the game should be played. But you're talking about someone who coached during the '60s, during the '70s, during the '80s, during the '90s. You get a different type of mentality among student-athletes. You get different types as far as physical ability is concerned. For someone to be successful through those different periods of time is just unbelievable to me. At one time, he was dealing with young men who were concerned about the Vietnam War. At another time, he was coaching men who were listening to LL Cool J.

Race relations was one of the things we talked about the first time we met, although at that time Coach Smith did not mention to me that he had sat in certain restaurants with African Americans to integrate those restaurants. That's something I learned later. He's so humble. He would never brag on himself. But that was a big deal. Growing up in North Carolina, Charlie Scott was my hero. I think Charlie Scott was a hero not only to a lot of African American kids, but to a lot of white kids as well. He was such a great player. And I remember in junior high school my teachers bragging on him about how he was a good student. But to be like Charlie Scott, you had to make good grades, too.

Later on, I came to understand about Coach Smith's role in integrating Chapel Hill. That means a lot to me. In the '60s, it wasn't cool. That was a stance that wasn't very popular. But if you know Coach Smith, he really doesn't take a stance because it's popular. He takes a stance because it is right. And if he believes something is right, he's really strong about that feeling.

We stayed very close after I went to the NBA. I did go through some very tough times personally. Coach Smith was there for me when I went through the bad times as well. That's what a lot of people don't understand. They think Coach Smith is just there for the good times, just there for the young men that make All-America, for the ones who play professional basketball. Coach Smith is there for us when we go through the good times, but also the bad times, too.

He called me every day (when Ford was battling alcoholism). He learned more about my disease, helped me to deal with it. I had been out of the program six or seven years. For him to have that much interest in me, my personal life, it made me feel very good. He helped me recover.

EDDIE FOGLER

Fogler, a point guard at North Carolina from 1967-68 to 1969-70, returned to work under Dean Smith as a graduate assistant in 1971, then became a full-time assistant in 1973. He was named head coach at Wichita State in 1986, Vanderbilt in 1989 and South Carolina in 1993.

Recruiting for Coach Smith was easy. Selling him was a piece of cake. There was a lot of jealousy of North Carolina's success, jealousy of our ability to recruit. We didn't get everyone we wanted. But we certainly had a very good percentage return on the student-athletes we recruited. We didn't get Ralph Sampson after recruiting him for two years. We didn't get Danny Ferry. We lost some along the way. But we got our share.

I remember being in Danny Ferry's home, recruiting Danny. His father, Bob, was the general manager of the Washington Bullets. His wife, Rita, was there. And I remember Bob saying to Coach Smith: "I've been in the NBA. I talk to just about everyone who played for you. And I can't find one guy who doesn't worship you, think you're the best."

Then Bob said: "But you know what? That sucker is going to be out there one day. And I'm going to find him." Bob was kidding. What he was really saying, in front of his son, was: "I can't believe how respected you are by the players who played for you." It blew his mind.

A lot of people are enjoyed the Lakers' downfall in 1999. A lot of people like it when the Yankees lose. The people on the outside who had a hard time with North Carolina's success wanted to think it wasn't true—the family atmosphere, the almost-unanimous respect for the coach, the university and the program. But down deep, they knew. And that made them even more jealous. They had a hard time coming to grips with the fact that he was getting so many good players, and they all worshiped him.

I went to play for Coach Smith in 1966. There was a track record of kids from New York going to North Carolina. I had heard about that. But that was a very small part of it. I went to the North Carolina basketball camp the summer before my senior year of high school. I was in Chapel Hill for a

Eddie Fogler

week. That pretty much made my decision about where I wanted to go to college. I liked the low-key approach, the first-class manner in which Coach Smith ran the program, the fact that my parents were very approving, the fact there was tradition, the school, the campus—the entire first-class manner with which Coach Smith recruited me.

There was never a point where he wasn't going to call or write or be back in touch. He was always on time. He always followed through in terms of what he said he would do in the recruiting process. Players came to understand very quickly, you could always count on what he tells you. You learn that he's incredibly dependable, reliable, professional, confidential. As you mature, you realize what an incredible man he is. He cares about your personal life and basketball career. You know he'll be with you forever.

The adjustment my freshman year was not so much to him as it was to college basketball. We had freshman teams then. Larry Brown was my freshman coach. The work and conditioning involved, the intensity level, the physical nature of the game—it was a rude awakening for me, as it was a rude awakening for everyone. That is very vivid. When I got there, it became quite apparent that the best way to get playing time was to know what to do. Knowing how to play was very important.

I was a freshman with Charlie Scott. It was certainly a unique situation. I can remember being at other schools where Charlie was not well received. I can recall a number of times where Charlie and Coach would go off to the side and visit. I have memories of my freshman team reunion a few years back. Charlie came back, and I wish I could have tape-recorded what he said about what Coach meant to him, and what the University meant to him.

It was a very interesting time at North Carolina. Chapel Hill had a black mayor in the 1960s—Harold Lee. Coach Smith was one of the first to integrate. He has always been at the forefront, working with people of different races, different religions, different backgrounds. He doesn't see color. He just sees people.

Like most coaches, he mellowed somewhat as the years went on. We used to kid him that he didn't run the later teams as hard as he did the ones from the early years, when the program started to take off. My former players tell me the same thing. You get that way as you get older. And kids today are different.

He would periodically ask: "Eddie, what do you want to do when you get out?" I said: "Coach, I'd like to get into coaching." I always had that in my mind. I went to DeMatha (Maryland) H.S. as an assistant for a year. But Coach Smith always took care of his own first. He gave me a chance to finish my master's and become a graduate assistant. And when John Lotz became the head coach at Florida (in 1973), the timing worked out great for me to move up and become a full-time assistant.

I remember the 1977 final against Marquette. It was an interesting game. First of all, Phil Ford was hurt. That was a huge negative for us. He had hyperextended his elbow in the regional final against Kentucky at College Park. He didn't have the ability to do his thing. I can still remember Mike O'Koren getting a defensive rebound all by himself, and the ball slipping out of his hands. That was a pet peeve of mine—they always used new balls for the Final Four. It was just one of those games. But I really thought we had the better team.

The thing I recall about the '82 final was how Coach Smith was so incredibly calm, under control emotionally, prepared to coach that team. He had been to the Final Four so many times, and had not yet won a national championship. But he did not get overly wound up or emotionally involved with that. He understood it was a lot more difficult to get to the Final Four as many times as he had than it was to win a national championship. He was very excited when we won, very emotional, very happy—mostly for his players.

My feelings for him have never changed. I talked to Coach Smith before I went to Wichita State. I talked to him before I went to Vanderbilt. I talked to him before I went to South Carolina. I respected him enough and trusted his judgment enough to discuss those situations with him. But they've been my decisions. Since I've been a head coach, he probably has called me more than I've called him, just to see how I'm doing. But I don't call him unless I'm really struggling with a decision. I'm a decent problem-solver. The only time I called him this year was when we had to decide how long to suspend a player. I talked to him, and I also asked Roy Williams how to handle it.

I wanted him to break (Adolph Rupp's) record. My feeling was: "As soon as you break the record, I don't care if you walk out the next day. I'm selfish enough to say that I wanted to play for the winningest coach in the history of college basketball." All of us felt the same way. I told him: "I want you to break that record, and the next day you can walk out into the sunset and say: 'Hi ho, Silver.'"

He always said when October came around and he didn't have the desire to put in everything he had, that's when he knew he would get out of coaching. This is total conjecture, but he took each October one by one to see how he felt about the upcoming season. He said at his press conference that he was retiring because of April, May, June, July, August and September—all the speaking engagements, all the alumni, all the players and coaches he helped to get jobs, being in the public eye.

I don't think coaching was the major factor. It was the off-season, the demands on his time, the 100 to 200 people he continues to help. My opinion was that he shouldn't have to speak anywhere, shouldn't have to recruit—he could just coach. But that's not him. He's a very hands-on person. He was going to continue to work, and not let anything through the cracks.

There's no one in my life that I've respected more. There's no one whose judgment I trusted more. There's no one else who has done as much for me as Coach Smith.

MATT DOHERTY

Doherty played at North Carolina from 1980-81 to 1983-84 and was a sophomore on the '82 team that won Dean Smith's first national championship. He spent seven years as an assistant to Roy Williams at Kansas before being named head coach at Notre Dame at the age of 37 on March 30, 1999.

I told (Notre Dame) in the interview that I felt I owned the rights to a Dean Smith franchise. Just like McDonald's is successful wherever it ends up, Dean Smith's former players and former coaches are usually successful. There's a system in place that is highly effective. I definitely talked about that.

Coach Williams and I would talk about Coach Smith in different ways. Every once in a while during practice, Coach Smith would catch his toe on the ground. He'd be walking, and stumble a little bit. Guys would notice, and chuckle to themselves. Once in a while, Coach Williams or I would do the same thing in practice. We'd look at each other and think: "It's Coach Smith all over again!"

You start finding out that you're saying some of the things your parents told you, stuff that used to drive you crazy. I'd tell our players: "Turnovers only happen because of carelessness or selfishness." Coach Smith used to tell me that all the time.

My first memory of him is from the 1976 Olympics, when there were four Olympians from North Carolina, coached by Coach Smith and Coach Guthridge. Then, in '77, they went to the Final Four, and I fell in love with Mike O'Koren. I was in ninth grade. I always wanted to be 6-foot-7, and able to play many positions. Mike O'Koren was from Jersey. I was from New York. I even wore number 31 in high school.

The first time I met Coach Smith is when he came into my home on the official visit. I just thought he was very unassuming, very down-to-earth, very humble and kind. My mom loved him. She felt comfortable that he would take care of her son.

I visited Duke, then Virginia, then North Carolina. I was actually going to visit Notre Dame, too. When I came back home from North Carolina and landed at LaGuardia Airport, my mom was there to greet me. She said right away, without me saying a word: "You're going there, aren't you?" I said: "How do you know?" She said: "I could see it in your face."

At first, it was difficult being away from home. My roommate, Jimmy Braddock, was from Chattanooga, Tennessee. When I first met him, it looked like someone had punched him in the face. But I realized he had a dip of tobacco inside his lower lip. It was tough at first. But once the running program started, once practice started, your four years just blow by.

I remember waking up in my room the day of the (1981) NCAA final and hearing that Reagan was shot. I wasn't sure if we were going to play or not. I remember James Worthy

Matt Doherty

getting his third foul, and I didn't think it was a good call. We were in good position, then all of a sudden, we lost a lot of ground. I remember that Indiana's pressure defense was incredible. And Isiah Thomas just went berserk. It was very disappointing (North Carolina lost, 63-50), but that was my freshman year. I was stupid enough to think we'd get back there and win it—and we did the next year.

Our goal every year was to win the national championship. To have that as a goal, and to accomplish it in 1982, was very satisfying. Jimmy Black was our verbal, vocal leader. James Worthy was our playing leader. James was the man. But everyone was so unselfish. No one cared who scored. That came from Coach Smith and the type of players he recruited. He always preached that no one remembers who led the nation in scoring, but everyone remembers who won the national championship. If the team wins, everyone wins. And if the team loses, only a couple of guys get recognition.

Look at that team. Worthy averaged 15 or 16 points per game. Sam Perkins averaged about 14, Jordan about 13, Black and I about nine apiece. I remember playing N.C. State in the ACC tournament. They played a triangle-and-two. I think it was against James and Sam. James came to me and said: "I'm going to find you. Just shoot the ball." That gave me a lot of confidence. It was just fun basketball.

We all wanted to win for Coach Smith. What was the only thing you could knock him on? That he hadn't won a national championship. We all knew how lucky you had to be in college basketball to win a national championship—one loss, you're out. Coach Williams would talk about how Michael Jordan and the Bulls got to lose two games (in the NBA Finals), and still won the world championship in his final season. But in college basketball, you're not allowed to lose.

I remember visiting the Raleigh jail that same year. We went to the jail because Coach Smith wanted us to realize how fortunate we were, realize that you have to pay the consequences for the mistakes you make—and also to put smiles on the prisoners' faces. I think that's the only time I ever saw Coach Smith intimidated. A pretty mean-looking guy looked down and said: "I recognize you." Coach Smith wanted to get out of there.

During the scrimmage, we were surrounded by prisoners. A guy sitting behind the bench tapped James (Worthy) on the shoulder. He said: "Hey, James, remember me? I went to high school with you."

The loss to Indiana in the second round of the NCAA tournament my senior year was the most devastating loss of my athletic career. We were the best team in the country that year. We had suffered some injuries late in the year. Brad Daugherty had dislocated fingers. Kenny Smith had a broken wrist. The injuries broke our rhythm a little bit. We were 21-0. Kenny Smith broke his wrist against LSU (on January 29). Then we lost at Arkansas (on February 12). Then we lost to Duke in the ACC tournament.

Kenny came back the last week of the regular season, and he was playing pretty well. We had Indiana down big. (Steve) Alford got open shots, and knocked 'em down. It was devastating. That was probably the best team I ever played on. You could make a case that it was the best team ever at Carolina. Because we didn't win it, people don't remember it as such. But you were talking about six guys who played in the NBA (Jordan, Perkins, Daugherty, Smith, Dave Popson and Joe Wolf), two coaches (Doherty and Buzz Peterson) and a doctor (Steve Hale). You had a very smart team, a very deep team, a very talented team.

I remember when Coach Smith retired. We would go down to Chapel Hill each fall to talk basketball—George Karl, Larry Brown, Roy Williams and others. But that time, there wasn't a whole lot getting done. We had some free time. Something was going on. I didn't know what.

It turned out there was free time because Coach Smith was telling everyone he was retiring. I remember Coach Williams saying: "We've got some free time. What would you like to do?" I said two things: "I'd like to go to Carmichael. And I'd like to walk on campus." I don't think I had done that since graduating.

I remember walking on campus thinking to myself about how lucky I was at age 17 to make a really great decision to go to North Carolina. This place, these people, impacted my life in such a positive way. Without going to North Carolina, playing for Dean Smith, working for Roy Williams, I don't get the Notre Dame job.

I once said: "I honestly don't believe Coach Smith ever does anything wrong." I don't think he ever has done anything wrong. He's as close to perfect as I've seen, just an amazing man.

ROY WILLIAMS

Williams, a 1972 graduate of North Carolina, was an assistant coach under Dean Smith from 1978 to '88, when he became the head coach at the University of Kansas. He entered the 1999-2000 season with the highest winning percentage among active Division I coaches (.809).

I went to T.C. Roberson high school in Asheville, North Carolina. My high-school coach was a guy named Buddy Baldwin. Buddy played on the freshman team for Coach Smith at North Carolina, when he was an assistant to Frank McGuire. He was always a huge North Carolina fan.

I made a decision the summer between ninth and tenth grade that I was going to be a coach. My high school coach was extremely important to me, still is today. As it got close to the end of my high school education, I was trying to decide where I wanted to go. He was pushing North Carolina quite a bit.

He thought that if I wanted to get into coaching, I could make the freshman team at Carolina, get to know Coach Smith, learn something from Coach Smith about coaching that might help me later on. I was accepted there, got some scholarships—not athletic. But enough that I was able to afford to go.

I made the freshman team and played for Bill Guthridge. I wasn't good enough to continue playing for Coach Smith and Coach Guthridge. But they allowed me to come in and watch practices of the freshman team and varsity. I would sit there and take notes—I still have those notes today.

I was working in the intramural department. I was in charge of officials. We would play basketball at intramurals from four in the afternoon to ten at night. I'd make sure we had officials on every court, then watch 15, 20 minutes of varsity practice. I'd go back and check on intramurals, then go back and observe practice. Woollen Gym and Carmichael—there was only a wall separating the two.

My senior year, they wanted me to keep statistics—the points-per-possession statistic that Coach Smith talks to his team about at halftime, and that I still use today. I stayed an extra year getting my master's. I had done so much officiating; he asked me to work at the camp that summer. There were good prospects at the camp, including Phil Ford. They wanted someone to referee, and referee the right way. They asked me to come do that, and I did.

Joining the staff in 1978 was a big thing for me, but it was a difficult decision to leave Charles D. Swannanoa (North Carolina) High School. The position was part-time assistant. What that meant, in Coach Smith's words, was full-time work, part-time position. I took the job for $2,700. I was married, and had a one-year-old boy. We picked up and went to Chapel Hill. My wife

Roy Williams

didn't have a job. But the reason I did it was that I had complete faith in Coach Smith, complete faith it world work out.

In the early years, I was just in administration. I spent so much time going through past clippings and records, getting an idea how they recruited. At first, it was like research for me. At the same time, I was included in the staff meetings, the discussions about basketball, something a young former high-school coach could only dream about.

I worked as hard as Bill Guthridge and Eddie Fogler, and in some ways harder with the other things I did, selling calendars, things I had to do to make a living. In everyone's eyes, it was a full-time job. It just didn't have the title from the NCAA. During the summers, I would do a lot of different things, trying to make enough money to feed my family.

The reason I was hired was to have another guy on the road recruiting. The first two-and-a-half years I did that. Then the NCAA changed the rules, and part-time assistants couldn't recruit off-campus. I had the opportunity to leave even as early as after my first year for a full-time assistant's spot. I didn't take it. I thought it was best to stay at North Carolina.

I never made a decision in my life based just on finances. For me, it was easy to pass up other assistant jobs. After my sixth year, I was offered a head-coaching position. After my eighth year, Eddie Fogler left to take the head-coaching position at Wichita State, and I moved up to full-time assistant.

I trusted Coach Smith completely. I had a lot of faith in him. And I had a lot of faith that regardless of what it took, I was going to make it work. He always told me to be patient. He always told me that if I wanted to leave, to make sure it felt right. It got to the point where I wouldn't take a job unless it truly did fit, unless it had Roy Williams' name on it. The last four years I was there, I turned down head-coaching positions every year. Then, all of a sudden, Kansas came along.

I didn't think I had any chance. The athletic director called Coach Smith, asking him to come back. Coach Smith told him since they had named a building after him at Carolina, it was better that he stayed. He gave him my name. I remember him coming back to my office saying: "Don't be concerned about it. At the end, I think you'll have a chance." He walked out of my office, and I said to myself: "Coach has finally lost it." I thought there was no chance whatsoever that I would get the job at Kansas.

Four weeks later, things started happening, and I thought maybe I had a chance to get the job. It was only because of Coach Smith. I was going to be patient, wait for the right job. But he allowed me to have that confidence, to be that patient. He gave us responsibility, made us feel part of the program. Every day, I felt I was taught how to be a head coach.

What made him so special was his concern for the entire program. That meant he was concerned about every facet of his players' lives. It was a lifetime commitment for him. His satisfaction came from trying to be the best, but not just winning and losing games. He wanted to help his players to improve mentally and physically as basketball players. But he also helped them prepare mentally, socially and academically, so they could be productive members of society.

When we won the national championship in 1982, he said that he didn't feel like he was a better coach because of it. It had never been his entire dream. Of course, it made him feel good. But it was not the ultimate game. The ultimate game was to help young people move on and become successful. That was more important to him than either of the national championships that he won.

Yes, he was very hard on Michael Jordan. A strong leader doesn't say: "We're going to treat everyone the same." A strong leader says: "We'll treat everyone fairly." It's a cop-out to say you're going to treat everyone the same way. Coach Smith didn't do that. Some of the little things that Michael would do, the slight mistakes, Coach Smith would make sure he pointed them out. He saw what Michael had, and wanted him to push to be the best that he could possibly be.

Every time you talk to Michael about his success in the NBA, he will point back to the emphasis on fundamentals he had at North Carolina. It gave him a good foundation. Then he was able to build on top of that. It's just like with a house—you've got to have a good foundation. Coach Smith gave him that foundation. Coach Smith also instilled in him the importance of team.

Not many people realize it, but Michael's senior year in high school, his team lost seven games. His great desire to win came after he got out of high school. His mother and father were a very important part of that. Coach Smith was a very important part, too. He pushed him to put the team first— he could still be an individual, but not if it detracted from the team. It was just like in the NBA when Michael had great individual performances. His greatest moments were when his individual performances helped his team win.

I could have stayed at North Carolina another 20 years and I would have been perfectly happy. But deep down inside, I always wanted to know if I could be a good head coach. In 1991, we reached the Final Four—and I had to coach against Coach Smith. I was able to block out the distraction. I was able to block it out because of what he had taught me in the past.

The goal was the game. Don't be distracted by everything else. Focus on the game. Once we got to the arena, I treated it like we were playing any other team, and any other coach. There were six days of media buildup because it was the semifinal. It was a huge distraction. But it didn't change anything with my team in practice that week. And once we got to the site, we treated it just like any other game.

I was surprised he got ejected—surprised, and very disappointed. It was a 50-50 thing. I was disappointed because I didn't think he deserved it. But I was also disappointed because I knew it would take away from a great win by my team (79-73). Coach Smith felt the same way. He said at his press conference that he didn't want what had happened to take away from a great performance by my team.

We speak every two or three weeks during the season, get together in the late spring to play golf. I enjoy playing golf with him. He has so much pride. I was a high-school golf coach. My handicap is lower than his. But he has so much pride, it's really hard to get him to take shots—he wants to beat you without taking shots.

I love being his partner when the two of us play someone else. He's going to find a way to get the ball in the hole. Sometimes, it's not going to look pretty. Sometimes, he'll be playing poorly. But if it's close at the end, he's going to hit a much better shot than he had the rest of the round. I've told him before that he's not a good chipper, and not a good putter. But from eight to ten feet on the last hole to win a match, if I can't take the shot myself, I'd rather have Coach Smith do it than anyone else.

It was a great experience having my son, Scott, attend North Carolina, but a very sad one, too. My son played J.V. the first two years. Coach Smith retired before his junior year. So, Scott didn't get a chance to be coached by Coach Smith. That was a dream for me—I would have loved for my son to have an opportunity to play for Coach Smith. Bill Guthridge is one of my favorite people in the world. It still worked out fine. But I would have loved for Scott to play his junior year for Coach Smith, and his last year for Coach Guthridge. It would have been the best of both worlds.

I wasn't really surprised that he retired. We had talked about it. The last three or four years, the stuff on the periphery took its toll on him. He still enjoyed the coaching profession, practice, working with the kids. But all the stuff on the periphery got to be a burden. The last three or four years, he would get invigorated over the course of the summer, re-enthused about coaching. But I saw that become more difficult for him to do.

My mother, my high-school coach and Dean Smith are by far the most influential people in my entire life—my mother and high-school coach when I was younger, Coach Smith once I got out of college. Even now, at 48, he's still the most influential person for me.

LARRY BROWN

Brown, the point guard at North Carolina from 1960-61 to 1962-63, was the first Tar Heel player to compete in the Olympics, winning a gold medal with the U.S. squad in 1964.

He later served as an assistant coach under Dean Smith before becoming a three-time All-Star in the ABA. He has spent the past 27 seasons as a head coach in the NCAA, ABA and NBA, winning an NCAA title at Kansas in 1987-88.

On May 5, 1997, he was named head coach of the Philadelphia 76ers.

We were at an outing in the summer of '98. I grabbed Michael Jordan. I said: "Michael, look. I've offered Coach Smith a job." The day he resigned, I offered him a job here as president or coach—whatever he would want to do, and I would do the other thing.

I was teasing Michael. I said: "Michael, if you come back, I'll get Coach to be coach, I'll be his assistant and you can play." Coach smiled when

I told him that. He always laughs. But it's an open invitation. If ever he gets antsy, he can have my job in a minute.

I was there the day he resigned and missed my first preseason game with the 76ers. I got crucified for that in Philadelphia. My first thought was that there was something physically wrong. I didn't know what to think. But one of the greatest feelings I've had in my life is to see the way Bill Guthridge has allowed Coach to continue to be part of it. And the way Coach manipulated it to where Bill couldn't turn it down, it's one of the most selfless stories you can ever have, from both people's perspectives. It's pretty wonderful.

Larry Brown

I wanted to be there. The first thing he said to me was: "Larry, I saw your practice. I don't have the same enthusiasm you have." That blew me away. He never lost his enthusiasm. The thing I still believe is that when he got close to the record, so much attention was being placed on him, he wasn't allowed to be the coach he wanted to be. His thing is, he wants to be with the kids, be teaching. He always put the program way ahead of himself. I really believe that got overbearing with everyone saying how many wins he had, how close he was.

At one time, when we were down meeting in the summer, there was some talk that he wouldn't continue to coach as he got close to the record, because of the attention that was placed on him. He always said all along: "The players made the program." I don't think any of the players have ever felt that. Eddie Fogler, Roy Williams and I, we all talked. I don't know if we could have talked him out of it, but I really felt that it was a legitimate thought by Coach Smith. And none of us wanted that. The bottom line is, all the players felt so special that they were part of it with him. We all wanted him to understand that.

I never wanted to see this man stop. He's the greatest coach. He was that program. Through the years, there has always been talk of who's going to replace Coach. I never wanted him to be in a position where he had to choose. I wanted him to stay forever, for him to do it his way. Even though I love that school so much, and it would always be an honor to coach there, it couldn't have worked out any better in my mind. The way the transition was made, the fact that the guy who is there now has the integrity and the character to allow Coach to do it on his terms with dignity, it's been phenomenal.

I was a junior at North Carolina when he became the head coach in 1961. Before that, he was an assistant. I used to practice with the varsity a lot as a freshman. Coach McGuire was on me hard. Coach Smith was there to kind of pick me up. He was a terrific complement to Coach McGuire. Coach Smith was really well organized, a detail kind of guy. Coach McGuire was a guy who kind of coached by the seat of his pants.

When Coach McGuire left, I was devastated. It had nothing to do with Coach Smith. It was just a devastating feeling. On top of that, Kenny McComb flunked out of school—he was probably the best guy we had left in the program. And Yogi Pateet became ineligible. Two guys who were going to start were taken away. Coach Smith couldn't recruit because there were a lot of NCAA sanctions. And a really good sophomore we had hurt his ankle the first game—Bryan McSweeney. Coach was left with virtually nothing.

That first year, it was kind of tough. Our schedule was cut. We had limited players. It wasn't what I envisioned my career at Carolina to be. My coach leaves, we had sanctions, we're not able to recruit. Dean inherited a really tough situation. My senior year, Billy Cunningham became eligible. It was fun, even though we still had limited recruiting ability and a limited number of games. We lost six games (finishing 15-6), but we were in every one of them.

He was a lot different than Coach McGuire. Coach McGuire could walk into a room with 100,000 people, and it would almost be like there was a spotlight on one guy. Coach Smith was just entirely different. He was hands on, hard working—and I'm not saying anything against Coach McGuire, I idolized him. But Coach Smith, he was from the Midwest. He demanded a lot from you. He expected a great deal. He had a different way of approaching things. But he was prepared for everything.

He's the biggest influence in my life—and I didn't realize it until I left. Coach McGuire was my hero, along with Jackie Robinson. Coach Smith, I didn't understand all the things he was teaching me until I got away. From the day I left Carolina, he never stopped trying to help me. I was drafted by the pros, but they said I was too small. If you tried out to be a pro then, you couldn't play amateur ball again—it's not like it is now. So, I didn't even try out.

I was supposed to go with Phillips 66 to play AAU ball, but it didn't work out. At the last minute, Coach Smith scrambled around and got me to Goodyear, another team. I was going to be a high-school coach. But I still thought I could play. He got me with Goodyear, and lo and behold, I ended up playing on the Olympic team because of that. Then he asked me to come back and coach with him. So my whole life changed.

I had interviewed for a high-school job. I even took an exam to go into the Navy or Marines. I didn't know what I was going to do. I really thought I could play in the NBA. So did he. Buddy Jeannette of the Bullets came to see me. I was sitting with Coach. I'll never forget it. Buddy said: "You're smaller than I thought you were when we drafted you." He said it in front of Coach Smith, "How are you going to guard Oscar Robertson, Jerry West or John Havlicek?"

I remember looking at Coach Smith and saying: "I looked in the paper, they were all averaging 30. I didn't think anybody was guarding them too well." Then, when I made the Olympic team, they invited me to come back. I had a commitment to Goodyear, so I stayed one more year. That's when Dean asked me to come back. That was like the greatest thrill. I think that's the number-one thrill I've had in basketball—being able to go back to the University of North Carolina, the place I graduated, and coach with the man who coached me.

I'll never forget something that happened my first year as an assistant. We went to the NCAA tournament at College Park. Coach took me up to a hotel. I walked into the room and Mr. Rupp was there, Mr. Iba, Coach McGuire, Ray Meyer, Pete Newell. They just were talking basketball, sharing ideas. I was just mesmerized. They all knew Coach Smith. They really liked him. You could see a real fondness for him.

My first year as an assistant, we had that really good recruiting class, which kind of established Coach. It was the first time we were allowed to go out and really recruit. My second year, I remember he sent me to Lebanon, Indiana, to see Rick Mount. You couldn't even get close to him. *Sports Illustrated* was in the stands, and I don't know how many coaches. I wasn't even allowed to say hello.

I got on the plane, and Coach called me and said: "Larry, I want you to go to Laurinburg Institute. There's a kid at Laurinburg who supposedly might be going to Davidson, but he hasn't signed, and I hear he's pretty good." The kid was Charlie Scott. I remember watching Charlie play. I called Coach Smith and said: "Coach, you're not going to believe me, but he's better than Rick Mount." And I thought Rick Mount was pretty special.

He allowed me to grow as a coach. A lot of us back then got to be freshman coaches in terrific programs. The head coach not only helped teach you, but he enabled you to learn by coaching your own team. Coach afforded me that opportunity. He was always there for me as a freshman coach, but never came to practice, never was standing over my shoulder. I didn't have to feel his presence, but I knew he was behind me.

And then, as an assistant coach, he never allowed me to miss a practice. A lot of guys, their assistant coaches are just recruiters. He wanted me to become a basketball coach first. That was all my responsibility, to learn how to coach and teach. That's where I'm most indebted to him.

When I left to play in the ABA, Coach said I had a terrific opportunity. He said: "Look, someday you're going to be too old to play. If you still can play, go ahead." That was hard. I knew at the time I wanted to be a coach. As a matter of fact, I was offered the Connecticut job when I was 25, while I was Dean's assistant. The AD at Connecticut was an ex-football coach at Carolina. Coach told me to take it. I just didn't feel mature enough.

It's funny how life happens, things happen. I enjoyed so much being an assistant at Carolina. But I just had a real desire to play. I played all the time. I was still getting better. The New Orleans team in the ABA asked Doug Moe to play. He was in Italy at the time. Doug said: "I'll play if you sign Larry." They didn't know if I could play or not. They just wanted Doug. But I ended up getting to play. And Coach told me that I could always come back and coach.

We always get together down at Carolina before the season starts. When we share ideas, I'll offer input. He always says: "I'm getting a lot out of it." I never once went there feeling I could give back anything, compared to what he has given me. Yet, he has a way of making you feel like you've added something. It's always been unique going back there in the summer. He's always opened it up for anybody involved with the program. And if I had guys who weren't involved in the program—John Calipari, R.C. Buford — he's always allowed me to bring them. I've been careful about imposing. In his own way, I know it's not something that he feels completely comfortable doing.

We have a responsibility to the other guys who are part of the program. I'll never forget this—I was trying to recommend R.C. for the Tulsa job. I've never asked Dean to do anything that he hasn't done for me. But his first response is always: "I've got to see if McAdoo wants it, Jimmy Black . . ." He'll go right down the list. Which is the way it should be.

Now my team practices down there. He allows us to run our training camp there. He's always involved. He comes to all of our practices. I always run into him and talk to him about things. He always acts like: "Larry, you know what's right." But he's the best coach in any team sport, period. You can dispute that. But from every aspect—teaching, game coaching, being there, running a program—he's got it all. And I'm not unique in what I say about him. And I've been through hell with him. I wasn't the easiest kid to coach. I wasn't the easiest assistant coach. I have not taken the path a normal coach's career would take. But he's always been available to me.

It always bothered me when people said he couldn't win the big one, couldn't win the national championship. I used to argue all the time with people about that. His teams had major injuries. And he allowed guys to come out early. I coached Danny Manning at Kansas. You don't want to be selfish. Danny told me he wanted to graduate, wanted to win the national championship, wanted to be the number-one pick. I didn't know what to tell Danny Manning. And I was thinking of Coach Smith, how many times he had to go through that situation. Never once did he waver in trying to figure out what was best for the kid. It's pretty unselfish.

There have been a lot of phenomenal coaches who never even went to the Final Four. I was with him the first time in Louisville when we lost to Dayton (in 1967). I realized what a magical ride it is, how lucky you need to be. Then in '80, my first year as a head coach at UCLA, I walked into that arena at the Final Four, and the first man to come to me in practice was him. And I started to think about all the things he had accomplished, and how lucky we were. Ray Meyer was the second man to come over to me, and he had never been there.

It bothered me. Year in and year out, the excellence of that program was right there in front of your eyes. And the conference was not a weak conference. And the other thing that people don't realize is that prior to the '80s, you had to win the conference tournament just to go to the NCAAs. It wasn't like it is now, even though now you've got to win six games to win the national title. When somebody says you can't win a big one, they ought to be in an ACC tournament final or a regional championship. That's much more pressure than being in a final game. The final game is gravy.

If you look back on my career, you can see how many Carolina guys I've had. From Steve Previs to Dennis Wuycik to Donald Washington to Darrell Elston—I've had 'em all. There's not a guy from Carolina that if he says take, I wouldn't take. Don't ever ask him scouting reports about Carolina guys, either. As loyal as he is to me, if I ever ask him about somebody, he'll say: "The guy's the best, the guy will help you." But I'll take any kid from his program. And he's relentless in his efforts to see that all these kids are taken care of.

He's been calling me about Brian Reese, I don't know how many years—"Do you have a place for him?" That's just him. I don't know how anybody could be that involved with so many people. He's every bit as intense helping Brian Reese as he would be helping a Jerry Stackhouse or Rasheed Wallace.

I just got a note from him saying how thrilled he was that we have George (Lynch). He put in parentheses: "George is one of my special ones." But I always laugh with Coach Smith. I know who his special ones are. But no one else does. He'll never allow anyone else to know who his favorites are, which is kind of unique.

I've been involved with a lot of people that if you need help, you'd have to probably call. I never have to call him. He's always there for me. And it's not just me. I used to hear a lot of guys who aren't from the Carolina family who looked at Coach a little differently. Maybe he didn't extend himself to them. But he doesn't have enough time. His responsibility, he always felt, is to all his players, his managers, the people who work with him. That's all time-consuming. I like to joke that he's still doing expense accounts from the David Thompson Era.

He has had an effect on my life every single day. He writes me a letter and asks about my son and daughter, my wife—handwritten notes. He never stops calling me on the phone. I wouldn't be here if it wasn't for him.